Meeting the Shadow
on the
Spiritual Path

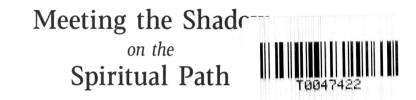

T0047422

"Many of us fondly imagined that spiritual practice would do it all: with enough meditation or yoga we would swiftly awaken to abiding love and light. But then we ran into problems: ourselves and our shadows—those powerful inner dimensions and dynamics that remain unconscious but can overwhelm and humble us. These shadow dynamics are best recognized and healed with the help of wise friends, counselors, and guides, people like Connie Zweig—a master guide and illuminator of the shadow, our inner world, and the spiritual path."

ROGER WALSH, M.D., PH.D., PROFESSOR OF
PSYCHIATRY AT THE UNIVERSITY OF CALIFORNIA AT IRVINE
AND AUTHOR OF *ESSENTIAL SPIRITUALITY*

"This book is vital for anyone who yearns to fully awaken. Skillfully drawing upon her hard-won contemplative insights and expertise as a depth psychotherapist, Connie Zweig offers us a brilliant road map for navigating the inevitable peaks and valleys of the Great Way. I highly recommend this book to new seekers and seasoned spiritual veterans alike."

DAVID CHERNIKOFF, M.DIV., LCSW, AUTHOR OF
LIFE, PART TWO AND GUIDING TEACHER FOR
THE INSIGHT MEDITATION COMMUNITY OF COLORADO

"If consciousness is a sea of limitless depth, Connie Zweig is a deep sea diver who brings back treasures for us. By examining the spiritual, psychological, and emotional dynamics between mentors and students, she demonstrates how shadow-work can help us move into deeper self-awareness and wholeness. This book is a compelling read—I couldn't put it down!"

ROBERT A. JONAS, ED.D., AUTHOR OF
MY DEAR FAR-NEARNESS AND FOUNDER OF THE EMPTY BELL,
A CHRISTIAN CONTEMPLATIVE SANCTUARY

"The shadow has emerged as a key concept in contemporary spirituality as communities wrestle with the recurrence of sexual violence and various forms of abuse across traditions. Rooted in depth psychology, *Meeting the Shadow on the Spiritual Path* offers a comprehensive, much-needed treatment of how the shadow and spiritual abuse operate. Updated with attention to the impact of the #MeToo movement, this new edition provides practitioners with the tools for both understanding and transforming abuse dynamics in a spiritual context."

ANN GLEIG, ASSOCIATE PROFESSOR OF
RELIGION AND CULTURAL STUDIES
AT THE UNIVERSITY OF CENTRAL FLORIDA

"Most spiritual traditions have a dirty little secret: when you surrender to an authority, you will face the dark side of human nature. At last, this book explains why and how to recover."

AARON KIPNIS, PH.D., AUTHOR, PSYCHOTHERAPIST,
AND PROFESSOR EMERITUS OF PSYCHOLOGY
AT PACIFICA GRADUATE INSTITUTE

"True spiritual wisdom invites all the energies within, including the darker ones. Blessings to Connie Zweig for shining a light on our shadows, allowing insight and joy to move our consciousness toward wholeness."

ROSHI PAT ENKYO O'HARA,
COFOUNDER AND ABBOT OF THE VILLAGE ZENDO

Meeting the Shadow

on the

Spiritual Path

The Dance of
Darkness and Light in
Our Search for Awakening

Connie Zweig, Ph.D.

Park Street Press
Rochester, Vermont

Park Street Press
One Park Street
Rochester, Vermont 05767
www.ParkStPress.com

Text stock is SFI certified

Park Street Press is a division of Inner Traditions International

Originally published in 2003 by Tarcher Perigee under the title *The Holy Longing*.
Paperback edition published in 2004 by Sentient Publications.
Revised edition self-published with iUniverse in 2008 and in 2017 under the title
Meeting the Shadow of Spirituality.

"The Holy Longing" by Goethe (translated by Robert Bly) was reprinted from
News of the Universe: Poems of Two-Fold Consciousness, edited by Robert Bly,
published by Sierra Club Books, San Francisco, 1980. Copyright © 1980 by
Robert Bly. Used with permission.

Cataloging-in-Publication Data for this title is available from the Library of Congress

ISBN 978-1-64411-722-4 (print)
ISBN 978-1-64411-723-1 (ebook)

Printed and bound in the United States by Lake Book Manufacturing, LLC
The text stock is SFI certified. The Sustainable Forestry Initiative® program
promotes sustainable forest management.

10 9 8 7 6 5 4 3 2 1

Text design and layout by Priscilla Harris Baker
This book was typeset in Garamond Premier Pro with Blacker Pro, Gill Sans, and
Legacy Sans used as display typefaces

To send correspondence to the author of this book, mail a first-class letter to the
author c/o Inner Traditions • Bear & Company, One Park Street, Rochester, VT
05767, and we will forward the communication, or contact the author directly at
ConnieZweig.com.

To Neil,
who wears the face of the Beloved for me

⁓ᴏᴇ⁓

As the deer pants for streams of water, so my soul pants for you, my God.

PSALM 42:1 (NIV)

Could the longing for a god be a passion welling up from our darkest, instinctual nature, a passion unswayed by any outside influences, deeper and stronger perhaps than the love for a human person?

C. G. JUNG

When the Guest is being searched for, it is the intensity of the longing for the Guest that does all the work. Look at me, and you will see a slave of that intensity.

KABIR

(TRANS. ROBERT BLY)

Contents

PREFACE TO THE NEW EDITION

A Call for Spiritual Awakening   xi

A Call for Shadow Awareness

PROLOGUE

My Longing for the Light   1

A Meditation on Up

❦

PART I

Before the Fall

A Guide for Faithful Believers

ONE

The Holy Longing   17

Awakening to Holy Longing   22

God Longs for Us as We Long for God   27

The Inner Marriage:
A Story of Holy Longing in the Sufi Poet Rumi   31

TWO

Longing for God   39

The Hidden Object of Desire

The Changing God Image:
Involution or Down   42

The Changing God Image:
Evolution or Up   51

The Inner Marriage:
A Story of Holy Longing in the Hindu Master Ramakrishna   55

THREE

Longing for the Human Beloved   61

The Search for Romantic Union

Beloved as Parent:
The Psychology of Love   66

Beloved as God:
The Archetypes of Love   70

The Inner Marriage:
A Story of Holy Longing in the Sufi Lovers Majnun and Layla   74

FOUR

Longing for the Divine Human   81

The Search for Spiritual Communion

Priest or Teacher as Parent:
The Psychology of Spirituality   83

Priest or Teacher as God:
The Archetypes of Spirituality   93

Priest or Teacher as Divine Human:
The Teacher/Student Relationship   102

The Inner Marriage:
A Story of Holy Longing in the Christian Saint Catherine of Siena   104

PART 2

After the Fall

A Guide for Disillusioned Believers

FIVE

Meeting Spiritual Shadow   113

Darkness on the Path

Encountering the Spiritual Other:
The Breakdown of Communion   118

Tales of Religious and Spiritual Abuse   126

SIX

Understanding Spiritual Abuse   169

Detecting the Patterns across Denominations

The Consequences of Spiritual Abuse   179

Who Is Susceptible to Spiritual Abuse?   184

Meeting the Shadow of Addiction   190

Death and Transcendence   193

MIDLOGUE

My Longing for the Dark   196

A Meditation on Down

SEVEN

Rekindling the Flame   201

Shadow-Work for Spiritual Abuse and Disillusionment

Communal Shadow-Work   203

Individual Shadow-Work   211

EPILOGUE TO THE NEW EDITION

Through the Shadow to the Light   245

Acknowledgments   249

∽∾⊛∾∿

APPENDIX ONE

The Association for Spiritual Integrity (ASI)
Code of Ethics and Good Practice   251

APPENDIX TWO

The Code of Ethics for
Insight Meditation Society (IMS) Teachers   254

Bibliography   255

Index   266

About the Author   274

A Call for Spiritual Awakening

A Call for Shadow Awareness

The first edition of this book, *The Holy Longing: The Hidden Power of Spiritual Yearning,* appeared during the peak of the Catholic Church's child sexual abuse scandal. The second edition, *Meeting the Shadow of Spirituality: The Hidden Power of Darkness on the Path,* appeared in 2017, just before the #MeToo movement launched. Since the publication of those earlier editions, the world has turned on its axis. We are observing urgent interconnected global crises at the same time as we are witnessing thousands of people report spiritual awakenings.

In addition, this new edition appears just as an epidemic of political indoctrination via misinformation breeds political wars over the very nature of truth. Social media has caused a collective shift from personal privacy to personal disclosure. National media reports, books, and online firsthand accounts continue to describe the eruption of the human shadow, both in the political context and in the religious/ spiritual context, our topic here. These continuing reports should make it more difficult to believe in human infallibility. But, instead, many true believers continue to trust in the perfection of their spiritual leaders.

The intention of exploring the shadow in our search for awakening is not to negate the profound and precious transmissions of our teachers and invaluable gifts of our communities. We don't want to deny the light of consciousness any more than we want to deny the dark side of human nature. Instead, my intention is to offer ways for readers to hold the tension of both—the dance of darkness and light on the path.

Power, Sex, and Money Shadows

As we will see, our spiritual teachers, even when enlightened, are still human—and most certainly not perfect. As their egos become inflated with success, some may come to feel that they deserve to sit on a golden throne, build empires, and increase their authority and fame without limit. As they use power to serve the ego's agenda, the danger grows. Soon, they do not have power; power has them. And that power becomes an unconscious complex, acted out on the stage of the most sacred arena of life. Acting out this power shadow, teachers may subject their followers to verbal abuse, physical violence, emotional control, withholding of love and approval, and threats of punishment or expulsion.

Power and sex go hand in hand; they are a matched set. Some teachers or clergy may use sex to express power, intimidate others, and feed their own emptiness. They may use sex to control others while satisfying their selfish impulses. In particular, a culture's deeply ingrained traditions of misogyny and objectification often engender in male teachers and clergy a shadow that allows them to use others (women, men, girls, boys) as objects for their own gratification.

Some teachers use strategic transparency to defend themselves: "I'm not celibate, so this is not inappropriate behavior." Or "This is crazy wisdom to awaken the student." In these cases, the shock of hypocrisy—celibate clergy or gurus having sex—is lessened. But the shock of trauma is not.

Like sex, money can become the ego's tool. It's "the root of all evil"; it's the grail we seek. It, too, carries the projection of divine energies and can be worshipped like a false god in the same form as a shiny

Rolls Royce or a sleek private jet. Many clergy and teachers convince their followers to tithe, then eventually to turn over their entire financial inheritances. The reports of so many spiritual teachers living lifestyles of excess and abundance, in great contrast to their teachings and in even greater contrast to those who serve them for no pay at all, are deeply disheartening.

These religious leaders may claim that salvation or enlightenment lies in giving them sex or money. They may promise that these actions will carry their believers to heaven or to higher stages of consciousness. In either case, the broken promise can be devastating.

Religious or spiritual abuse results in an identity crisis. Victim, survivor, muse, consort—who am I? Victimizer, abuser, predator, dominator, perpetrator—who is this teacher? And who am I if not his devotee or her acolyte? Who am I if not a special member of a special group? Who am I if I have been abused by the very person with whom I needed to feel safe? Am I a victim? Am I a fool? Am I alone, unloved, and without purpose?

Most of all, who am I in relation to my god or the gods or my own divine nature? Sadly, most inquiry does not get this far. Despite the widespread search for identity in our time—political, religious, racial, gender, sexual orientation—for most people, identity remains a concrete concept, rooted in genetics, beliefs, preferences, behaviors, or tribal groups.

Yet the perennial question—Who am I?—is most essentially a spiritual question. Advaita teacher Ramana Maharshi built his entire spiritual path around this inquiry. Nevertheless, today the search for the relative and concrete forms of identity, though necessary developmentally, obscures this deeper quest. Humanity has taken a developmental step with its expanding view of ways of being in the world: "I am a queer Latina" or "I am a political progressive" or "I am a survivor of religious abuse." But let's not stop here. Let's extend the search for identity to our deeper spiritual nature. Let's heed the call for awakening that is ringing around the world, while learning, at the same time, to hold shadow awareness.

Since the first edition of this book, humankind's exploration for the meaning and experience of enlightenment or awakening has both broadened and deepened. The democratization of practices in every tradition, including those that were previously hidden or esoteric, has enabled millions of people to find a teacher, a practice, and a community of their choice.

The podcast *Buddha at the Gas Pump (BATGAP)*, started by my friend Rick Archer, gets tens of thousands of listeners a day. Rick has interviewed more than six hundred "ordinary spiritually awakening people," as he calls them, in a conversational way that allows them to disclose their inner worlds and confront controversial questions about the nature of their experiences. As Archer told me recently, most teachers are not perfect. He has had to take down a few videos due to interviewees being inappropriate—that is, acting out their shadows, or dark sides, destructively. "Some have charisma and *siddhis* [yogic powers], but they are half baked. Even some eloquent spiritual prodigies are not qualified to be teachers. No one gets a pass," he concluded.

In addition to BATGAP, *Spirit Matters* podcast has posted hundreds of interviews with spiritual teachers of all traditions.

At the same time, the brilliant work of Ken Wilber, in the field of integral philosophy, continues to spread around the globe. Integral's key insights into the nature of human consciousness have helped me immensely. In particular, in the context of our exploration here, Wilber suggests that a devotee or a teacher can experience any state of consciousness while living in any level of consciousness. In other words, one can have a peak experience, even a nondual state, while living in a lower level of development or stage of awareness. But that advanced-state experience will be interpreted through the worldview of one's level of development.

We can use this insight as a lens through which to examine some of the teachers described here, who appear to have spiritual gifts but express them through ego mania, greed, aggression, and sexuality. They are interpreting their fleeting awakened states through the framework of their development, which includes a lack of self-esteem, lack of empathy, or narcissistic injury (need to be seen). In other words, in Wilber's terminology, they may have some experience of spiritually Waking Up but little experience of Growing Up (emotional work) and Cleaning Up (shadow-work). Waking Up, on its own, does not encompass emotional repair and relational development; it does not require moral development. This frame allows us to see how these states and stages of development can coexist in one person. It also leads to a startling conclusion: one may be awake at some level and still be a sociopath.

Andrew Holecek, in an essay titled "The Evolution of Abuse," puts it this way: "Many practitioners become 'state junkies,' always searching for the high of spiritual experience, and forget that coming back to earth fully incorporating those high states—as stabilized and embodied traits—is the 'low' (but final) point. It's not about what you experience. It's about who you become. And that becoming is not so much about what you say; it's about what you do."

In *The Religion of Tomorrow*, Wilber makes another point: Shadow material typically remains lodged in every chakra. As the kundalini rises through the chakras toward realization, unconscious material may not be fully cleared. This provides a map. So, for example, as we move through the stages of spiritual development, the remains of shadow material in the second chakra may lead someone to act out sexually. The remains of shadow material in the third chakra may lead him or her to act out in an abuse of power. This means that even someone who is highly developed, spiritually speaking, may still have layers of self-deception.

Since the publication of the earlier editions of this book, the Religion and Sexual Abuse Project has gathered scholars to understand the dynamics of sexual abuse and misconduct in religious communities, especially in their cultural, social, and historical contexts. It is holding conferences (with presentations available for viewing on YouTube), collaborating with advocacy groups, and developing teaching resources and an online resource hub.

Yet other critiques attempting to understand spiritual abuse focus on feminist analysis, which sees patriarchy and sexism as core to the violations. For example, in her book *Traveller in Space*, June Campbell wrote about her experience as a secret consort to Tibetan Buddhist teacher Kalu Rinpoche in the context of patriarchal authority and appropriation of the divine feminine. And Tibetan Buddhist lama Tsultrim Allione has developed a teaching that focuses on feminine wisdom energies in her tradition, which she places in the context of "recent feminist resistance."

Other critiques focus on race, sexual orientation, and class privilege. In his book *Love and Rage*, Lama Rod Owens, who identifies as a Black queer tantric teacher, looks at how patriarchy and racism interact in abusive *sanghas* (spiritual communities). He calls on male and masculine-identified practitioners to explore "sacred masculinity," which is rooted in collaboration with the feminine, rather than domination over it.

In a 2015 report published for *HuffPost*, Jaweed Kaleem tells us that many of the mostly White meditation-oriented traditions have not integrated with traditional Asian-American Buddhist communities. These traditions are now being challenged by Black, Latino, and Native American converts to Buddhism, and BIPOC sanghas are forming around the country to address issues of race in meditation communities.

In 2011, An Olive Branch was formed, as a project of the Zen Center of Pittsburgh, to offer greater understanding and reduction of ethical misconduct on the part of religious leaders. Their website states: "We help everyone recognize the trauma caused by unethical relationships between spiritual leaders and their followers; promote understanding and healing; and strengthen the organization's board, policies, and procedures to reduce the likelihood of future misconduct." Acting as a third party for spiritual communities facing allegations of abuse, their consultants have complementary skills related to training, facilitation, governance, and intervention.

In 2018, the Association for Spiritual Integrity (ASI) was launched "to encourage spiritual teachers, leaders, and guides to approach their work in the most competent and ethical manner—and to help safe-guard the sacred teacher-student relationship." ASI holds presentations online. (The ASI code of ethics can be found in appendix 1 of this book, while the code of ethics for the Insight Meditation Society can be found in appendix 2.)

Enter the #MeToo Movement

This edition also appears after the #MeToo movement went viral in October 2017. Started by Tarana Burke, a Black activist, with the intention of raising awareness about sexual harassment and violence, the movement has enabled survivors to speak out and push for systemic changes in the workplace, the military, universities, and other settings—including spiritual communities. #MeToo has helped survivors and wit-nesses of exploitation by spiritual teachers to connect online, empower each other, and encourage whistleblowers to expose decades-long abuses. Overnight, all-powerful teachers in many denominations could no lon-ger control the narratives about their isolated kingdoms. Investigative journalists and attorneys lurked. Stories went viral online. Many fled the country or lost legal battles. The list I recount in chapter 5 has been expanded and updated as the wave of reports and memoirs continues to roll in.

My litany of teachers in that chapter is not comprehensive. But it does explore how some religious and spiritual communities, formed with positive intentions, can become fundamentalist and cultlike. It focuses on those groups that are rooted in the teacher/disciple relation-ship, which is based on unconscious projection. And it examines the consequences of that projection for both teachers and students. It also examines the challenges of breaking that projection, letting go of who we want teachers to be, and seeing them for who they really are.

The disturbing stories in chapter 5 are not intended to bash gurus or clergy. Rather, they are intended to highlight the psychological dynam-ics in these relationships, as well as the hidden structural or systemic issues that allow people in power to abuse others with impunity in religious settings. In some cases, an individual's destructive behavior is a symptom of these built-in issues, and the elimination of that person does not eliminate the problem.

It seems evident that we need a spiritual justice movement, much like the social justice movements against racism, sexism, ageism, and homophobia that call for social, legal, and psychological change. However, as of this writing, only thirteen states and the District of Columbia have penal statutes that, in at least some circumstances, support the criminal prosecution of clergypersons for having sexual relations with a coerced congregant.

According to a 2019 report by Anna North, several positive changes have resulted from the broader #MeToo movement. The states of California, New Jersey, and New York have banned nondisclosure agreements (NDAs) involving sexual harassment or assault. Typically, when a case is settled for a financial payment, NDAs are used to silence the accuser, a practice that fails to protect others against the perpetrator.

We can ask how this shift in attitude toward NDAs might be applied in religious or spiritual settings. In the Catholic Church, for example, children who are sexually abused, who are incapable of giving consent, are threatened with theological danger to their families and to themselves. They are exhorted to keep the secret of abuse. What if the Catholic culture rewarded other clergy to become whistleblowers on behalf of children, rather than to maintain a brotherhood of silence?

In the same way, a guru might demand secrecy about his or her behavior, threatening abandonment, punishment, or humiliation. That pact of secrecy can become systemic, leading to years of lies and acts of deception, or it can be used as leverage against a devotee.

Some traditions, such as Tibetan Buddhism, require vows against disbelieving or disrespecting the master, revealing secrets, or criticizing the teachings (which include the guru's behavior). Like an NDA, this vow, known as *samaya,* keeps survivors bound to silence and unable to heed their own intuition about wrong behavior or to act on their own behalf. What if *samaya,* a vow to the guru that was imagined centuries ago as part of an empowerment initiation, were updated to include a vow to conscious commitment of no harm and relative empowerment, rather than blind obedience to a perfected master? Does this idea uproot the foundation of the guru/disciple relationship? Does it lead to the breaking of the projection that holds the relationship in place? I suggest that it would create a more mature spiritual relationship dynamic, with both people accountable for their words and actions.

As Lama Willa Miller suggests, "The essence of *samaya* is not blind faith. It is a promise to uphold one another in mutual goodness, while recognizing our human potential to go astray."

Many federal laws don't protect independent contractors or low-wage workers from sexual harassment. So, in many states these workers, when facing abuse, have no legal recourse. Similarly, many churches and ashrams have dozens or hundreds of people doing service or *seva* for low wages or no payment at all. They believe that selfless service without expectation of reward will bring them other benefits: closeness to a divine human being, a special sense of belonging in a group, a higher purpose through self-sacrifice for the benefit of others. But, like low-wage workers in secular settings, they may be unable to protect themselves from exploitation or have legal recourse against abuse.

#MeToo accusations of sexual harassment, trafficking, and financial corruption have spread to political leaders. There have been some efforts to reform the response to staff allegations against members of Congress. The waiting period to report has been eliminated, and legislators have been barred from using taxpayer funds to settle cases. In a similar way, religious leaders could be barred from using disciples' donations for abuse settlements with those very disciples.

The high-profile cases of producer Harvey Weinstein, sex trafficker Jeffrey Epstein, and U.S. Olympic gymnastics team doctor Larry Nassar have alerted the public to many of the issues involved in exploitation. How do we think about power and gender? Who has the power? Who doesn't? What leads men, especially, in positions of power to abuse it?

Of course, this is not a new discussion among feminists, whose critique of patriarchy has been an ongoing cultural conversation for decades. But the blatant and graphic abuse of power that has come to light has renewed discussion about consent. Can a woman consent to sex if her career, education, mental health, financial well-being, or spiritual well-being is controlled by the person who desires sex? Can she consent if she is told that she will be excommunicated, her family will go to hell, or her karma will be damaged for many lifetimes if she refuses?

Psychiatrist Peter Rutter, in *Sex in the Forbidden Zone*, concluded that she cannot. Consent means actively agreeing to sex, including setting boundaries. How can she agree under threat, intimidation, or coercion?

I would suggest that the issue is a bit more nuanced. A teacher's move into the "forbidden zone" may range from careless to aggressive and from subtle to traumatic. A student's response may range from feeling special and chosen to feeling assaulted and alarmed. Some women *do* choose to have relations with spiritual teachers. Perhaps they are blinded by devotion; perhaps they have promised to serve unconditionally. In a few cases, these liaisons lead to marriage, though we do not know the consequential power dynamics in these relationships.

In most cases, I believe the power differential renders consent questionable. But I don't want to reduce the issue to a moralistic outsider's point of view, in which both predator and victim are condemned. Rather, I want to bring the lens of depth psychology to examine some of the unconscious components of this dynamic.

In addition to a reexamination of power and gender, #MeToo survivors saw that they were not alone. They gathered and bonded online, some forming a lineage of survivors in particular denominations. They supported one another across race, class, and industry. And a larger audience saw the devastating consequences for them.

#MeToo has alerted the public to another factor: the crucial role of bystanders or witnesses. In every tale of spiritual abuse in this book, staff members, community members, and even other clergy, including popes and the Dalai Lama, knew about the violations—and failed to act for decades to save face. They colluded with spiritual rationales, propped up their teachers, disbelieved or dismissed the accusers, or remained in group-think denial. In addition, they ignored their own traditions' ethical guidelines. In my opinion, their silence made them complicit.

From Bystander to Whistleblower

How does a person make the shift from bystander to whistleblower? An encounter between a charismatic religious leader, citing a long lineage of initiation into esoteric knowledge, and a naive, uninformed Westerner, who is eager for spiritual experience, is not a meeting of equals. Together, they create an isolated world composed of two opposing cultures: a traditional, typically non-White, often patriarchal, feudal culture of the leader, steeped in blind authority, hierarchy (especially gender hierarchy), and secrecy, mixes with post-modern, typically White, individualists, prone to question authority and support gender equality, openness, and consensus.

But in the unconscious shadows of those Westerners lies a desire to relinquish agency and responsibility for decisions, so that another, wiser person can tell them what to do, and to relinquish the questioning, analytical mind and follow devotion to a more evolved human being. This is the flip side of the Western heroic ego that lies in the shadow.

In psychology, this transference, as it's called, describes the unconscious tendency to attribute feelings about someone in the past, such as a parent, onto someone in the present, such as a therapist, clergy person, or spiritual teacher. This tendency may leave us in a childlike position in relation to the other person, subordinate in power and authority, even seeking dependency.

When we feel lost and wounded and meet a charismatic spiritual leader, we may be desperate to find meaning and direction. We may be looking for validation of our own value or a way to transcend our psychological injuries with spiritual practice (spiritual bypass). This is a setup for archetypal projection or transference—that is, when we come to believe that the priest alone can perform the sacraments, for example, with divine authority, or that the guru alone can initiate disciples into secret practices and carry transcendental power that is out of our reach. If our spiritual leaders personify our highest yearnings, then we will do anything to be close or special to them and to participate in their divine knowledge or higher consciousness. In our yearning, we will give up our capacity to set boundaries, discriminate between right and wrong behavior, say no, or express doubt and criticism. Many devotional teachings of guru yoga in Hinduism and Buddhism support this surrender of the devotee's discrimination.

Buddhist practitioner Rob Preece put it this way: "My idealism not only blinded me to my teacher's human fallibility but was also reinforced by the teachings. I was even given the message that to see flaws in the guru, or to criticize him, would lead to dreadful suffering."

The Dalai Lama has tried to counter the impact of this teaching. In his book *The Path to Enlightenment*, he stated:

> The problem with the practice of seeing everything the guru does as perfect is that it very easily turns to poison for both the guru and the disciple. Therefore, whenever I teach this practice, I always advocate that the tradition of "every action seen as perfect" not be stressed. Should the guru manifest un-Dharmic qualities or give teachings contradicting Dharma, the instruction on seeing the spiritual master as perfect must give way to reason and Dharma wisdom. . . . I could think to myself, "They all see me as a buddha, and therefore will accept anything I tell them." Too much faith and imputed purity of perception can quite easily turn things rotten.

The Risk Goes Both Ways

So, this is the dilemma, the perilous risk of the teacher/disciple relationship in any tradition. Despite profound insight or spiritual realization, the teacher also has wounds, unmet needs, and unconscious motives.

He or she even may have what we call in psychology a personality disorder. But a believer's blind faith requires the teacher's integrity. When a clergy person or guru acts out a power, sex, or money shadow, one of two results can ensue for the student: either the projection pops, and she moves from faith to disillusionment, or the projection is reinforced by spiritual rationale, and she defends or even accepts the teacher's abusive behavior, leaning into masochistic tendencies. (We'll discuss this scenario in chapter 4.)

The clergy person or teacher is also at risk. When hundreds or even millions of people treat teachers as if they are godlike, perhaps from birth, they may buy into the projection, unconsciously believing they are above ethical codes, above spiritual codes, above the law. Or they may believe that, from their level of consciousness, they cannot do wrong. They may believe that, with their inner nonattachment, they are not the doer of these deeds. These beliefs are reinforced by teachings: Zen priests who have realized their true nature are free to follow conventional morality or not; the same is true for Tibetan Buddhist teachers. This choice emerges out of the realization that social morality is a cultural or intellectual construct, a product of relative mind and, therefore, essentially empty.

But we have seen, again and again, that many teachers are not free from the bonds of self-centeredness. Regardless of their level of realization, they cause suffering. And we see, again and again, that they feel impunity to the consequences of their destructive actions. Perhaps their awakening is not integrated enough to reshape old habits; perhaps it is a transitory nondual state experience, which is mistaken for a more stabilized stage of realization. Perhaps, as Ken Wilber explains, their spiritual line of development may be advanced, but their moral or social development may be delayed.

These teachers (like therapists) may be caught in countertransference, unconsciously projecting onto their students their own unresolved issues, such as the need to be seen and valued. In this case, critical feedback and reminders of ethical codes will go nowhere. Leaders may continue to act out power, money, and sexual shadows due to their own unconscious feelings of superiority or inferiority, emptiness, compulsiveness, and entitlement. They may also feel isolated, unable to speak about their own needs or unable even to admit to themselves that they have emotional needs.

And teachers often collude with this unconscious dynamic of transference/countertransference. Instead of completing the transference relationship and returning power, authority, and self-definition to their students or disciples, and instead of finding a colleague with whom to share their own needs, leaders often prop up the interconnected systemic structures that give them full authority and reinforce the projection. And they deny the harm they cause, again and again.

In a rare acknowledgment by a teacher of how this dynamic of transference/countertransference feels, the late Zen priest Yvonne Rand said, "In our understanding of the Zen tradition as coming from Japan, we include robes from Tang-dynasty China, shaved heads, formality in meeting," and more. "If I give a lecture in my traditional robes, I can feel an increase in the degree of authority which the people listening attribute to me. They edge toward accepting what I say as true, without really examining and questioning it. Subtle changes, but they go deep, begetting a kind of handing-oneself-over. This is sometimes useful in a learning process, but it is also dangerous to student and teacher alike if it's not conscious and within clear boundaries." (Cited in *Meetings with Remarkable Women: Buddhist Teachers in America* by Lenore Friedman.)

In the cases reported in chapter 5, this unconscious dynamic goes unexamined by the people involved. The teachers' charisma and success prevented the followers' critical thinking and prevented institutional change. The teachers were not merely lonely and reaching out for contact; they were too narcissistic or sociopathic to feel empathy for those they harmed. They were too convinced of their superiority and privilege to care about the consequences of their actions.

On the other hand, the followers, students, or disciples became so identified with their dependent roles, and with the specialness of their teachers and their fortune of living in close association with them, that they enabled clearly abusive behavior for years. They knew—but didn't want to know. To break through their denial, to end the unconscious transference and become a whistleblower, would mean that they themselves had been fooled; they had wasted time, money, even their lives on a fraud. Who are they then? This terror of loss of identity, loss of community, loss of secret knowledge, loss of meaning prevents people from speaking or even thinking the truth. So, this world of projection, secrecy, ritual, and group think is frozen in place, while children, women, and men suffer unimaginable harm.

And the unasked question, buried in the unconscious shadow, becomes: Am I wrong about this teacher or clergy? Is this person not who I thought she or he was? Or is my religion or my spiritual promise of awakening not what I thought it was?

When all is said and done, followers live in a double bind: an awake teacher, chosen by birth or lineage, or a clergyman chosen by god cannot behave in this horrific way. Yet he or she does.

To become a whistleblower in this situation is to risk it all— identity, meaning, purpose, community, beliefs, hope. To become a whistleblower and recover from the heartbreak of spiritual disillusionment means to break free of delusion, withdraw the projection, reclaim independent thinking, reclaim intuition, and reclaim action on our own behalf. At the same time, it also means cultivating mutual respect for the spiritual essence, true nature, Spirit, Emptiness, pure awareness, or Christ nature of one and all.

This dilemma is like a *koan,* a question that stops the mind: Can we feel devotion, even love, for a teacher, yet not idealize him or her? Can we follow the teachings of another person, yet maintain our own discrimination or inner intuitive guidance?

Further, can we build spiritual relationships of mutual accountability? Can we create support communities for teachers and students alike? We will explore some examples in chapter 7.

The shift of identity from, for example, "I am a devotee of this teacher," "I am a Buddhist," "I am a nonduality student," or "I am an Evangelical or Catholic" to "I am a survivor of religious or spiritual abuse" is a long and winding road. It requires a shift from a childlike position to an accountable adult position. It asks us to do our emotional homework without leaning on religious belief or spiritual practice to do it for us. It calls on us to cultivate the capacity to question, call out, even challenge verbal, emotional, physical, sexual, and financial abuse—in the moment, when it is happening.

This is a relative kind of waking up, a capacity to be present to the shadow within us and within others—and to break free of the delusion of a perfect human. Shadow awareness asks us to attune to ourselves more deeply and take more responsibility for our own blind spots. It asks us to attune to others more vigilantly and with heightened awareness. And, finally, it asks us to make choices that prevent us from falling into the grip of the shadow.

A Global Identity Crisis

Today's widespread identity crisis has several other dimensions. For example, most religious and spiritual communities reinforce binary gender stereotypes in both identities and roles. This setup reinforces patriarchal institutions. But today a rigid separation of genders is giving way to a spectrum in which a person's gender expression (as distinct from sexual orientation) can change over time or in different social settings.

Stories of fluid gender identities can be found in the tales of many traditions. Hindu mythology has many examples of deities manifesting as different genders at different times or combining to form androgynous or hermaphroditic beings. A god may manifest as an avatar of the opposite gender in order to facilitate sexual contact. Hindu saint Ramakrishna exhibited gender fluidity in his worship of the goddess Kali, as described in chapter 1.

As detailed by Peter Jackson in "Non-Normative Sex/Gender

Categories in Theravada Buddhist Scriptures," Theravada Buddhist texts contain numerous references to individuals who could be identified as hermaphrodites, transvestites, transexuals, and homosexuals. Most accounts of nonnormative gender and sexuality are found in the *Vinaya,* the clerical code of conduct for monks, which identifies four main sex/gender types: male; female; hermaphroditism, including both psychological and physiological traits; and non-normative male sexuality, which probably includes gay males, voyeurs, and eunuchs.

Of course, Buddhism espouses the teaching of freedom from a fixed, independent "I." In a 2014 column in *Buddhadharma* magazine called "Ask the Teachers," a Buddhist student posed the question: "I was born male, but I've come to the conclusion that I'm actually a woman, and I'm now seeking sex-reassignment surgery. As a Buddhist, I feel conflicted by the teachings of no-self and this unshakable feeling that there is a deep, hidden truth about me that I need to express. Am I wrong to embrace this sense of true self?"

In response, Zen teacher Sallie Tisdale makes the distinction between the relative "authentic self" and the "true self," our essential spiritual nature: "The incongruence you feel is not that uncommon. I would advise only that this 'felt identity' is not your 'true self.' That self is not dependent on the physical body, intellect, spiritual practice or relationship. It cannot be obstructed by anything phenomenal."

Andrew Holecek, a teacher in the Tibetan tradition, responded to the question in this way: "To become a Buddha (absolute) we first have to become fully human (relative). Your question suggests to me that you're homesick for the absolute [i.e., holy longing], and that homesickness is expressing itself in this relative way. This is not to dismiss your desire to find a true form but to help you put it in perspective. Sex reassignment could be one step toward the recovery of the true self."

Holecek continues: "Until we wake up to who we really are, we're all victims of a primordial identity theft. You originally thought you were a man, only to find you're actually a woman. . . . But the finite cannot contain the infinite. If we identify with that form, it will always feel like something is missing. . . . If you properly identify yourself as no-self, you will naturally express that selflessness as compassion and fulfill your longing—in any form."

What happens in this context of gender fluidity when we meet the shadow on the spiritual path? What happens to the standard male/female power dynamic if one person involved is nonbinary or trans? The universal internal image of a man in power and a female survivor no longer holds sway in the collective imagination with our expanding view of gender.

In her book *Buddhism beyond Gender,* Rita Gross explores "the prison of gender roles" from a Buddhist point of view. What has a greater hold on people's imaginations or limits them more, she asks, than ideas about biological gender? But if clinging to gender identity does, indeed, create obstacles for us, why does the prison of gender roles remain so inescapable? In revealing the inadequacies of identifying with gender identity, Gross illuminates the suffering that results from clinging to any kind of identity at all.

Our widescale identity crisis has another crucial dimension: the climate crisis. Professionals of ecopsychology are demanding that we expand our awareness to include our habitat, the earth, and all living beings. As we recognize our interdependence with the web of life, we extend our identity to include more and more of reality.

An expanded environmental identity is intimately connected with the spiritual realization of nondual awareness: there is no separation between self and object. At that stage of awareness, how can one cause harm to another? If we recognize the Self (or no-self) in another person, animal, or tree, how can we not recognize that its suffering is our suffering? Ideally, the realization of this stage of awareness leads naturally to compassion, not to a moral rule.

As one teacher said to me, "Love is always directed to the Self." In other words, there is only the Self (or non-self), so love and compassion should be inherent with the realization of nonduality.

The story of religious/spiritual practice in America is the story of human beings, after all. It is we who seek priests, teachers, practices, fellowships, *sanghas, satsangs.* It is we who become teachers, embody practices, run communities. So, in the end, this is our story. And, to state the obvious, we are human, which means we have shadows, unconscious parts, impulses, feelings, desires that we act out in ways that harm ourselves and others. Sometimes in ways that are unthinkably harmful.

But the shadow is not the whole story. This investigation has a mystery at the center of it—the human soul's longing for transcendence, awakening, union with the divine beloved. I call this our holy longing.

The Holy Longing

To follow our holy longing, then, we must ask: What is spiritual integrity? The Latin root of *integrity* means soundness, wholeness, completeness. The French root means innocence, blamelessness, purity.

How can we learn to detect a violation of spiritual integrity before we are blinded by devotion or belief? That is, how can we cultivate shadow awareness, maintain our internal warning systems, and be guided by those higher voices, rather than by past wounds that keep us in traumatic patterns?

In professional religious or spiritual domains, this means the creation of institutions that honor both the autonomy of individual life and the interdependence of all life. If as teachers we don't have the direct experience of this stage of unity with all life, we can hold the knowledge of it, build systems that respect it, and act accordingly. I suggest that leaders and their institutions also focus on teaching moral development, rather than assuming it will emerge with spiritual development. It clearly does not.

For individual believers in religious or spiritual settings, this antidote would include cultivating shadow awareness in ourselves and toward others, so that we are attuned to our own susceptibilities and to those of our teachers or clergy. If there's a whiff of violation of spiritual integrity, we can turn within to trust our own intuition, and we can turn without to speak up to others. We can study moral development for ourselves as well. Our integrity would include speaking and behaving with honesty and transparency, not secrecy. It would include living with congruence (we do what we say), not hypocrisy. It would include cultivating our personal shadow awareness—that is, uncovering our blind spots that leave us at risk of acting out. And if we do make a hurtful comment or cross a boundary inappropriately, it would include taking full responsibility for our intentions and actions as either teachers or students. In addition, it would include listening to and supporting survivors of spiritual abuse, as well as whistleblowers who report survivor accounts.

Why, then, do we continue to imagine a religious or spiritual life without an encounter with darkness or a meeting with the shadow? Why do we continue to be shocked and betrayed when it erupts?

I am calling for a reimagination of religious and spiritual life—and a revised understanding of enlightenment or spiritual awakening—that expands to include the human shadow. It is not absent in anyone. It is not going anywhere. It is an inevitable part of the human search for identity and of the journey toward union with the divine.

My Longing for the Light

A Meditation on Up

As a meditation practitioner for fifty years, I have been insane for the light. Like a moth diving into the flame, I sought to be consumed in the burning, cooked, turned to ash.

At times, on my knees, arms outstretched to the heavens, I beseeched my god. At other times, sitting still like a yogi for hours on end, my senses switched off, I turned an ear within to hear my god. Occasionally, for moments, the timbre of a celestial voice suggested itself; the horizon of another realm shimmered. But, at other times, disappointed and exhausted, I suffered the indifference of my god.

At the age of nineteen, I turned toward the East. The turn back did not begin until twelve years later. Today, in certain ways, I am still struggling to make the turn.

A student at UC Berkeley at the time, enjoying an intellectual, politically active, experimental lifestyle, I learned meditation for no holy reason or higher motivation but to date a man who would not get involved with me unless I learned the practice. I had no idea how this seemingly lighthearted decision would radically alter the course of my life.

After about a year of sitting, eyes closed and legs crossed, several internal changes had taken place: My chatterbox mind, usually highly

1

active and alert, was quieting down. At bedtime, it was not full of obsessive or random thoughts that kept me awake. My breathing, too, was quieter, softer, and gentler, so that my body felt calm rather than agitated much of the time. Emotionally, I felt more stable. Friends commented that I seemed less angry.

As my emotional turmoil subsided, I grew less engaged politically with "the enemy" out there and more engaged with the battleground within. I also grew less interested in saving the world through social activism and more interested in saving myself through the development of consciousness. Increasingly drawn to the meditative state, to the ocean of silence that pulled me away from complicated relationships and toward the simple goal of making that silence permanent—enlightenment—I began to long for god.

I signed up for a monthlong retreat that involved meditating for many hours each day and listening to long lectures at night. Sitting in the hall that first morning, in the company of several thousand others whose own restless eagerness could not be detected in the stillness, I awaited the guru. I wanted to be calm yet alert, open yet unattached—in the correct state of mind for him. I wanted to please him already.

A door opened, and a tall, stately man in saffron robes glided into the room. A bushy beard, just beginning to gray, covered his face. He folded his knees beneath him on the couch and nodded to the room.

I beheld the image of serenity, depth, and self-sufficiency. He embodied freedom from suffering, ignorance, even death. I felt certain that I witnessed a complete, self-realized human being whose mere presence implied that I, too, could be free.

After several weeks, I was at home. I had found a small community of dedicated, like-minded seekers, an intellectually sophisticated and compassionate teacher, and, best of all, a simple practice that emptied my mind of trivial thoughts and filled my heart with love.

Almost without noticing it, I adopted wholesale a philosophy that ran counter to everything I had been taught. This philosophy held that the "real" world is an illusion. The only reality is consciousness.

Pure awareness—big mind—can be reached only through meditation. Enlightenment or liberation from suffering is a result of the regular experience of pure awareness in meditation.

I began to believe that the way I led my life was the source of my pain. My attachment to people and things caused my suffering. The high stimulation of my lifestyle produced the stress in my nervous system, which agitated my mind, which triggered more desires, which led me to seek more stimulation, in an endless cycle of frustration and desire.

Like a key fitting into a lock, this teaching fit into some unknown part of me. As the message held a growing numinosity, the rest of life held less shine. The satisfaction of desires through personal love or creative work seemed futile. Working only to save money to go to more retreats, and socializing only with people who shared my worldview and my goal of enlightenment, I burned for god.

Very quickly, the spiritual group became my new family, harmonious and aligned, unlike my family of origin. My parents, from this new perspective, seemed lost to the world of materialism; my old friends seemed lost to the illusions of politics and romance.

I read voraciously in Eastern philosophy, assimilating its ideas until they were a part of me, flesh of my flesh. I found my life purpose and, like an arrow heading for the target, went off to a long retreat, where I meditated . . . and meditated . . . and meditated. When my back ached and my concentration faltered, I wondered what latent, nagging, restless urge led me to shut my eyes to the beauties of the world. But then my mind quieted for a moment, dipping into a delicious silence, and the questions evaporated.

After two months of a rigorous routine, I cast aside any remaining doubts and chose to become an instructor. I could hardly believe my good fortune. Like many before, I felt chosen—and certain that I had found the Way.

Again, I attended a women-only meditation retreat for several months. During that time, I practiced yoga, meditated, and ate simple meals. I did not get distracted by other stimuli. For all intents and purposes, I led a monastic life.

Near the end of that period, I was in an altered state of consciousness: deeply rested, yet hyper-awake inside. I did not need to sleep or dream—that is, to go under into unconsciousness. Instead, the inner wakefulness simply continued, whether I was lying down or walking around.

However, something else had changed as well. When I had joined this spiritual army, there had been no signs of regimentation, authoritarianism, hierarchy, or even rigid adherence to dogma. Perhaps because I knew nothing of the dark side, I couldn't see it. But I believe that in its early years this organization was fairly tolerant and open-ended.

Slowly, this attitude shifted, stricter guidelines set in, and eventually an institutional hierarchy arose. There was no dramatic violation of my rights, no singular spiritual abuse from which to recover. I simply began to grow uncomfortable with what I observed in the group dynamics.

I spoke to friends about my growing discomfort. But no one wanted to hear. Growing alienated from those I loved most deeply, I began to question the teachings to which I had devoted my life. The more I questioned, the more the pain increased. And the questions kept coming:

- Why doesn't this community feel like home anymore?
- Why is there a gap between the group's public persona and its inner workings?
- Why doesn't anyone else admit that something is subtly wrong?
- What would my life be like without my spiritual family?
- How can I live without the hope of enlightenment or salvation?
- If I leave, can I continue to meditate, separating the practice from the organization and its beliefs?
- How do I work through the grief of having invested more than a decade of my life in this community that I no longer trust?

Just as the outside world had become unreal and dreamlike (maya) upon my discovery of Eastern philosophy, so now my spiritual world seemed like a bad dream.

At the end of the training, I stood at a fork in the road, about to make one of those major life choices that quickly rules out other options and forms a certain destiny: to continue my cloistered life with its sole focus on raising consciousness, or to return to the quotidian world, to ordinary people and ordinary dreams. Even then, the choice seemed to mean taking only one of two directions: up to the life of spirit or down to the world of matter; up to god or down to earth.

With a heart clouded by uncertainty, I boarded the next plane home. I never took official action, but other members knew that I had stepped out of the circle. I expected my closest friends to understand; they did not. More than that, they would speak to me no more. I returned to Los Angeles an apostate, without a friend, without a job, without faith.

Over the next ten years, I suffered a deep disillusionment with the meditation community and its teachings. I slowly began to look at each philosophical assumption from every angle, turning it around and around, examining it as if my life depended not on hanging on to it, but on seeing through it. I applied the discipline of mind I had developed through meditation to questioning the basic premises of the practice.

I tried desperately to understand what aroused this intense longing in me, this hunger for spiritual sweets, this thirst for the nectar of the gods, this desire to dissolve. I sought answers in the twists and turns of my family dynamics and in the sweeping vision of transpersonal psychology. I studied the timeless mystical traditions in an effort to find my predecessors there—Krishna's devoted *gopis,* the dancing Baal Shem Tov, Sufi poets Rumi and Kabir, the Hindu ecstatic Mirabai, the nuns Catherine of Siena and Julian of Norwich.

And, although my disillusionment with my teacher and his teachings was heart-wrenching, I suffered an even deeper disillusionment with god, who, I believed, had set me on the path only to betray me. For a long time, I railed at my god, pointing a finger of blame at the heavens.

I had believed that a spiritual commitment would save me from shadow suffering. Like a child who believes that if she prays fervently enough, her petitions will come true, I thought that if I meditated diligently enough, fulfillment would result. And not only that: fulfillment without sacrifice.

I had held a simple image of a spiritual path—do your daily practice, purify your lifestyle, open your heart in love—that ended in certain rewards. How was it possible that my practices, my devotions, would leave me with empty arms? How was it possible that god would give me stone when I had earned bread?

I fell headlong into a well of despair, slipping into the underworld that I had struggled so hard to evade. I disappeared into a great blackness, living for a while at the bottom of a dark hole, looking up.

Eventually, groping in the dark for a thread to lead me out, I found a guide, a Jungian analyst who was familiar with the backstreets of the underworld, and who knew that my next key could be found in the darkness, not in the light. She helped me to pierce the innocence that held me in thrall to my teacher, which eventually enabled me to withdraw the spiritual projection onto him and reclaim my own radiance. She helped me to dissect the simplistic framework that held me in blame, which eventually enabled me to think more independently and to hold a more complex, nuanced view of spiritual life. She introduced me to the many gods living in my own soul, so that my former conception of a singular, all-mighty god appeared naïve and childlike. She initiated me into the sacred shadow side of life, where the hidden power of darkness shines like gold.

Today I see my awakening to this longing in my soul as my awakening to a conscious life, as a second birth. I see it as the fuel that drives my ongoing quest for greater understanding and for ecstatic experience. I see this longing behind my other deepest longings. I see it behind my images; I hear it behind my words. I see this longing before me, before I was, and before I become. My goal is not the end of longing; the holy longing itself is my guide.

Perhaps you, too, feel a yearning beneath your other yearnings that gnaws at you, despite the fulfillment of so many other desires. Perhaps you also fled the traditional religion of your childhood and, like me, joined an alternative community, hoping to find spiritual values and practices that would deepen your inner life. Perhaps you continue to be a believer but find yourself in exile from the traditional forms in which your faith is expressed. Or perhaps you have suffered spiritual or religious abuse and disillusionment at the hands of teachers or clergy, resulting in a loss of faith, hope, and trust.

And yet . . . your holy longing stirs. You feel a restless desire for something more, but you lack the words and images to describe your quest.

In my counseling work with hundreds of clients, I have found that this essential yearning—a secret feeling with many disguises—lies hidden at the source of each person's life story. It is the seed of a soul's desire, which spurs us to take certain actions, which in turn evoke more desire and again more action.

In part 1 of this book, you will read many stories of longing and how the object of our desire calls us to follow it, like a whispering echo. We respond, even unknowingly, perhaps by pursuing a romantic union that we imagine will fulfill our deepest needs. Or we seek a spiritual communion with a mediator for the divine, in a twinship that promises to surpass human limits. Or we serve a fellowship community, a dedicated group of believers who form a surrogate family in which we feel at home. In this way, the obscure object of our longing, like a hidden compass, determines the course of our lives, pointing us in its direction. And our life story unfolds, invisibly shaping our destiny from moment to moment.

We will explore some of the invisible images at the center of the archetype of holy longing, the fantasies of the soul longing for the divine. Together, they help account for our indescribable yearnings for something Other, something beyond the bounds of ordinary life. Like Carl Jung, who suggested that the gods are in our own souls and appear to us spontaneously as archetypal images—the beloved parent, the beloved partner, the beloved home, the beloved teacher or god—I suggest that by contemplating our own sacred images of holy longing, we can uncover our own gods.

Is there a transcendent God blazing behind the image? That is a question for theologians and people of faith. I am not advocating a position here concerning the metaphysical reality of god. That is why I use the small "g" for *god*—to indicate the *imago dei* (divine image) as it lives within our souls and as it mobilizes uncanny power in our lives.

With the help of this book, you can begin to detect the whispering call of your own soul. You can begin to acknowledge your longing and to reflect on it. You can explore what fuels it and what derails it, what ignites it and what numbs it.

You can discover the particular ways that you override your spiritual yearning by misplacing it onto concrete objects—wealth, status, online "likes," food, alcohol. When you fail to discriminate between these "idols" and your true object of desire, you are left feeling frustrated and dissatisfied. You silence the urgent message of your soul and hear only the voices of distraction, addiction, and compulsion. Instead, you can learn to attune to your holy longing, to hear its echoes of the past and its portents of the future.

In part 2, we will explore the painful and dark side of holy longing—the inherent pitfalls that can result when spiritual yearning goes awry. Countless recent headlines have highlighted the forces of destruction and annihilation that lie dormant in religious fundamentalisms and blind faith of all types, whether Christian, Jewish, Muslim, Hindu, Buddhist, or New Age. As a result, today we see the painful consequences of religious abuse and disillusionment on the faces of believers everywhere. I will attempt to shed light on this dark corner of religious life by exploring the roots of charismatic personalities, as well as those who are susceptible to them, and by uncovering universal patterns in spiritual abuse that can be used as wake-up calls for the purpose of prevention.

Clearly, the encounter with spiritual darkness throws believers into the fires of doubt. And these fires can either consume us or transform us. As Fyodor Dostoevsky put it, "The ideal passes through suffering like gold through fire."

The work of recovery, which I call spiritual shadow-work, cannot save us from suffering. It is not offered as a solution to a problem. When we enter the night sea journey, as Jung called it, we are not off the path; we are on it. In fact, we may be spot on it, right where we belong—ready to face spiritual shadow in ourselves or others.

If that is the case, then our disillusionment or loss of faith is an innate part of the inner journey. And our psychological work to recover our faith and to reclaim parts of ourselves that were sacrificed during periods of spiritual naivete is part of the larger spiritual task. In the same way that our cultural innocence was betrayed by the events of September 11, 2001, and January 6, 2021, and our religious innocence was betrayed by the epidemic allegations of abuse by Catholic clergy, each of us undergoes the betrayal of our own naivete when we face the spiritual shadow.

Later in part 2, we will explore those parts of ourselves that we typically sacrifice in order to participate in a religious community or to obey religious doctrine. By doing spiritual shadow-work, we can reclaim those lost parts and, as the mystics of all traditions teach, become more whole, developing through the stages of religious innocence toward a more mature spirituality.

By doing so, we can build bridges between our emotional and our spiritual lives, which are all too often perceived as separate means for separate ends. Today the inner journey needs to include psychological growth—that is, ego development and shadow awareness—so that our spiritual practices can be augmented with the safeguards of psychology. But psychological growth and spiritual awakening are not the same animal; spiritual shadow-work does not lead inexorably to enlightenment. In the final section of this book, we move through the shadow to the light, through the deafening betrayal and heartbreaking disillusionment back to the continuing longing of our souls, and to the continuing evolution toward union with the source.

In the epilogue to this edition, I share a few of my discoveries since finding and befriending a number of awake people. And I describe some popular misunderstandings of enlightenment that many seekers hold. We need to expand our understanding of awakening to include the shadow.

To sum up, this book explores the deeply felt desire for union with the divine in whatever faith or language it appears in you. This hidden yearning lies at the root of religious belief and faith. It is the heart of religion, not the mind. It is a *feeling* for the eternal, a taste of the infinite that sweetly lingers or emotionally seizes us with rapture or despair.

Religion, wrote William James, is the feelings, acts, and experiences of individuals as they stand in relation to whatever they consider the divine. Theologies grow out of these felt experiences, he added. And I suggest that it is the strength of these feelings of yearning and desire, of longing and hope, that determines the degree of our religiosity and the depth of our soul's desire.

This book will not examine the content of theological or philosophical beliefs. Instead, it examines the inner worlds of those who feel holy longing, the experience of the holy, which promises participation in the greater mystery. Therefore, as the inside story of religious longing, it cuts across denominations and links them to a more universal experience. And it does not examine the validity of practices. Instead, it examines how clergy and teachers behave in the context of transmitting those practices. That is, how do they speak and touch disciples as they transmit the world's sacred traditions?

William James also wrote that as each of us grows in self-awareness, we may begin to be influenced by another dimension through a longing or desire for it: "There is an unseen order, and . . . our supreme good lies in harmoniously adjusting ourselves [to it]. This belief and this adjustment are the religious attitude in the soul."

This inherent need of the soul—to turn to face the holy and to be changed by an experience of it—is purposeful and meaningful, according to Carl Jung. It is an inborn striving to open our limited personal selves to the archetypal and transpersonal realms. Just as Sigmund Freud posited a will to pleasure, Alfred Adler wrote of a will to power, Viktor Frankl advocated a will to meaning, and Abraham Maslow postulated a will to self-actualization, I suggest that there also lies within us a will to transcend, a longing for the eternal.

Although psychology is my lens, this book does not reduce spirituality to psychology or the ineffable to words. Instead, I intend to use psychology to explore spirituality, rather than to explain it. I believe that our early personal histories and unmet emotional needs influence our adult spiritual quests and religious desires. They are a necessary part of our exploration, but not a sufficient explanation.

The same is true for biology. In the early part of the last century, before the advent of neuroscience, William James pointed out that "medical materialism" attributes St. Paul's conversion to an occipital lesion due to epilepsy, St. Teresa's ecstatic visions to hysteria, and St. Francis of Assisi's asceticism to a bad gene. Today we know that there are neurobiological correlates to our emotional experiences, such as depression and anxiety. And there are brain correlates to heightened spiritual experiences as well.

In *Why God Won't Go Away,* neuroscientist Andrew Newberg and his coauthors described using brain-scan technology to map the inner worlds of Tibetan Buddhists in meditation and Franciscan nuns in prayer. Whether the subjects called their experiences loss of self or unity with god, respectively, they felt a sense of transcendence when activity in the frontal lobes increased and activity in the parietal lobes (which define our feeling of orientation to a physical self) decreased. That is, when this latter area is deprived of information for drawing a line between self and other, we feel a sense of boundless awareness.

This machinery of transcendence can be set in motion by ritual behaviors such as chanting, singing, and drumming, as well as prayer and meditation. That's why, Newberg concluded, god won't go away even in our age of reason.

Hard-core rationalists may use this data to support the thesis that god is merely a perception generated by the human brain. Hard-core religionists might argue that these findings offer evidence that the brain is wired to experience the a priori reality of god. But I suggest that neuroscience has not explained away the mystery after all. Biological correlations are not the same as causes. The soul's longing is embodied, perhaps even wired into the brain. But that doesn't mean it's caused by fleeting chemical events in the body/mind, even though it is reflected in those events. Thus the revelations of high-tech brain images can deepen, rather than dispel, the mystery of god in the human brain.

At the same time, this book does not romanticize spiritual experience by singing its praises and cleansing it of all dangers and darkness. Instead, it aims to acknowledge the pervasiveness and worthiness of our holy longing and to place it in the broader and deeper context of human evolution: you will see that your soul's desire is not separate from the vastness of life, but that it participates as an innate and vital part of it.

In *Healing Fiction,* archetypal psychologist James Hillman posed a guiding question for this book: What does the soul want? He suggested that the soul wants something that is not what we think it wants. So, we seek the wrong thing—and turn up empty-handed. We are left, again and again, with the ineffable, the mystery. And our yearning burns in us.

Words—such as *holy longing*—evoke feelings and images that activate meaning for us. Goethe, in fact, titled a poem with those two words (see chapter 1), and when I first saw them, I felt startled. He had found language to signify what I had always felt: my longing *was* holy; my longing was *for* the holy. The words lived in me for many years before this book was born.

Yearning, a cousin of *longing,* means to long persistently, wistfully, or sadly. It's related to a Latin word meaning to cause to wish. It's also related to a Greek word that means grateful and is tied to the word *eucharist,* the holy sacrament. Therefore, yearning is related to a wish being caused by an Other, as well as to being gratified by a symbol of the divine.

When we glean these root meanings of *longing*, we can contemplate again the question: What does the soul want? And we can understand more deeply the hidden power of spiritual yearning. It does not involve finding the object of our desire and satisfying our hunger, like being satiated after a rich meal. Rather, it means holding the tension of our longing, returning it again and again to our own souls, so that ultimately it may reveal its secrets and lead us to the next level of consciousness. It means tracking spiritual desire like a faint footprint, not to trap an object but to catch its scent and follow it deeper into the landscape of the soul.

Although at times it may be frustrating and even painful to hold the tension of your yearning rather than to submerge it, when you align with it, you align with the force of evolution itself.

And my wish for every reader is that your holy longing guides you home.

PART I
Before the Fall
A Guide for
Faithful Believers

One thing I ask from the Lord, this only do I seek: that I may dwell in the house of the Lord all the days of my life, to gaze on the beauty of the Lord, and to seek him in his temple.

PSALM 27:4 (NIV)

I long for a single glance from your eyes of pure love. To you alone I consecrate my entire existence without ceasing.

HINDU SACRED HYMN

A Hasidic rabbi noticed that an old man didn't follow the meaning of his discourse. He summoned the man and told him to listen to a melody instead. The rabbi hummed a song without words, a poignant melody of trust in god and of clinging to him. The old man proclaimed, "Now I understand what you wish to teach. I feel an intense longing to be united with the Lord."

HASIDIC TALE

ONE

The Holy Longing

In every mystical tradition, saints and lovers speak eloquently of the soul's search for the beloved, its yearning for the gods, its longing for communion. The bride in the Hebrew Song of Solomon sings her erotic yearning for her bridegroom, desiring to kiss him because his love is better than wine. The bride proclaims fervent union at last: "My beloved is mine and I am his."

The Greek maenads, or madwomen, dressed in fawn skins and ivy crowns, carried lit torches and danced wildly around Dionysus, desiring nothing but union with him. The Egyptian divine queen, Isis, lamented and longed for her murdered husband, Osiris. After finding his body parts and rejoining them, she united with him. Osiris was resurrected a god, king of the dead. In the Hindu tradition of devotion, milkmaids, known as *gopis,* long for union with Krishna, the dark blue god. Krishna's sixteenth-century devotee Mirabai wanted to be turned into a heap of incense, burned into ash, and smeared on Krishna's chest.

I wonder why the metaphor of burning recurs again and again in the words of mystics, saints, and devotional poets in their attempts to describe the ardor of human-divine love. St. John of the Cross said he was fired by love's urgent longings for Christ, the divine beloved. Jewish mystics declare that burning ecstasy unlocks the meaning of life. If we fulfill the commandments but don't feel the burning, they say, we won't feel the burning in paradise either. Rumi, the thirteenth-century Sufi poet, declared that a burning of the heart is more precious than everything else because it calls god secretly in the dark.

More recently, eminent psychologist Carl Jung proclaimed in *The Psychology of Kundalini Yoga*: "A man who is not on fire is nothing; he is ridiculous, he is two-dimensional. He must be on fire even if he does make a fool of himself. A flame must burn somewhere, otherwise no light shines; there is no warmth, nothing."

The master poet Goethe spoke of it in his poem "The Holy Longing," in which he said,

> *Tell a wise person, or else keep silent,*
> *because the massman will mock it right away.*
> *I praise what is truly alive,*
> *what longs to be burned to death.*
>
> *In the calm waters of the love-nights,*
> *where you were begotten, where you have begotten,*
> *a strange feeling comes over you*
> *when you see the silent candle burning.*
>
> *Now you are no longer caught*
> *in the obsession with darkness,*
> *and a desire for higher love-making*
> *sweeps you upward.*
>
> *Distance does not make you falter,*
> *now, arriving in magic, flying,*
> *and, finally, insane for the light,*
> *you are the butterfly and you are gone.*
>
> *And so long as you haven't experienced this:*
> *to die and so to grow,*
> *you are only a troubled guest*
> *on the dark earth.*
>
> TRANS. BY ROBERT BLY

I suggest that it is because of this holy longing for something Other, this timeless yearning for union with something beyond ourselves, that human beings sit still, cross-legged, eyes closed, as the splendors of spring pass us by. It is because of this longing that we strive to lose ourselves in one another in ecstatic embrace, like Shiva and Shakti weaving creation. It is because of this longing that we build Sistine Chapels, sculpt the *David,* and compose the *Messiah.* It is even because of it that we search intensively for the smallest bit of matter, the "god particle," which might be the ultimate building block of life.

It is also because of this holy longing that Islamic fundamentalists fighting a jihad, or holy war, eagerly sacrifice their lives to go to paradise. It is because of this longing that cult fanatics, such as those at Jamestown, commit group suicide to attain the other world. It is because of this longing that monks and nuns wall off the difficult demands of bodily life and bury their emotional wisdom like hidden treasure. It is because of this longing that faithful churchgoers and aspiring meditators refuse to see what appears before them as spiritual abuse, perpetrated in the name of god.

In my earlier book *Romancing the Shadow* (with Steve Wolf), I explored several forms of human longing: the longing for family soul, the yearning for the ideal partner, the desire for the sacred friend, the hope for meaningful work, and the search for meaning at midlife. In this book, I explore an even more primary hunger: the drive toward self-transcendence that fuels evolution itself in the physical, mental, and spiritual worlds.

In the physical realm, for example, those physicists who developed thermodynamics observed that physical systems tend to deteriorate, moving from order to disorder, like a car becoming a heap of rust. But a more recent theory suggests that a self-organizing capacity, which was previously invisible, is inherent in physical systems. Nobel Prize winner Ilya Prigogine demonstrated that open systems are characterized by self-organization, self-renewal, and self-transcendence. Although simple physical systems appear to fall apart, some actually fall together, transcending their previous level of development and reorganizing at a higher level.

The sciences of complexity suggest that the end point of a physical system pulls its development in that direction: an acorn inevitably becomes an oak, a zygote grows into a human being. When a system becomes unstable and chaotic, an internal force (known as an attractor) reconfigures it for a new and higher level of stability. The system unfolds according to its end point, driven toward greater levels of integration by the physical analogue of the holy longing.

In the mental realm, the holy longing is at work in individual development as the soul longs for manifestation. It attaches to form and conception takes place, beginning the downward journey from unconscious unity to ego consciousness, the journey toward a separate self.

Pre-personal stages of individual development find their fulfillment in the personal stage of a fully consolidated ego. For most psychologists, this is the goal or end point of human growth, exemplified in the myth of the hero who follows his path alone, combats his adversaries, and ultimately wins a boon.

But for mystics of all traditions and for transpersonal psychologists and philosophers, who intuit the larger story of the holy longing, this moment is another stage in the cycle of consciousness: the beginning of what the Sufis call "the great return." The holy longing is transformed from a yearning for separation and individuality to a yearning for ego transcendence and union.

In the spiritual realm, this desire or will to transcend is built into the human soul as spiritual aspiration. This yearning can be felt as a restless hunger to unite with a holy Other, something greater than ourselves. It drives the *telos* or direction of the journey from ego consciousness to Self-realization, from personal to transpersonal life, just as the silkworm emerges a butterfly, to use St. Teresa's metaphor.

Christian mystic Meister Eckhart put it this way: Now the seed of god is in us. The seed of a pear tree grows into a pear tree. The seed of God grows into God. Or as Rabbi Abraham Joshua Heschel put it, "Let there be a grain of prophet in every man." Buddhists teach this too: they believe that a seed of Buddhahood lies at the core of every sentient being, and its realization is the end point of our evolution.

The glories of the "downward" arc of involution—from unconscious transcendence to immanence in incarnation—have been extolled by scientists and psychologists for hundreds of years. The glories of the "upward" arc of evolution—from immanence to conscious transcendence in enlightenment—have been extolled by poets, spiritual teachers, and mystics for thousands of years.

But warring camps have emerged. In *Sex, Ecology, Spirituality,* Ken Wilber calls those who favor "up" puritanical ascenders, who tend to devalue nature, the body, and the senses. He calls those who favor "down" shadow-hugging descenders, who futilely seek the timeless in the world of time.

Rarely does a philosopher present the full cycle. Wilber pointed out that Plato saw the big picture: he traced the outflowing of the One through god into the mental world of Forms and into human minds, then bodies, then matter. He also traced the return journey of the soul from its infatuation with the material realm through the realm of Forms to a spiritual immersion in the One.

However, his descending vision became associated with the dark shadows of the cave. As a result, the ascending vision became the goal of Western civilization: up and away from the flesh toward spirit; up and away from the world toward heaven. Aristotle, Augustine, Hegel, Schopenhauer, de Chardin, Novalis, Coleridge, and others perpetuated that bias, with devastating long-range consequences: the devaluation of nature, the body, and the feminine.

The ascending and descending paths also appear in microcosm in us in our kundalini, a subtle energy that is imagined in tantric yoga and Eastern medicine as a serpent coiled at the base of the spine that ascends to the top of the head with meditation practice. As it rises, kundalini opens the seven *chakras,* which are energy vortices that attract life force from its source. At each level, the chakra acts as an interface between individual awareness and the energy frequencies of that level. As kundalini energy is activated and chakras open, the individual incorporates ever-higher frequencies into the self, as it identifies with each level, is transformed by it, and then transcends it.

Yoga masters have mapped the progress of energy up from primitive stages in the lower chakras to reunion with its divine source in the highest or crown chakra. In ancient China, Taoist masters taught "circulation of the light," in which sexual energy is generated in the lower spine, sent up to the top of the head to become spiritualized, and directed back down the spine to complete a circle and begin again.

The holy longing fuels the ascent of kundalini—the upward arc—as the individual longs for higher levels of unity. At the same time, the magnetic pull of the higher chakras draws up the evolving self.

Conversely, the holy longing fuels the descent—the downward arc—as the individual yearns for embodiment, sexual union, and immanence. The magnetic pull of the lower chakras draws down the evolving self.

I suggest that by making conscious the descent, development, and ascent of the soul, we can participate more consciously in evolution. Through allying with our holy longing, rather than resisting it, we can learn to hear the call of the soul. Through fidelity to our yearning, rather than betrayal, we can fuel evolution in our own lives and in the life of our species. This is the greatest promise of uncovering and attending to our religious yearning: our will to transcend aligns us with the collective drive toward self-transcendence.

Awakening to Holy Longing

A famous Jewish mystic, Rabbi Abraham Kook, pointed out that the person who tries to sustain himself only from the surface of life will suffer terrible impoverishment. "Then he will feel welling up within himself a burning thirst for that inner substance and vision which transcends the obvious surfaces. . . . From such inner sources he will seek the waters of joy which can quicken the dry outer skeleton of life." (For the full passage, see Herbert Weiner's book *9½ Mystics,* page 4.)

This innate burning thirst can be felt in many ways. For some, the holy longing can be detected as a nagging awareness of a lack or a fleeting sense of something more. At the age of fifty, one client sat across from me with a challenging glare: "I feel a constant, gnawing ache inside. Time is passing. I *know* this is not all there is."

Her statement implied unspoken questions begging for answers. I recalled Jung declaring that every patient he saw over the age of thirty-five was suffering from a religious problem. My client's pressing desire for something more pointed to her unconscious need for meaning and value, a need that was essentially religious because it revolved around her relation to larger forces, higher powers, or what we may call the gods.

Early childhood experiences of abuse, grief, and loss lead many people to seek relief from suffering, but more as well: Caught in feelings of anger and bitterness, they seek compassion and forgiveness. Trapped in feelings of isolation, they seek communion. Entering therapy to minister to past wounds, they begin to ask spiritual questions of meaning and depth. The pain that had seemed so purposeless and arbitrary is the very thing that sets them on the path.

Other people hear what mystics refer to as the still, quiet voice, or what the Sufis refer to as the call of the beloved. After that, they intuit that this world of the senses is not all there is. They wander restlessly from place to place, relationship to relationship, church to church, guru to guru. Their relentless hunger drives them here and there, but the smorgasbord of tastes never satisfies.

Many people experience their longing as a yearning for romantic love. Their hunger for the ideal loved one compels them to place relationship on the altar, above all other things. And, believing in the sacred power of love to heal them, even to save them, they anoint the lover with special gifts and unknowingly ask him or her to stand in for the divine.

Some women long for a divine child to redeem them. I have met women who, since their own youth, have yearned for the birth of a special child whose unconditional love will reward them. Or, disillusioned with a romantic beloved, a parent may unconsciously channel holy longing toward an innocent child, who becomes the family savior.

Others set their longing in a spiritual framework and feel it as a yearning for the light, which compels them to purify themselves of darkness. They may attempt to achieve this through strict diets and fasting or yoga and meditation. They may seek a teacher who is ahead of them on the path and who can relieve them of sins through practice or good deeds. They may imagine their objective as a desired shift in consciousness, which offers an end to isolation through a direct experience of unity with all of life.

As good Buddhists, they may give up their back support and sit upright for extra hours of meditation practice. As good Christians, they may redouble their efforts to take up the cross and follow Christ. As good Jews, they may strive harder to fulfill the commandments with the proper intention. As good Muslims, they may recommit to following Sharia, or sacred law. In each case, believers channel their fervor into form, turning it into an effort toward greater perfection, a striving toward a remote goal. The form of their striving is determined by the form of the holy Other, the object of their desire.

For some, the goal is an ideal home, whether a community of like-minded seekers or a paradise in the other world. Many mythic heroes—Odysseus, Gilgamesh, Dionysus, Heracles—are wanderers who follow a restless urge that never finds its object. James Hillman referred to this urge as *pothos,* the longing toward the unattainable, ungraspable something that drives our seeking for home.

This motif of paradise recurs in every generation. In an earlier time, human beings lived in unity with the creator and in harmony with nature. The Hindus' Vedic age of enlightened seers, the Hebrew Garden of Eden, the Greek golden age, the Viking warriors' Valhalla, the Australian Aboriginal Dreamtime, the Chinese Taoist Age of

Perfect Virtue, the Muslim paradise in which the Prophet awaits his martyrs—all are local variations on the universal theme of a long-lost time and place of perfection.

Some traditions encourage a longing for this other world. It can be felt in the poignant yearning of Black gospel music for Jesus and his salvation. It can be seen in schools of Jewish mysticism that teach that a believer who does not savor the world to come, but whose soul still yearns and thirsts for god, will not quench his thirst with the water of the Torah that is in front of him. Rather, he is like a man who stands in a river and cries for water to drink.

Even today this image of paradise—of home and happiness—beckons us with archetypal power. But it may remain just outside the boundaries of our awareness. Like a forgotten hypnotic suggestion, it compels us to leave home to find home, and yet it remains hidden from sight. Perhaps, as some literal thinkers believe, its source is a memory of history, of an actual time and place. Or perhaps, more symbolically, paradise harks back to an earlier psychological state.

Freud spoke of it as a return to the womb. In his early work, Jung thought it stemmed from a desire for the forbidden parent, which can never attain its goal. Therefore, we long eternally for the unattainable. Later, Jung viewed it as the ego yearning for the Self, the archetype of wholeness. Transpersonal and integral psychologists believe it refers to a higher level of consciousness that we have not yet realized.

For a select few, an object of longing appears at once, as in Paul's revelation of blinding light on the road to Damascus, or Dante's sighting of the young Beatrice, or Ram Dass's instantaneous recognition of his Indian master, or St. Catherine's first vision of Jesus. That vision takes over the emotional life of the person like a possession. For example, Paul, formerly a Jew who fought against the teachings of Jesus, became the main advocate for a life in Christ.

When this happens, all earlier commitments are relativized. Dante contemplated the image of Beatrice as his anima, or soul image, for years to come. And she fired the poet's imagination.

And all former values lose their foundation. Richard Alpert, a professor at Harvard, became Ram Dass and spent his life teaching the value of Indian mystical practices. For him, and for Paul, Dante, and St. Catherine, meaning gathered around the beloved object like iron filings around a magnet.

For some, the holy longing is felt with the sweetness of hope and the ideal of communion with others. "I long for a community of souls," a friend said, "where I'm like one lit firefly among thousands in the dark skies." For others, it is suffered with the bitterness of isolation and disillusionment. An encounter with our lower nature, our sins or shadows, may evoke a deep desire for repentance and healing. When we see our own cruelty or face our unconscious limitations for the first time, we may yearn for the light of consciousness and the forgiveness of higher forces. As we awaken to our longing for transcendence, our love of family may seem to bind us to attachments and responsibilities, which keep us tethered to this world. Work may feel purposeless and seem to separate us from our higher aims. Our human limits and longings for material comfort and love seem to conflict with our religious yearnings. And the object of our longing appears forever elusive, trapping us in promises for the future and robbing us of the vitality of the present moment.

"It's always out there, in front of me, just out of reach," a client said to me. "I feel no gratitude for what is, only hope for what should be and fear that it will never come."

Many individuals turn a deaf ear to the whispers of the soul. Myths tell us of heroes who do not heed the call. Today, too, despite their spiritual thirst, some people retrench in established patterns, too fearful to risk changing a life of comfort. Or they find substitute gratification in an addictive substance, which appears to quench their thirst for a moment. But their holy longing is simply held captive by that substance. On the other hand, stories of the mystics and saints in every tradition give us a glimpse into the lives of those who follow their longing to its source.

God Longs for Us as We
Long for God

The inner urge that sets us seeking is itself the thing we are looking for.

KARLFRIED GRAF DÜRCKHEIM

Like the individual soul longing for manifestation and completion on the downward arc, creation myths tell us that the unmanifest god desired manifestation, and so spirit descended into matter. Some religions view "down" as a fall from grace, an irreparable loss of original unity. But if we keep in mind the complete cycle of consciousness, as the mystical traditions tend to do, we see that it is only half of the story: descent into matter is occurring simultaneously and continuously with ascent to spirit. Unconscious unity is leading to conscious unity everywhere and always.

In Hinduism, Brahma, the creator, manifested life to dispel the enveloping darkness. He created the waters and deposited a seed that became a golden egg, which was divided into male and female. For Hindu mystics, the purpose of life is to realize consciously the unity that was present in the beginning unconsciously.

Hindu myths of gods and goddesses retell this universal narrative of the human soul, often depicted as feminine, longing for the divine beloved, portrayed as masculine. For example, the milkmaid Radha adores her consort Krishna, an incarnation of god. He performs superhuman feats to destroy the powers of evil and is renowned for his skill as a flute player. When he plays, spreading the melodies of love through the cow pastures, peacocks strut, cows adore him, clouds let the rain fall. And Radha and the other devotees dance about him, burning for his love.

From a human level of interpretation, Radha, a woman married to another man, directs her fervor to an unattainable object of desire, in apparent disregard for social convention. As in the courtly love tradition of English troubadours, it is the lovers' separateness that fuels their desire for union.

From another level of interpretation, Radha is the ultimate female devotee, or bhakta, who seeks complete identification with her image of god. At this level, there is no question of morality, but of a worshipper's desire for union with her beloved or, more symbolically, a soul's desire for union with god.

Finally, from the point of view of unity, Radha and Krishna never were separate. Pure consciousness or spirit divided itself into two— Krishna and Radha, or the masculine and feminine face of god—only in our limited perception or level of consciousness. In the final stages, duality is an illusion.

In Jewish mysticism, the light of the absolute source, or Ein Sof, descended, degree by degree, into the world through many "garments," which screened its light, until the material world emerged as darkness embodied. The purpose of this downward gradation of light into creation is transformative: one day, with the coming of the Messiah, the light of the Ein Sof will shine in the place of greatest darkness.

But this fulfillment depends upon human action. When believers follow the commandments with the proper intention, or *kavanah,* they bring down the light from above into matter, which was previously dark. The Hasidic text *Tanya* tells them that their hearts should truly desire this higher union—the joining of the soul with the light of god—and that they should habituate themselves to this intention, which puts them into harmony with god's will.

Jewish prayer is in part a crying out of holy longing to god, a calling for the divine presence to come nearer. As Psalm 141 (NIV) says, "I call to you, Lord, come quickly to me; hear me when I call to you. May my prayer be set before you like incense; may the lifting up of my hands be like the evening sacrifice."

When believers focus on learning the Torah, they intend to bind their thought to god's thought, their speech to god's speech. They call to the holy one to come closer, just as a person calls a companion or a child calls a father to join him or her and end their separation. As Psalm 145 puts it, "The Lord is near to all who call on him."

As the Kabbalah put it, in the beginning, there was only god. With an in-breath, it withdrew into itself and, contracting, left a space where there was no god. With an out-breath, god reentered that space. During this process, the light of god scattered. Some holy sparks returned to their source; others fell into the mineral, vegetable, animal, and human realms, destroying the original divine harmony. Those sparks that fell forever yearn to return.

It is the human task to repair divine unity by lifting the sparks through our deeds, which are spelled out in the commandments. This work of repairing the world, or *tikkun olam,* is the hidden purpose of Jewish life, and it may carry us far into the darkness of descent. Some Hasids suggest that gathering those sparks that have fallen farthest from god is the greatest *tikkun.* However, this task also presents the greatest danger: the risk of getting lost in the darkness.

This Jewish story of individual mission parallels the collective story of Jewish life: Just as god withdrew from existence initially, some Jews suffer the absence of god now. This condition of exile in the soul is like the exile of god from the world. For believers, this exile requires the mission of gathering sparks. The longing for god is proof of the possibility of reunion.

In the late 1700s, Rabbi Nachman of Breslov, who suffered a perpetual restless yearning, told his followers that a person can shout very loudly to god in the silence of his or her own small inner voice. No one will hear because no sound is emitted. Therefore, a person can stand among many people and cry out loudly, longing for god. Even today, when we sit in a synagogue during services and listen to the ancient melodies, we can hear the soul's bittersweet yearning to end separation, to climb to the higher realms, and to return home to the holy land.

Reb Nachman believed that this spiritual restlessness was a sign that a renewed effort was now required to reach another level of consciousness. For him, to sin meant to remain on the same level for too long. He would repent and beg god's forgiveness for not attaining a higher rung on the ladder. For him, this process meant that he was moving with the will of the universe, or the natural course of progress in the human soul.

In Christianity, Paul spoke (in Philippians 3) about *epektasis,* reaching forth to the things that are before us and forgetting the things that are behind. We might interpret Paul's description of dying each day (in 1 Corinthians) as transcending the level of the past and being reborn to a new consciousness.

Early Christian saint Gregory of Nyssa wrote commentaries about *epektasis,* which he translated as straining toward god. For Gregory, this human effort, which stems from free will, takes place within the context of the soul's movement of perpetual ascent toward god, who is immovable. The soul is drawn by desire for god like a lover is drawn by the scent of the beloved, as described in the Song of Songs. Or, as Philippians 3 put it, he who always stretches forward will never cease his ascent, ever guided to comprehend transcendent reality.

The sixth-century *Rule of St. Benedict* prescribed behavior that led each monk to share in the sufferings of Christ so that he deserved to share in his kingdom. But these behaviors are empty without straining forward with hope in Christ, by whose spirit we participate through grace in the nature of god. As his divine image is restored in us, we are ever more capable of giving and receiving love.

Contemporary Christian teacher Gordon Dalbey takes a more psychological approach to god as the father. He told me, in a personal communication, that most Christians don't acknowledge their holy longing because, as children, they called out for their father and he failed them. He may even have scolded them—"Stop crying or I'll give you something to cry about"—when they yearned for him. "Our fathers didn't come when we called, so we learned not to trust them. Some of us awaited their arrival with fear and dread. As a result, it's not safe to long for God the Father today. It's not safe to be like a little child, dependent on God. But that's exactly what we need for healing. Rather than choosing out of pride to be our own masters, we need to become a child who is dependent on Him, to take his saving hand, and to surrender to his plan. He will forgive us and restore us to life."

On the other hand, Christian chaplain Jeff Utter told me that, for some people, disappointment in their fathers only increases their longing for god. The reason we feel unsafe in turning to god, he said, is that we fear what god will ask of us.

This unconscious intent—to meet an absent father/god via religion—plays out in other traditions as well. For example, the biblical story of God's abandonment of Ishmael has led some scholars to view Islam as a tradition of orphans in search of a lost father, Allah.

In Islam, Allah is the hidden treasure who longs to be known. A longing arises spontaneously within the hiddenness of Allah's transcendence and without disturbing its perfect unity. This divine longing is the first light to emerge from the source of light. It shines prior to time and prior to eternity. It gazes everywhere, perceiving only divine unity illuminated by its own light. It calls out, "*Il ilaha illallah* [there is nothing other than Allah]."

The individual Sufi's journey is symmetrical: when divine yearning emerges, one begins the great return, the path of the soul from union with god through the Sufi stations (or levels of consciousness) to reunion with god, in which one consciously realizes that there is nothing other than Allah.

We can recognize these ideas in the lived realities of seekers and saints, in their narrative stories of poignant yearning for the divine beloved. Whether Christian, Jew, Hindu, Buddhist, or Sufi, whether theistic or nontheistic, they long for union with something transcendent, something beyond themselves.

∾ THE INNER MARRIAGE ℮

A Story of Holy Longing in the Sufi Poet Rumi

In the year 1207, in what is now Afghanistan, a boy was born to a family of Sufis, those Muslim mystics who call themselves lovers of god. As an infant in his mother's arms, Jelaloddin heard stories of the Prophet Muhammad and his saints. As a toddler at his father's side, he learned to keep the names of god between his teeth, to repeat "Allah" with every breath.

One morning, following the dawn prayer, seven-year-old Jelaloddin felt restless. The open sky beckoned him. He stretched out on a grassy knoll, arms flung wide, the green carpet prickly beneath his muslin pants, the sun bathing him in warmth. A circle of cypress trees swayed around him. He gazed up at the feathery wisps of white clouds and watched them float freely, thinning to invisibility and dissolving into the blue canopy. He imagined that he, too, could rise, float, and hover above the hills.

Just then, his body seemed to float up, and the mud-brick houses below receded into miniatures. He rose higher, became cloud, then air, then nothing—yet everything at once, a wind through all things, a spirit.

An ant bit his ankle, and the sting jolted him back to himself. His head felt heavy on the ground, his bare neck itchy, his throat scratchy with thirst. He had ascended to the celestial world! He had known god's grace.

The mystical flight stirred in the boy a spiritual yearning, which Sufis call himma. It slowly detached him from the passions of other men, from the wanting animal that lives in the body and keeps men tied to the earth. From an early age, it helped him to still his desires—except for the desire to lift off and dissolve. And his spiritual wanting became an ardent desire for god, a passion for god alone.

The community of Sufis left their home and wandered for many years, finally settling in the town of Konya in south-central Turkey. When Jelaloddin was twenty-four, his father, who was also his teacher and guide, left this world for the next. Jelaloddin stood on his father's pulpit before the community and gave a sermon for the first time. From that day on, he was known as Rumi, after the land of Rum, whose residents he would now guide.

The young man inherited his father's pulpit, his disciples, his position of great influence. Secretly, he knew that although he was intellectually prepared, spiritually he was a novice. He felt a gnawing discontent, a yearning for something more. His wife did not fill this hole. His sons didn't fill it. His knowledge didn't fill it. Even his practices of ablutions, prayer, and fasting were not enough.

For thirteen years Jelaloddin fulfilled his duty. He cared for his followers'
spiritual lives by leading prayers, interpreting religious law, resolving conflicts,
and mediating for them with local sultans. But one afternoon, as he rode his
donkey through the streets, surrounded by his loyal followers in tattered blue
robes, their questions darting about him like arrows, their turbans bobbing,
he felt particularly restless. No one among them knew of his secret longing; no
one among them could still it.

Suddenly, a wild desert dervish appeared out of nowhere and grabbed
the reins of the donkey. The dervish, his head and eyebrows shaven clean, was
dressed in rags and covered with road dust. He wore a black cloak and a pointed
felt hat and carried a massive wooden staff. His gray hawk eyes probed Rumi's.

The dervish stepped closer and asked an impertinent question. When
Rumi responded, the stranger cried, "Praise God!"

Rumi slipped from the prickly back of the donkey and fell with a thud
to the ground. He gazed up at feathery wisps of white clouds floating freely,
thinning and dissolving into the blue canopy. Just then, his body seemed to
float up and hover above the hills, the men and shops below receding into
miniatures. He rose higher, becoming cloud, then pure air, then nothing—yet
everything at once, a wind through all things, a spirit.

The dervish came forward, lifted his wooden staff into the air, and touched
Rumi between the eyebrows. Rumi felt his body jolt against the hard ground.
A blazing heat rose up his spine and burst into a white light in his forehead.

A moment later, his neck itched against the gritty dirt. He lifted his head
to see the dervish towering above him. Rumi recognized the man, though he
had never seen him before. He rose and, without bothering to look around,
took the stranger's hand and marched off with him.

From that day, Rumi stepped off the path of knowledge and onto the path
of love. From that day, he knew that his rank, his knowledge, and his family
were all veils that separated him from god. The dervish would wear for him the
face of god, and he would become a servant of love.

In the presence of the dervish, sitting knee to knee, it was easy for Rumi
to love. No wanting, no striving, no wishing for this love to be different—but
as it was, here, now. Rumi began to wonder if his devotion to the dervish was

merely a human attachment. Was he a secret idolater? Or was he seeing the face of Allah in the dervish?

When the dervish disappeared without a trace, Rumi's life became a hymn of homesickness. If his beloved was in Damascus, then Damascus was home. If he was in Samarkand, then Samarkand was the only sanctuary. Rumi longed to see him with every fiber of his life. He yearned for the sharp clarity of that voice, the tapping sound of that staff, the scent of musk coming around the corner. And as he longed for the dervish, he longed for god. As he burned for him, he burned for Him. Everything else was gone—everything but this himma, this yearning for Him.

Distraught and alone in a dark room, his green robe and turban tossed aside, Rumi lit a small taper, which cast an arc of light on the ceiling. Suddenly, unbidden images flooded him like a storm whipping through the house. They poured down in a ceaseless rain. He swooned at their hidden meanings. He folded his legs beneath him on a cushion and contemplated the inner images as they arose, entering each one's mood and landscape.

When he opened his mouth, verses flamed out. Rumi, the scholar, was long gone. The wise man, who once thought poetry was a waste of time, was taken over by these images, the pawn of a greater force.

Eventually, Rumi's loyal son found the dervish and brought him back to Konya. Again, Rumi sat face to face with his beloved, his gaze lost in those bottomless pools. Again, he rose to the sound of the dervish's viol and turned and turned on his left foot, his arms in the air like wings.

And again, the dervish disappeared. The color drained from Rumi's face. He refused food and became as thin as the dervish's staff. He refused work and wandered aimlessly through town. He ran to the city gates and accosted every visitor, without the customary greeting of peace, demanding the whereabouts of his beloved. A current of grief wrapped itself around his body.

At home he paced the room that had belonged to the dervish. Everything remained in its place: the rugs piled neatly, a few clothes in bundles. It was all there, except him. All at once, Rumi could hear the dervish's footsteps growing louder as they neared. He could hear the tapping of his staff as it touched the floor—tap, pause, tap, pause. He rose and turned toward the curtain, arms open, expecting to see him standing there. But nothing. No one. Silence.

Forty days later, he ordered mourning robes and ripped open his shirt at the chest. He stepped into the garden, placed his right hand around a post, and began to turn round and round, whispering a name of god. He leaned into the movement. The post beneath his hand disappeared. He gave himself up to the whirling, and verses, swift and startling, poured out of him.

As Rumi whirled and vanished, he became still inside. His spiritual exile was coming to an end. In the first separation from his beloved, a poet was born. That longing, that burning for the beloved, gripped him and drove the poems out of him. But desire remained—desire for the beloved.

Now, he died even to that desire. His beloved was in him; he was in his beloved. His gaze turned inward toward the brilliance of a million suns.*

⟋∽⟋∽⟍

I suggest, then, that there is an archetypal basis for the spiritual impulse in human beings, for the soul's yearning for union with a beloved or a home in the archetypal realm. Our natural longing can lead to ecstatic, numinous experience, communion, and wisdom. Or it can lead to a dark possession, emotional despair, even death. The holy longing is a two-faced archetype, with a light side and a dark side.

In our demythologized world, the holy longing persists in reminding postmodern humanity of another realm, another time, another life. It's like a finger pointing upward to Olympian heights, to our divine mirrors, to our own futures. Or downward to chthonic depths, to Dionysian splendors, to the soul breathing beneath our skin.

The burning of the holy longing brings us into the incandescence of the present moment, into the revelation of light when the veil of darkness parts. Like the bush that burns without being consumed, the seeker is alight in rapturous ecstasy.

But sometimes, in the grips of the holy longing, the dream of

---

*See my novel, *A Moth to the Flame,* for a more detailed retelling of Rumi's life story.

dissolution may take over. Then, we are infantilized in our helplessness, in the Other's omnipotence. Then, religion is a dark womb.

What is the proper stance toward our holy longing? We might take refuge from it in our rationality, attempting to think away the discomfort of the feeling or to rationalize it as an impossible dream. Or we might embrace it with open arms but closed eyes, innocently grasping at teachers or teachings that promise transcendence, while leaving ourselves open to destructive personal or group dynamics. Or we might try to relinquish the desire to go up to spirit and seek only to go down to soul, valuing body over spirit, darkness over light, immanence over transcendence.

Feminists might critique the holy longing for something Other as a sacrifice of individual power, becoming like an object to the divine subject and achieving fulfillment only at the price of autonomy and reason. Certainly, our religious institutions and creeds have been forces for social conservatism, appalling sexism, and even genocide. In fact, they have used our holy longing as currency, promising salvation or higher consciousness in exchange for obedience.

Postmodernists might critique it as a holdover of the modern era, when beliefs could simply be believed and egos could simply be taken to have substance. Certainly, our growing capacity to see through beliefs and our growing awareness of the mythic stature of the ego will, in the future, alter the way we describe religious experience.

But I propose that, for many of us, the holy longing carries the seed desire of a life story. If planted deeply enough in the soul, if allowed to gestate, if nurtured carefully, it may yield a rich harvest. Certainly, if you follow the seasons, this seed desire may lead you to the myth at the center of your life, the story that unfolds beneath your yearnings and wanderings.

However, the road is often crooked and narrow: the spiritual dream carries many believers neither into the blue sky of clarity nor into the waters of absolution; instead, it delivers us into the cloud of ambiguity, into the chaos of dissolution. With spiritual shadow-work, this very ambiguity can become a way out of the prison of spiritual innocence and into a life of greater spiritual maturity.

To the degree that we do not take our longing into our own souls, where it truly belongs, and suffer through it as a rite of passage, we will be compelled to live it out literally to the bitter end—and to live only and always in painful longing. But if we can acknowledge our religious yearning and even befriend it, and if we can detect the hidden objects of our desire, perhaps we can follow our holy longing to a higher end.

Invoked or not invoked, the gods will be present.

ORACLE AT DELPHI

Tell me what you yearn for and I shall tell you who you are. We are what we reach for, the idealized image that drives our wandering.

JAMES HILLMAN

Whether you follow the ideal of the Personal God or the impersonal Truth, you will certainly realize the One Reality, provided that you experience profound longing. The same cake tastes sweet from every direction.

RAMAKRISHNA (IN *GREAT SWAN*,
BY LEX HIXON)

The union of the soul with the light of God, this is what every member of Israel desires with all his heart and all his soul . . . to cleave to God and not to be separated from his blessed unity and oneness.

TANYA, A HASIDIC TEXT BY
RABBI SCHNEUR ZALMAN

The thing we tell of can never be found by seeking, yet only seekers find it.

BAYAZID BISTAMI

TWO

Longing for God

The Hidden Object of Desire

When you imagine god, what do you see? A stern, bearded male perched on a throne with angels circling his head? A beatific madonna seated with an innocent child at her breast? A black, four-armed goddess dancing on a corpse? Indra's net, as it weaves through and interconnects all living beings? The letters of a holy name, a colorful mandala, a sacred mountain, or a sparkling void?

Each organized religion comes with its own images of god full-blown. They may inspire awe, love, fear, guilt, or doubt. They may carry potent and life-restoring energies for a believer, or they may remain life-less and inert for a skeptic.

According to Genesis, god created human beings in its own image. Therefore, that image is a link between humans and god. Pope John's zealous imitation of saints is an example of the imitation of Christ as the divine image. It's an effort to remove the obstacles that separate lover from beloved in the Christian tradition.

In the Hindu Upanishads, the god images, or *ishta devas,* also mediate between the human world and the divine world. The scripture says, "He is, indeed, initiated whose gods within him are initiated, mind by mind, voice by voice."

Islam permits no personified image of god. But the Koran urges believers to repeat without ceasing the name of Allah and to celebrate its praises night and day. In this way, they attempt to awaken and cultivate the attributes of god, as exemplified in its ninety-nine names: mercy, compassion, light, love, sovereignty, holiness, faithfulness, peace.

Buddhism teaches that the Self is an illusion (a no-self or *anatman*); therefore, divine images are illusory. But Tibetan Buddhists use contemplation of a god or goddess as a stage of practice that promises to result in the seeker's transformation into the nature of the divine being. For instance, one contemplates Chenrezig, goddess of compassion, to become more compassionate, green Tara to remove inner obstacles, or Manjusri to sharpen the intellect. In the final stages of practice, however, the images dissolve into emptiness or non-dual reality.

In Bodhisattva Buddhism, the aspirant moves beyond the ego's longing to avoid suffering and gain happiness and yearns for the happiness of all beings. To achieve this goal, she desires to attain Buddhahood, to be purified from the veil of conflicting emotions and the veil of objects of knowledge. She desires only to be perfected by ultimate knowledge: the union of emptiness and compassion, which is beyond all concepts and images.

At a mythological level, we are what we imagine. The form we give to our divine ancestors in our collective and personal imaginations is the form we aspire to become. So, these images are, in a sense, architectural: we are building our own futures in the world of imagination. When gods are divorced from matter, seekers will disdain their bodies and the earth. When gods are perfect, seekers will strive for purity. When gods are erotic, seekers will see sexual practices as holy. As Episcopal priest Morton T. Kelsey put it, "The love and celebration of Wotan can produce Hitler and Nazism; the love and celebration of Christos, a St. Francis of Assisi."

If our self-images evolve but our god images do not, they may haunt us like ancestral ghosts. From deep within the unconscious mind, they may sabotage our conscious desires. For example, a transpersonal image of the Bodhisattva, who sacrifices all gain for the enlightenment of humanity, may serve Buddhist monks well. However, for some people with family, economic, and political responsibilities, it may interfere with the needs of a personal life. When one American Buddhist teacher prepared to marry, he found that the inner *imago* of the Bodhisattva kept him from acting on his conscious intentions to build intimate personal attachments, which inevitably involve dependency and suffering.

The ghost of a static god image also may feed feelings of shame and failure. An ex-Catholic woman approaching sixty called me because she could not recover from the shame and guilt she felt about having an abortion in her twenties. Although she no longer consciously believed in the religion of her childhood, unconsciously she carried remnants of the same unforgiving god image, which threatened to punish her for eternity. Like a water lily, that *imago* drew its life force from hidden roots in the waters of the unconscious.

The image of god also evolves in tandem with the image of the archetypal shadow in us. As we imagine the divine, we reject certain traits, which get banished into the demonic. And in this way we disown both the light of the god image and the darkness of Satan. Therefore, if our god images do not evolve, our shadow images remain static as well, narrowing the range in which we can live our conscious lives.

This chapter explores the development of human consciousness through the development of this god image within. These images emerge naturally in the human soul in response to changing circumstances that require distinct symbolic solutions. In contrast to collective symbols of established traditions that are given to us in doctrines or historical events, these images arise spontaneously in our dreams, fantasies, and projections onto other people. And they evolve continuously, offering direct access to the soul, which is not mediated by an institution.

The *imago* is not a conscious image; it's an unconscious symbol, formed by a mix of inner and outer representations of divine figures, beginning with our parents, and our unique temperaments and circumstances. And because it tends to remain hidden from conscious awareness, it carries great charge, often steering the direction of our holy longing.

The spiritual seeker yearns to touch that which is just out of reach or to see that which is just out of sight. In this way, our holy longing points the way toward an image of god, and it, in turn, can guide us in the direction of the ineffable, ungraspable, unknowable realm behind the image.

The Changing God Image
Involution or Down

[Humanity's] helplessness remains, and along with it [our] longing for the father and the gods.

SIGMUND FREUD

At each stage in the growth of human consciousness, the holy longing fuels development via a god image. The changing imagoes reflect changing modes of human experience as our holy longing goes through successive stages of projection, from early childhood figures to idealized internal figures to representations of god to, finally, nondual reality, in which the images themselves are transcended.

For some individuals, an early image carries symbolic latency. Like a seed, it holds a potential for meaning that cannot be fully grasped by childhood awareness. But, with developing consciousness, it yields sweet fruit.

In his autobiography, *Memories, Dreams, Reflections,* Jung recounted such a compelling image from his early life. As a child he carved a small man, dressed it in a coat of wood, and set it in a pencil box with a smooth, black stone from the Rhine, which he painted with color. In his imagination, the stone belonged to the wooden man. He hid them in the attic of his home, a secret that gave him a feeling of security for a year.

Many years later, Jung said, he read about soul-stones in indigenous cultures and realized that he had a clear image of one. The wooden man of his childhood was a little god of the ancient world whose life force derived from the river stone. To his surprise, he realized that as a child he had spontaneously tapped into archaic levels of the psyche via this potent image. It had captivated him, although he had not understood its meaning for many years.

It's unclear when this process of accessing the deep psyche begins. Most psychological theorists discount the possibility of consciousness in the womb or during birth, proposing instead that infants are born with a blank slate and shaped only in their early years. But recent evidence suggests otherwise. At three months, a fetus's five senses operate; its head moves away from light, and it responds to loud noises. It is stimulated by the mother's heartbeat and digestion.

The fetus floats, kicks, sighs, cries, and even does somersaults in its fluid environment. Freud imagined this prenatal sensation of union with the mother as the infant's "oceanic feeling." He viewed the later holy longing for mystical union as a childlike wish to re-merge with the mother, a regressive yearning for lost eternity.

Other psychoanalytic thinkers describe this adult fantasy as a wish to have needs met in a perfect relationship that makes no demands. The fantasy may arise in a romantic bond, a therapeutic relationship, or a spiritual liaison. In extreme cases, the individual turns to a world beyond this one for ultimate fulfillment, waiting to be rescued by an idyllic union with an all-loving Other.

But for Freud this mother-longing is not the primary source of the religious impulse. Rather, Freud believed that the origin of the religious attitude can be traced back to an infant's feeling of helplessness and consequent longing for the father's protection.

From two to six months, the infant slips in and out of unconscious unity, or symbiosis. It feels no boundary between itself and the mother's breast. Longing for fusion with the breast, the infant is soothed by it as part of itself. Does the breast carry the imago for the sucking infant? It certainly remains a powerful image throughout the life cycle of many men.

Inevitably, the infant's frustration grows because the mother cannot soothe ideally at all times. Much of psychological theory describes the results of unfulfilled longing at certain stages, where development stalls or the individual tries to skip steps. For example, if a man's symbiotic needs were unmet, he may try to get them met as an adult, yearning for an endless supply of love from his wife. But she cannot fulfill his early needs, no matter how nurturing her behavior. Thus his holy longing is displaced onto the wrong object, creating problems in his marriage.

At five or six months, the baby begins to move out of unconscious unity and distinguish between mental images and physical reality. It slowly gains a sense of self, which includes feeling, memory, and bodily awareness. At the same time, it gains a sense of Other—the ideal mother, an imago of the perfect soother. In fact, the coherence of the child's growing self-image depends on the presence of an ideal imago.

From eight months to two and a half years of age, more separation occurs, which we observe in a toddler's persistent drive to walk, despite falling again and again. During this stage, the child comes and goes from the parent, while seeking constancy from her and, at the same time, fearing abandonment. The child may alternate between clinging and rejecting behavior, as he both yearns for reunion with a permanently present imago and fears it as well.

Throughout these early stages, the baby's object of longing commonly has maternal qualities. If the infant feels nurtured at the breast, seen and recognized, she will more likely develop a sense of trust that eventually leads to faith and later experiences of transcendence. If she does not, she may feel lost and compensate by constructing a sense of her own omnipotence—a feeling of being *like* god that substitutes for the lost feeling of being *with* god.

By age three or four, the child spontaneously imagines a god who is both loving and hating, reliable and inconsistent, much like his mother. The child struggles with separation from the ideal, omnipotent god, just as he struggles with separation from the parent imago. He may submit, then rebel, placate, then reject, all the while testing his own powers through magical thinking.

(Drawing on the work of anthropologist Jean Gebser, Ken Wilber calls this stage, from ages three to five, magic because while subject and object are not clearly differentiated, the ego believes it can magically alter the world.)

On the other hand, if the mother or another adult severely traumatizes the child and her self fragments, she may fuse with god in a psychotic delusion. One schizophrenic girl whom I treated believed she was pregnant with Jesus. She had not only become the mother; she was the mother of god.

In the Oedipal stage, from age four and a half until seven, the mother image may be replaced by a representation of the stronger father, who is at once feared and hated, revered and envied. For Freud, this transition is rooted in a boy's sexual desire for his mother and his secret guilt and ambivalence toward his father, whom he wishes to kill. Freud saw this desire acted out on the stage of history when men killed their tribal leaders, from Cronos to Christ, and then idealized them as gods. To appease their guilt, they then performed repetitive rituals to propitiate the father god.

In this way, Freud linked the continual reshaping of the god image to the ever-changing parent imago. As the importance of the parents recedes, their imagoes become linked to teachers, heroes, and other authorities, including god.

Feminist researchers have pointed out that Freud's theory doesn't hold for girls because boys' and girls' Oedipal complexes are not symmetrical. A girl does not simply transfer her affection from mother to father and quickly give up her tender feelings for her mother. Instead, the bond is more likely to be sustained, and her relation to her father is added to it. Therefore, girls often come to define themselves more in relation to others, rather than as separate and isolated.

Beneath the yearning for the personal father, I suggest that we also long for the archetypal father, the father god, who alone can bestow his blessings. For some women, later in life, this masculine imago may become problematic, and the need for a feminine image of god or goddess may arise.

Between the ages of seven and ten, the child further distinguishes between god and his parents in the inner world as he faces their human limitations. In this way, god may become all that the parents are not. God may be utterly good and protective, while the parents are neglectful. Or the parents may be loving, while god withholds his gifts. For example, a boy who both loves and hates his father may isolate his tender longings and place them onto an all-loving god, leaving his father as the object of his hatred. Depending on his religious tradition, he may yearn for god the father and pray to him to intervene in his life. Or he may worship his father, despite his cruelty, and place his hatred onto Satan or another dark imago.

(Ken Wilber calls this stage, from ages six to eleven, mythic because the ego no longer believes it can perform miracles but calls on the gods to intervene through prayer or ritual.)

With the onset of puberty and hormonal changes, a teenager searches for her own identity. She yearns to separate from her family, identify with peers, and find sexual connections outside the family. Often rock stars and celebrities can carry the imago for adolescents because their unattainability permits sexual desire to erupt without danger.

In *Myths and Mysteries of Same-Sex Love,* Christine Downing pointed out that Freud saw sexuality as a vehicle through which we express our deepest yearning—our longing to be ourselves and our longing to lose ourselves. In other words, Downing notes, Freud located the holy longing in our sexual desire, making sex itself a god. So, Downing made the link between the body, the psyche, and the transpersonal realm that Freud resisted making.

During adolescence, a key period for the development of religious images, a teen may abandon the god of his childhood to separate from his parents. If he has a strong intellect, he may judge his faith as childlike and unworthy of an independent adolescent. If his feelings dominate, he may enjoy the music, ritual, or friendship in his religious community and continue to feel close to god in those ways. Or he may attribute to god the ideal qualities of his peers—friendship, loyalty, and an ability to listen. But in any case, his inner imagoes continue to be shaped by his outer experience, which in turn is interpreted by his inner world.

Researchers report conflicting imagoes during this period, perhaps reflecting our fluid gender roles. For some adolescents, the mother figure is dominant; for others, the same-sex parent is linked to god. In one study, boys emphasized objective, idealized qualities, such as purity and perfection, while girls emphasized emotional qualities, such as love and compassion.

For certain adolescents, a figure of god, such as the Virgin Mary, Christ, or Allah, becomes an ideal that, if not tempered, can lead to fanaticism. If a teenager needs to protect a vulnerable self by turning away from human imperfections and merging with a powerful god through religious belief, the seeds of fundamentalism may be planted.

I once had an older female client who had not resolved her Oedipal issues with her father and entered a cult to re-create that unfulfilled relationship with a charismatic leader. However, she remained stuck in the search for constancy and mirroring from an unavailable father figure when the teacher encouraged devotion and dependency.

(Ken Wilber calls this stage, from age eleven onward, rational because the mind dispenses with myth and tries to understand through evidence.)

From this brief review, we can see that Freud saw the holy longing as a backward pull, a means to express childlike or even infantile needs. For him, religious people are like children trusting a powerful god, who has replaced their parents. Freud believed that these needs should be overcome.

More recently, post-Freudian thinkers have expanded on his views, suggesting that the loss of boundaries in an ecstatic mystical state, for instance, may stem from a more advanced stage rather than an early, symbiotic level of development, as Freud would suggest. So, the health of the holy longing depends on our level of development. If we are caught up in primitive defenses, without a fully established ego, the desire to lose ourselves in another person may be a backward, even dangerous wish. But with the achievement of a cohesive ego, it may be a natural impulse to commune with something greater—an evolutionary will to transcend.

In addition, post-Freudians have cited multiple sources of the imago dei, insisting that it does not merely reproduce a parental figure. Other researchers measured the similarities between subjects' parental images and god images. They, too, found a complex situation: the image of god was closer to a parental composite than to a single parental image.

W. W. Meissner, an expert in the psychology of religion, pointed out that several aspects of a child's developmental experience are relevant for the shaping of an image of god. Early experiences of mirroring by the mother are key. If she is a loving and caring presence, and if the child feels recognized and cherished, he or she will more likely develop a sense of trust and acceptance that allows for religious faith. Meissner also suggested that some aspects of the imago dei derive from other significant family members, such as grandparents and siblings, or from cultural models, such as priests or rabbis.

While the holy longing pulls us nostalgically backward, it also pushes us purposefully forward. As early childhood expressions of benevolent or wrathful adults push up from the past and shape a child's image of god, the archetypal dimension calls to us as well, pulling us toward the future, toward reconciliation with the Self, toward higher levels of development.

Unlike Freud, who saw the body and its drives as the vehicle of life, Carl Jung recognized the centrality of spirituality in his patients and in the timeless myths of indigenous cultures. He viewed the religious impulse as a natural part of human life and believed that the unconscious has an authentic religious function, a special directedness toward god. Jung also saw religious issues as foundations of his patients' suffering, which often concealed a deep longing for god.

Jung even attributed to religious experience a purpose—an inherent move of the psyche that could be traced not only backward but forward, toward a future goal. That goal, individuation, is expressed by the Self, the transpersonal center of the psyche, which carries meaning, order, and value, and which belongs to the image of god. For Jung, the Self is the ideal imago, the dream of totality. It's the beginning of our inner life and the end point toward which we strive.

Jung wrote extensively throughout his thirty-year career about the psychological importance of the imago dei. He believed that psychic energy creates the god image by making use of archetypal patterns. As a result, we worship the psychic force within us as something divine.

In his early work, from 1902 to 1911, Jung agreed with Freud that religions were "fantasy systems" designed to resolve sexual problems and that the human-god relationship was rooted in the father-child bond. He saw religion as redirecting the incest wish by spiritualizing it as a relationship to transcendent realities. But, the son of a minister, he believed that individuals were cheated of their own personal relationship to the deity by traditional ethical commandments.

Over the next few years, as Jung studied mythology and began to posit the collective unconscious, he began to lessen his opposition to organized religion, thus weakening his alignment with Freud. In 1920 he referred to a religious attitude as a cultural achievement and to a symbolization of a god image as a great step beyond concrete thinking.

The foundations of Jung's thinking shifted even more as he ceased to identify the god concept exclusively with the Freudian drama of repressed wishes and began to suggest, instead, that it was a symbol of the unconscious itself. Jung soon introduced the term "god image," saying that, unlike the parent imago, which has an actual point of reference, the imago dei corresponds to nothing in the external world and thus cannot be reduced to subjective origins.

From 1921 to 1949, Jung came to see the contents of the unconscious as divine and viewed a direct, overwhelming experience of them as religious experience. In 1937 he adopted from Rudolf Otto the word *numinous* to describe an experience that seizes the individual and overtakes his or her personal will. Drawing from Otto, Jung described the archetype of the god image as having power, mystery, energy, and otherness.

As his concept of the archetypes, including the god image, developed, Jung suggested that, like all projections, the god image occurred spontaneously. He had become aware of the inadequacy of attempts to explain god images merely as symptoms of personal problems, ignoring the influence of the collective unconscious. And he recognized the god image as an archetypal symbol—as a bearer of meaning.

From 1950 to 1961, Jung revised his thinking about the link between an individual's personal history and his imago dei. He no longer saw the child-parent relationship as an adequate model.

During these years, Jung contemplated the opposites contained in symbols, including masculine and feminine, darkness and light. For instance, he saw the image of Christ as expressing the moral tension between conscious and unconscious, good and evil, human and god. But he viewed Christ as perfect, not complete; he would be completed only in relation to his opposite, the Antichrist or Devil. Thus, Jung believed that Christ and Antichrist together represent aspects of a greater totality, the original imago dei, which split into opposites in the process of Jesus's human incarnation and later Christian interpretation.

Unlike Freud, who proposed an "education to reality" in order to overcome religious thinking, Jung concluded that human beings cannot live without gods. The destruction of the god image, he believed, was followed by the destruction of the human personality.

Finally, Jung linked the religious imagination to the essence of religious life, claiming that we move in a world of images that point to something ineffable. However, we do not know whether there is something—what we call god—behind these images. We know only that, when an individual can survive as a separate person and the ego is stabilized, he or she begins to yearn for something more. For Jung, the holy longing is the ego's yearning to actualize the Self, to open the personal realm to the mythic or archetypal worlds. It's unclear whether he distinguished between the mythic and transpersonal realms. But I believe he conflated the two, unaware all those decades ago of the lived reality of nondual levels of consciousness.

The Changing God Image
Evolution or Up

All drives are a subset of that Drive, all wants a subset of that Want, all pushes a subset of that Pull— . . . the drive of God towards God . . . carried out initially through the intermediary of the human psyche.

KEN WILBER

Place your devotion whole-heartedly at the service of the ideal most natural to your being, but know with unwavering certainty that all spiritual ideals are expressions of the same supreme Presence.

RAMAKRISHNA (IN GREAT SWAN, BY LEX HIXON)

With the rise and consolidation of the ego, the holy longing is transformed from a yearning for individual separateness toward a radiant burning for union with the holy Other. It may emerge as a longing for another individual in romantic union or for a spiritual communion with a group or teacher or for a more unified state of consciousness.

Whatever the object of longing, this is a key turning point in the cycle of consciousness, where involution or "down" into matter meets evolution or "up" into spirit. Sufis call this latter leg of the journey—from individual back to source—the great return, while Jews call it *teshuvah* and more contemporary mystics and transpersonal thinkers might describe it as the evolution of consciousness from duality to nonduality. In the Christian mythos, it signals the end of the incarnation cycle of god becoming human and the burgeoning awareness of Jesus becoming the Christ in the Son/Father unity.

Traditionally, mystics and poets have pointed toward the unknown, unseen, shining source of desire. They ask: What is the dreamlike image that calls forth this intense yearning to lose oneself in order to find oneself?

The sacred traditions have mapped the ascent, which is fueled by the holy longing. They ask: Who am I? What is on the other side of the veil?

These sacred objects of longing often are imagined in spatial or temporal metaphors: above, below, within, without. Their inherent obscurity is built into our desire for them. The Latin root for the term *desire* is "ceasing to see." For this reason, the holy longing is paradoxical: it involves a blindness as well as a new kind of sight.

In Wilber's terms, this turning involves the shift from pre-personal to personal (ego) to transpersonal levels of development. Transpersonal experience, which he calls the integral stages, involves the extension of identity beyond (trans) the individual ego to encompass wider aspects of the mind, humanity, or the cosmos. In the context of transpersonal psychology, the holy longing is an innate urge to transcend the ego, to move up the ladder of evolution, to reach ever greater levels of awareness toward unity with the transcendent One.

In *Sex, Ecology, Spirituality,* Wilber described the four stages of transpersonal development—psychic, subtle, causal, and nondual—that complete the great cycle. The psychic level involves an intense union with the material realm and the natural world. For this reason, Wilber referred to it as nature mysticism. But unlike the infant's union with the mother's body, this is a conscious or transpersonal unity, not an unconscious or pre-personal one. (In more recent books, his names for the stages of development have changed.)

As Wilber put it, individuals at this stage are no longer exclusively identified with the ego. But because they preserve the ego, the force of the Self can flow through it. And with the Self, the observing witness arises on a vast expanse of silent awareness and transcends the isolated ego.

This stage is known in the spiritual literature as "cosmic consciousness," the beginning of the end of duality. Absorbed in this stage, the individual transcends senses, feelings, and thoughts and tastes union with the divine. He directly apprehends that the Self in him is the same as the Self in every other thing, a common essence. Therefore, the Self of the person and the Self of nature and the Self of culture are one and the same. And the split between subject and object, between self and world, is overcome.

Wilber pointed out that Ralph Waldo Emerson called this witness the Over-Soul and claimed that it runs through all life. So, when Emerson sang to nature, he actually sang to the Self or spirit that transcends and embraces all life. He was not, as some think, worshipping the natural world alone.

Wilber described this stage as the mystical union of matter, life, and culture. It's a result of self-development through self-transcendence; in this case, it's the result of going beyond the ego. And it entails a new ethic: because all sentient beings are expressions of one Self, they should be treated as one's Self. As Wilber said, that realization is the source of true compassion—not a moral imperative, but a natural outgrowth of the development of consciousness.

At the subtle level, another, deeper transcendence occurs: nature mysticism gives way to deity mysticism. The Self or spirit that is within and beyond nature, culture, and earth, that is the source and goal of evolution, comes forward. The person experiences subtle sounds and lights, raptures and ecstasies.

It is here that the object of our holy longing, in the form of an imago dei, becomes most consciously radiant. St. Teresa of Ávila chronicled the rapture, the visions, and the yearning on the way to the establishment of union in her sixteenth-century personal account, *The Interior Castle*. She described her first experience of transcendence with a famous metaphor: The ego, like a worm, emerges as a butterfly in this psychic stage. The butterfly yearns for the flame of spirit, in which it is extinguished in the next level of transcendence, the subtle stage.

At this stage, preliminary union is apprehended but not fully established. Teresa describes it as two candles that are joined to give off one light but can be broken apart again.

In the causal level, one becomes established in the direct experience of union with the divine, which Teresa calls the spiritual marriage. As the ego (worm) died and was reborn as the soul (butterfly), now the soul enters its final union and dies as a separate self—its end point.

We can observe in St. Teresa's evolution how the end point of each stage pulls development in its direction. As she establishes a level of consciousness, the holy longing, which had driven evolution that far, subsides. Then, slowly, a new force emerges, urging transcendence once more, and her level of consciousness becomes unstable. The soul's holy longing urges her toward the next, higher level of integration, and evolution unfolds toward its end point. At each stage, development proceeds as she transcends and integrates each earlier level of consciousness. In this way, each stage finds its fulfillment, and evolution moves toward complete union of the soul with god.

In the causal level, according to Wilber, the soul and spirit, previously united, are now transcended in the prior identity of formless awareness or pure consciousness. That is, the Self *is* spirit, Atman *is* Brahman. The Self is no longer united with spirit but fully identified with it.

In Vedanta, this realization is known as *nirvikalpa* samadhi, or awareness without any qualities or objects. We can observe it in descriptions of the later years of Ramakrishna's life, as told in chapter 1.

Meister Eckhart called this experience the naked existence of godhead. Here the godhead transcends and includes all worlds. It is, for Eckhart, completely free of all duality and, therefore, "empty," beyond images, concepts, or the witness, beyond intermediaries of any kind.

In this stage of union, the imago disappears. As Plotinus put it, "We must not be surprised that that which excites the keenest of longings is without any form, even spiritual form."

Going beyond this identification with formless, boundless, unmanifest spirit, we come to identify with all form. All manifestation appears as a perfect expression of the Self or spirit in the nondual ground of all stages and dimensions. The formless and the world of form are not two, but nondual; not two, but one, as the Sanskrit word *advaita* means.

In Vedanta, this realization is known as *sahaj* samadhi, which means "unbroken and spontaneous so." At this level, nirvana *is* samsara. Brahman *is* the world. Or, as Wilber put it, when all things are nothing but god, there are then no things, and no god, but only *That*. (Wilber's more recent work on stages now elucidates ten levels of consciousness; see his book *Integral Spirituality*.)

I have had the privilege of intimately knowing several people in these higher stages of awareness. One experiences the cosmos and everything in it within his own body. Another, whose sense of "I" is unbounded, can put his attention on the smallest or largest object, the closest or furthest object, and see only *That*. He told me, "I am not this body. I am not these thoughts. I am not my story. I am not the doer. I am *That*."

This, then, is the great cycle of consciousness—the "downward" arc (descent) into individuality and the "upward" arc (ascent) into universality or enlightenment. Although it may appear that spirit is the highest rung on the ladder of evolution, paradoxically, spirit is also the wood out of which the entire ladder and the rungs are made, to use Wilber's metaphor.

In other words, the two aspects of spirit are its transcendental nature and its immanent nature. In this sense, nothing is closer to spirit than anything else. Thus, spirit is the source, the course, and the goal of all evolution.

⚭ THE INNER MARRIAGE ⚭

A Story of Holy Longing in the Hindu Master Ramakrishna

Ramakrishna, a nineteenth-century Indian saint known as Paramahansa, or Great Swan, lived in a garden by the Ganges River near a domed temple dedicated to the goddess Kali, the mother of birth, death, and transformation. Before Ramakrishna's birth, his father had a dream in which the god Vishnu promised to be born as his son. His mother also had a vision of giving birth to a divine child.

When Ramakrishna was a young child, these omens appeared to bear fruit. When the boy portrayed various Hindu gods in religious plays, he lost himself in worshipful contemplation. As he grew, his intensely emotional and devout attitude grew, too, and he directed it toward the divine. Eventually, his bhakti or devotion opened him to a great yearning for a revelation of Kali, the divine mother. Leaving behind ritual duties, he simply sat before her stone image and sang devotional songs.

As Lex Hixon, in Great Swan, tells us, in his late teens Ramakrishna had a vision of his imago dei. Her black form rose out of a golden ocean, with waves rushing at him from all sides. He remained in an ecstatic state for several years, permeated by her radiance, unable to tell day from night. Observers called him the "mad priest of Dakshineswar," but he was mad with divine love.

Ramakrishna reported that for many years, in his painful yearning for god, he was like a bird shrieking for its mate, a kitten mewing for its mother, a cow lowing for its calf. The mention of a divine name would cause his body to catch fire with ecstasy.

He saw himself as a child of Kali, who projects the world from her own essence. He worshipped her through a young girl in the temple garden, or a passing prostitute, or an advanced practitioner. Later, he dressed in a red sari, and her divine manifestation passed through his form—he became her. All separation dissolved.

In the dawn light, the scent of incense filling the air, Ramakrishna bowed before a black basalt image of Kali adorned with colorful flowers, while chanting in Bengali the names of god. Then he sat on a white cloth, half naked and chewing spices, and welcomed his visitors as messengers of his beloved. They bowed and touched their foreheads to the floor upon entering.

Ramakrishna spoke of the path and goal of the mystic way: passionate immersion in god. Suddenly, this all-embracing love of which he spoke overtook him, and he urged his disciples to cry to the Lord God with an intensely yearning heart. Too many people shed tears for their children or for money, he said. Instead, cry to the Lord.

He likened our longing to the rosy dawn. After the dawn, the sun comes out. In just the same way, he said, longing is followed by a vision of god. Then his eyes rolled up, his breath stilled, and he disappeared into a state of absorption.

Ramakrishna sought to experience the divine presence through all sacred traditions, so he undertook practices from Tantra, Vedanta, Islam, and Christianity. Eventually he could embody the holy figures of these religions and transmit their energies through his own form. In this way, he expressed and transcended the gods and goddesses and merged into the greater spirit.

For example, when he practiced remembrance of the name of Allah and became absorbed in it, he had a vision in which Prophet Muhammad's radiant form blended with his own. When he concentrated on Christ, he merged with the divine form of Jesus.

A visitor belittled Ramakrishna's god images as figments of the imagination. The holy man responded by asking the visitor to consider the yearning of those who follow this path. It's like the attraction between lovers who long to meet and merge, he said. More than that, it's like the divine lovers Radha and Krishna, for whom this burning attraction is infinite. Those practitioners who commune with the divine through sacred icons shed tears of longing to be able to penetrate the outer forms of wood, stone, or clay. They long to experience divine reality directly. We can echo their cry and ignore the images they worship, he said. This is another path to god realization.

Eventually, Ramakrishna cut through his own personal image of the divine, the goddess Kali. Her form dissolved, and his self disappeared into her formlessness. For three days he sat in a high level of samadhi, united with god.

When his wife asked him not to remain in the formlessness of bliss but to return to the edge of individuality, he learned to operate in that gap between the pure consciousness of samadhi and the waking state. He moved in and out of the open sky of unity, impervious to duality.

Ramakrishna reportedly once said that young men and women who long for god from childhood are divine in human form. They are god nakedly longing for god.

⁊⟨◦⟩⁊

During both involution and evolution, the imago calls to us. It is the lure to consciousness. Whether the archetype is disguised in the clothing of the mother who cannot be won, the beloved who cannot be possessed, or the home that cannot be found, it is ours to continually approach, to approximate, to yearn for.

For many years, I have wondered why the theme of exile recurs in religious history. Today I see exile as a symbol for the separation from the divine, specifically from our images of god. During these fallow periods of exile, the holy longing of a people for a homeland and a new imago can be intense. With the destruction of the first Jewish temple in Jerusalem and the exile in Babylonia, the tribal deity of the Jews was transformed. Bishop John Spong suggested that the Christian community is undergoing a similar ordeal today: exile from an outdated Church and yearning for an updated image of god.

Likewise, for an individual, the separation from an imago, because it no longer holds holiness or serves the soul, leaves him or her feeling like a refugee in exile. When the Sufi poet Rumi could no longer gaze upon the face of his beloved teacher, which had become for him the face of god, he wandered aimlessly in a desert of thirst until he attained a new level of consciousness.

I had a similar experience: when the imago of the self-realized yogi who was my teacher became tarnished for me, I felt compelled to leave my spiritual community to maintain my integrity. I felt lost and alone, a homeless wanderer without direction or companionship until, eventually, a fresh imago emerged.

Therefore, as we develop, our image of the divine must evolve as well. If it remains all-powerful, we may remain feeling childlike. If it remains all-knowing, we may remain feeling ignorant. If we imagine a formless god, one that is not a being but a state of being, we may remain feeling inadequate and unenlightened, striving to attain the unattainable.

Today, at the height of the ego's reign, many people believe we have outgrown the gods. They can be explained away as projections or reduced to childhood fantasies. But I believe, with Jung, that the arche-type of god incarnates within us as the Self, a spark of the divine. And it will be present, called or uncalled.

If the imago remains unconscious, if it acts upon us outside the boundaries of awareness, then it can pull us like a magnet toward unknown territory. It can keep the heart in bondage to childhood rep-resentations. It can trap the mind in idolatry. It can cause the soul to wander endlessly, without rest.

With our overemphasis on rationality, the holy longing has been banished. In turn, this has resulted in the widespread loss of the imago dei. However, just as building a relationship with our shadow images can deepen and enrich our soul life, so can a meeting with the god image. In our society, that encounter often takes place when we fall in love.

Who is it we spend our entire life loving?

KABIR (TRANS. BY ROBERT BLY)

Who is your double in the extended realm of the soul? . . . Who or what is it that is yearning for you, calling to you; who is the Beloved you are always trying to remember?

JEAN HOUSTON

I tasted you, and I now hunger and thirst for you; You touched me, and I have burned for your peace.

ST. AUGUSTINE

The only beloved is the living mystery itself.

KATHLEEN RAINE

What is behind all this desirousness? A thirsting for the eternal. . . . Desire only burns in order to burn itself out, and in and from this fire arises the true living spirit which generates life according to its own laws.

C. G. JUNG

THREE

Longing for the Human Beloved

The Search for Romantic Union

Like a moth longing for the flame, insane for the light that will extinguish its very life, the lover longs for the beloved partner. To further paraphrase Goethe's poem "Holy Longing," given in chapter 1: As long as you have not experienced this loss of your self in another, you are only a guest on this earth.

This chapter examines the holy longing in the context of romantic love. In many relationships, one person is like a moth, yearning to dissolve boundaries and melt in ecstatic union. The other is like a flame, burning brightly on its own. The first person suffers terribly with separation, sensing even the slightest rejection as abandonment or loss. The second person suffers terribly with fears of being smothered or snuffed out, as if the partner could extinguish her light.

What is the relationship between this longing for a human beloved, or imago amore, and the longing for the divine beloved, or imago dei?

The Greek god of desire, Eros, helps us imagine our human desire as a divine power by giving it the name of a god. This naming honors the awesomeness of our experience of it. The ego cannot willfully direct our desire; it directs us. We cannot make ourselves desire one object over another; the objects of our desire choose us. We cannot even make ourselves stop desiring an object. Therefore, we are subject to it, as we are subject to a god.

Eros appears on the threshold between our reach and our grasp, drawing a thin line between subject and object, lover and beloved, and thereby stoking the fires of holy longing. We glimpse the beloved, and walls of separation crumble. We gaze into our beloved's eyes and recognize an ancient symmetry. We hear an obscure call to ascend, to leave our limitations behind in a flight toward the heavens. An instant later, we are jolted back to earth, inside our own skin, inside our own solitude, inside our own suffering.

The god Eros lives in this gap between what we have and what we seek, what we are and what we are becoming. He turns the object of our projection into the numinous Other, forever present, forever unattainable.

This god points to the root of human nature as desiring and longing. He speaks to an urge that is more fundamental than a desire for a person or a thing. I suggest that it's not people we crave; it's not sexual union; it's not material satisfaction. It's self-transcendence toward a higher level of spirit, toward union with god.

And Eros *is* that driving force in the cosmos. Eros is the holy longing of the human for the divine, the longing of the one for the holy Other. And when it appears in the form of romantic yearning, it is ultimately a spiritual desire for greater and greater union or completion.

Therefore, the erotic yearning of human love both conceals and reveals divine love. It is not simply individual longing; it contains or reflects cosmic longing. Within or behind the person we love, we seek an object of worship, an imago amore, a means to connect to the divine.

So, the purpose of love is not what it seems. It is not merely about forming partnership and family for love and security. Rather, its inner purpose is to evoke an image of the long-lost beloved, whose call initiates an unpredictable and sometimes painful journey back to the Self.

This motif has appeared many times in human history and legend. Between the eleventh and thirteenth centuries, the Christian tradition of courtly love emerged, in which knights and troubadours pined with ardent longing for married women. The woman's amiable smile charmed them; her gentle voice seemed celestial; her eyes shone like jewels. The knights felt their ardor from a distance and held the beloved's image in their hearts.

Because the object of their desires was unattainable, the knights' love could be spiritualized, their devotion refined and perfected. They submitted to the wound of unrequited longing, asking nothing of the beloved, and in this way their desires were purified of ego. They praised her and served her selflessly, cultivating the Christian virtues of patience, fidelity, humility, and faith. And internally, in an exchange of hearts, they united with her, resting their heads on her breast, just as St. John rested on Christ's.

In this context, the lady, the imago amore, stood in for something greater, something more transcendent, a mirror of the divine beloved. Therefore, she came to be called a "mystical queen." The knight's devotion to her prepared his heart for higher devotion. The aim of troubadour love was not to marry; it was to prepare the soul for union with god.

The same point can be made about Dante. He first glimpsed Beatrice when she was eight years old, and he was nine. Nonetheless, he claimed that, from that moment, love would govern his soul. Although each of them married another, Dante cherished Beatrice's imago and, eventually, it enabled him to ascend in the *Paradiso* toward divine love.

I confess that I, too, suffered the same rapture and torment as a young girl. While still very young, I went to school with a boy named Steve. When I first saw him, I knew, in my tiny heart, that one life had ended and another begun. When I watched him across the schoolyard, an inexplicable, wistful yearning descended on me. He seemed perfect, shining, godlike. Yet he was just out of reach. When, for brief moments, we spoke or danced together, I grew wings.

My parents became worried. Such an intense infatuation at such a young age seemed unnatural. They wanted to rescue me or fix me. But my longing only grew stronger. I was not content to contemplate his beauty from afar. I imagined that Steve and I would marry one day, and this terrible yearning would end when I shared life with him. No other images of union were available to me.

As the winds of life swept us apart through the years of middle school and high school, I continued to watch him, just out of reach across the classroom or the schoolyard. His blond curls, his freckled nose, his blue eyes haunted me. Until one night, lying on my back and reaching up to the heavens, I called out for help—and all of the radiant burning that had been directed toward Steve suddenly changed direction: I yearned for god.

The wrenching cessation of my romantic longing was the poignant beginning of my spiritual life. When I saw Steve the next day and the day after that, I still beheld a vision of beauty. I still felt the pain of separation from him. But something larger stirred in my heart. I began to see it through him, not merely in him.

When college took me out of town, I still carried Steve's image tenderly within me. But other images of the beloved began to appear. And when his life took a tragic turn and he was taken away finally and forever, I still loved that boy in the man fiercely. But I came to feel, as Dante did, that what I had fallen in love with at such a tender age was not Steve, but the divine beloved, the imago amore that lived in him.

Today I feel deep gratitude to the boy and to the divine image that he carried for me. Together they prepared my soul to love god and awakened in me the holy longing, the yearning that still stirs today and leads me to this moment in which I write these words.

Therefore, rather than focus on how to achieve a love union in daily life, which is a widespread preoccupation in our romance-obsessed culture, this chapter explores the separation that is inherent in any union, the impossibility of possessing the beloved. For those who feel they cannot find a worthy partner, the separation is all they know. Longing to be cherished, even ennobled in the eyes of a loved one, they may devalue their accomplishments and their other relationships, which seem meaningless unless they are shared with that special person.

For those who have known the beloved and lost him or her, whether through abandonment or death, the separation can be acute and consuming. If they believe that the object of their desire has been present and is then absent, their desire burns. Praying fervently for the return of the beloved who can grant fulfillment, they may feel that nothing else can quench this thirst.

For those who are graced to share daily life with their beloved, separation is also ever present. It is suffered in the very nature of our closeness and our distance, our sameness and our otherness. We sense it as we feel the press of skin on skin but cannot go deeper into one another. We know it as we hit the wall of a different opinion or the fortress of a separate reality and cannot find common ground. We intuit it as we watch our lives unfold in different directions, as if we follow two parallel paths that can never meet. In the end, we understand what the poet Rainer Maria Rilke meant when he said that love is two solitudes watching over one another.

Finally, for those who yearn for the divine child to redeem them from their own choices and limitations, separation is poignant. No matter how we cling, from the beginning it's evident that a child has a temperament and fate of his or her own.

Psychologically, we might say that consciousness grows through cycles of union and separation, through seeing the difference between ego and Other and transcending that difference. But separation can be a dark passage, accompanied by a painful yearning to return, to reconnect again with the source.

I suggest that, despite inherent separation, an image of the beloved can be accessed through an individual soul's desire. And, like the imago dei, the imago amore evolves as our consciousness develops. Therefore, as the tension of otherness ignites our yearning, love becomes a vehicle of evolution.

Beloved as Parent
The Psychology of Love

Behind the search for the Magical Other lies the archetypal
power of the parental imagos. Our first experience of
ourselves is in relationship to these Primal Others.

JAMES HOLLIS

We are conceived in desire. Our mouths salivate with desire. Our genitals burn with desire. Our hands grasp with desire. Our eyes gaze with desire. We yearn to melt into the beloved, to find our other half, and to lose ourselves in eternal union.

The romantic search today has taken on religious proportions. We long for the ideal partner, the beloved Other, as we long for god, the holy Other. It is in our intimate lives and our spiritual lives that we are most likely to meet the Self or imago dei. It is also in our relationships and our religions that we become most wounded and disillusioned.

Perhaps this occurs because, inevitably, we bring our early unmet emotional needs to a romantic union. Hidden within our erotic yearnings lie childlike yearnings—the desire to return to a lost garden of innocence, the longing for unconditional love and acceptance, the wish to depend on someone else to satisfy our needs. When we meet a potential partner and fall in love, all of these hopes are activated, and with them, an intense yearning to merge arises in our souls.

If we long to merge with a mother or father imago in a symbiotic union, we re-create the early, unconscious bond with a parent. For this reason, we unknowingly attribute highly positive traits to our partners and imagine that they will be the perfect parents, fulfilling the ideal parent imago in the exact ways that our own parents did not. For example, a young man imagines that his girlfriend always will be emotionally available and nurturing, unlike his absent mother. A young woman imagines that her boyfriend always will be kind and supportive, unlike her critical and controlling father. This is a natural and inevitable process of projection that allows the unconscious bond to form between two lovers and feels to them like a mysterious alliance, an echo of the past.

These fantasy images of the beloved—generous, pure, kind, selfless, controlling, abandoning, cruel—are, in part, made up of familiar parental qualities. When we feel a harmonic match with another person, a familiar resonance, we reawaken to our soul's dream of union, and we re-create early childhood patterns of loving and wounding.

These projections may take on mythic proportions, as we imagine that our partner is a hero or savior whose qualities will save us from the limitations of our parents. When one of my clients was an infant, her father died of tuberculosis. And as she grew, the secret promise of his love grew too. That promise became an emptiness inside her, a hunger for love or, more accurately, for union with the ghost of her father—an impossible union.

She soon found unavailable men to stoke the fires of her longing—married men, gay men, and other inappropriate partners for her. She believed that bonding with a man would end her yearning. But then who would she become? This unknown identity terrified her, so she chose the yearning over a loving relationship.

Eventually, she projected her longing onto spiritual teachers, but the emptiness remained. One would feed her mind for a while; another would receive her devotion. But in the end, their human flaws became apparent, and they fell from grace, shattering her ideal imago. She cried out in grief and rage at them, but they were just limited human beings, she told me. God was really to blame.

Slowly, this dream of union with her lost father/god loosened its grip. No human on the outside and no image on the inside could fill her up. She was thrown back on herself, on her own resources, on her own feelings. Eventually, she began to permit herself to feel the yearning without trying to fix it. She began to turn within rather than to external saviors. She practiced yoga daily, wrote in her journal each morning, and found words and images to tell the tale of her anxious restlessness and wistful yearning. Gradually, the psychic energy that she had been giving away all those years began to return home.

Jungian analyst Marion Woodman calls this archetypal pattern the ghostly lover. She tells the story of poet Emily Dickinson, who shared her father's pursuits and standards of perfection. In fact, she lived to please her father. As Woodman put it, he controlled her soul.

Unconsciously bound to a father/god, Dickinson fell in love with an unavailable man and projected her parent imago onto him. In her fantasy, she lived in a world that could never be, a life removed from reality. And she remained a child in her father's house, a maiden in white writing poems.

Although we are grateful today that Dickinson was able to turn her suffering into art, we feel dismay if we consider her actual life. Cut off from her bodily instincts and her capacity to develop maturity, instead she worshipped an imago from afar and displaced her passion onto the page. Confined by her cultural moment, unable to rebel or to live out her own life, she raged at god, who demanded her suffering and withheld her happiness.

In some cases, the yearning for an unavailable lover may involve an Oedipal imago, an adolescent desire for the opposite-sex parent who is bonded to someone else. These triangles are evident in some marital affairs, in which one dreams of killing off the same-sex spouse in order to win the other for oneself. And they are evident in family systems, in which a child intervenes between the parents and takes over the energy and attention of one of them.

The romantic longing due to separation also may occur when a parent was physically present but emotionally absent. This was the case for a couple in their twenties who came to me for marital therapy. The young man, who was initially drawn to his wife's independence, now suffered terribly when she pulled away to work, spent time with friends, or defended herself against his neediness. He felt neglected and abandoned, as he did as a child when his emotionally unavailable mother left him with a nanny each day. In order to fend off intense feelings of abandonment and loneliness, he sought to merge with his beloved through sexual intimacy. But these moments of pre-personal union were never enough to fill the emptiness.

Ever watchful for his wife's psychic or emotional withdrawal, he demanded that she open up more deeply and offer more nurturing. He seduced her into sexual contact more frequently than she wanted, and he criticized her for being distant and uncaring in a frenzied attempt to uphold his parent imago.

The result: She felt trapped, controlled, and inadequate as a partner. Somehow, she could never get it quite right for him. Remarkably, she had felt the same way as a child in the face of her demanding alcoholic father. Powerless when confronted by his mood swings and constant criticism, she learned to placate him, to try to care for his needs, and to withdraw when she failed. So, in her marriage, she yearned for separateness, for time alone to daydream and to feel free of control and caretaking.

While the husband—projecting his mother imago—needed more relatedness and felt traumatized with abandonment when he didn't receive it, the wife projected her father imago and felt traumatized with engulfment, as if she would be devoured. He drew close to her flame; she sputtered, fearing she would be snuffed out. As a result, they developed strategies to manage their anxiety and to attempt to heal their own childhood wounds. But they ended up in chronic crises around their respective unmet needs, while they simultaneously re-wound each other in repeating patterns. Unable to hold the tension between separateness and union, eventually they became resentful and hopeless.

This opposition between my clients appears to be a power struggle between two sets of needs, both conscious and unconscious. However, beneath a negotiation for time together and time apart, emotional union and emotional separateness, there lies a deeper impulse: the yearning for self-transcendence through a series of projections and disappointments, which constitutes the nature of every intense loving relationship.

When the partners learned to work with their own imagoes and withdraw their projections, their relationship evolved, moving through the levels of consciousness: from symbiotic to magic to mythic to rational to transpersonal. At the rational stage, an adult relationship emerges, in which each person has a consolidated ego that is independent enough to relate to the other through rational negotiation of differences. In my clients' marriage, the partners learned to experience their separateness as acceptable, even enjoying time alone. And they learned to join together (union) for reasons of compatibility to achieve tasks. At this rational stage, they could bypass difficult unconscious emotional material and function well together in a clear division of roles. But they often reported that although their union was harmonious, it was not juicy. It lacked a spiritual foundation.

Ideally, this rational level of development can become a platform for spiritual development beyond ego. A few years later, when they each learned meditation and began to detect their holy longing, they moved toward a more transpersonal connection with one another, beyond their roles to a deeper spiritual identity. In this way, human love promises to initiate us into divine love.

Beloved as God
The Archetypes of Love

Every lover is fain that his beloved should be of a nature like to his own god . . . his every act is aimed at bringing the beloved to be every whit like unto himself and unto the god of their worship.

PLATO'S PHAEDRUS

The man who identifies with his own ideal . . . cannot accept that the white radiance of his beloved can be stained by the humanity of her excremental functions.

MARION WOODMAN

Clearly, the parent imago is not the sole hidden object of our desire when we fall in love. On a deeper level, the search for the romantic beloved is a spiritual search, an attempt to return not merely to the oceanic feeling but to conscious, ecstatic union with the divine. This process takes place via the projection of the Self onto the idealized Other, who becomes soulmate, hero, goddess, savior. As a result, the imago amore appears to reside in the beloved, and the lover yearns for union with him or her.

In a case history of holy longing for the romantic beloved, detailed in *Psychology of the Unconscious,* Jung explored the written fantasies and poems of a young American woman named "Miss Miller." While traveling from New York to Europe, she spent long hours writing poetry in a dreamlike state on a ship's deck. When she caught a glimpse of a handsome officer on deck for the night watch, his image opened a new world to the girl, a world of erotic yearning.

Following her vision of the man, Miss Miller wrote a poem, "The Moth to the Sun," describing her glimpse of the beloved and her resulting longing that, like the moth's, could end only in a rapturous death. Jung suggested that she had to bury her sexual feelings and, to avoid that inner conflict, unconsciously wrote a hymn to a masculine god, thereby replacing earthly love with heavenly love. He pointed out that her hopeful tone could not be sustained because the longing returned again and again. Her hope was in vain, Jung said, because she was a mortal who was momentarily borne up on the wings of her longing into the light—and then sank down again to death.

But I suggest that disappointment and loss are inevitable in intense romantic relationships even when they are consummated in intimacy and marriage. During romance, the Self is activated, and we feel special, purposeful, and even exalted. The beloved seems to be divine because he or she provides access to the qualities of the Self, or imago amore.

But we cannot possess that moment; we cannot control it, for it is larger than us. It is not personal but archetypal. So, when a partner disappoints us or betrays us, which is inevitable, the projection of the

Self rattles. The guardian of the imago fails us in some way, and we feel emptiness and despair.

If we unconsciously believe that the Other is responsible for our experience of meaning and purpose, then we may try to coerce his or her words and actions to meet our needs. For a moment, for example, a woman may carry the imago again for her husband, and he may feel his fragmented self cohere with meaning and worthiness. But in the next moment, she fails him again, and he rages against the loss. So, he will try to get her to behave once more in ways that rebuild the projection and maintain his imago.

However, in this process he will not see her as she is. And she will feel used and controlled. Eventually, she may feel resentful and become unwilling to provide the Self for him.

Thus the risks for the lover are great. Those who project the ideal suffer diminishment and loss, identifying with the inferior, unworthy position in a relationship. In giving away the light, they fail to know it in themselves. They may suffer terrible cycles of gain and loss, happiness and despair, while continuing to believe that their partner is responsible for these swings.

In addition, if they project power and knowledge onto their partner, they may sacrifice their own authority and silence their own voice. In extreme cases, they may become hostages to love, believing that they can survive only when their relationship is enacted in specific ways.

The risks for the beloved are also high; those who carry the ideal Self for another may suffer under its weight. Unconsciously, they may feel the pressure to live out their partner's ideal imago, rather than live an authentic life. One woman, seen by her boyfriend as a goddess, told me that she felt idolized, not loved; she felt objectified, not seen. Individuals who are the target of such spiritual projections may get snared in identifying with them and become inflated, feeling themselves to be special or powerful, which may lead to narcissistic abusive behavior.

Those inner and outer figures who carry the Self or imago amore for others can appear via many archetypal images. They are shaped by our parent imagoes, the symbolic landscape of our play, the intellectual landscape of our education, and cultural messages about masculine and feminine beauty. If we feel needy or helpless and long to be saved or rescued, we may be attracted to the lover who appears as hero or savior. If we feel flawed and long for healing, we may be drawn to the lover who appears as healer. If we feel dry or empty and long for juicy, erotic passion, we may be drawn to the lover who appears as a wild, unrestrained Dionysus or Aphrodite or to a playful divine child. If we feel insecure and yearn for approval, we may be attracted to the lover who appears as a good mother or father, teacher, or mentor.

In her book *In Search of Woman's Passionate Soul,* Caitlín Matthews described the development of the inner image of her own masculine ideal. In early childhood, she played with invisible companions who were feminine. But with the onset of menstruation and her body's transition into womanhood, that inner figure became masculine, primarily a swashbuckling pirate who performed daring deeds on the high seas. Matthews attributed her early marriage to a man who lived outside the margins of society to the influence of this inner masculine ideal. Later, the inner masculine figure became an ancient Irish poet, who guides her creative life to this day.

One of my male clients recalled feeling his longing aroused at an all-boys college when he studied Renaissance humanists and poets. The world of imagination opened to him and a current ran through his body. At night, he peered up at the starry sky and called out to his poet-heroes, "Where are you?" He hoped that these eternal spirits would be his companions in the realm of creative imagination.

In this man's third year at college, women were permitted to attend for the first time. He remembered one woman in particular whose large breasts captivated him. From that moment, his longing became eroticized and directed toward the feminine ideal.

During a period of career building and marriage, he said, his holy longing was dormant, the fire banked. But later, when he met a woman whose life was dedicated to exploring creativity and consciousness, his longing burst into flame. Suddenly, he yearned for the freedom, openness, and creative potential that she represented for him. When he was with her, he felt alive, optimistic, and imaginative.

As long as this woman carried the feminine ideal for him, he felt liberated by her. His masculinity awakened at a deeper level, and at the same time, his hunger for the spiritual dimension increased. But when, through psychedelics and later through meditation, he began to have a direct experience of the Self, his reliance on her lessened. Instead of the woman acting as his guide to the soul, his own inner ideal became his guide.

Another client, who had little interest in dating and marriage, met her imago in a series of male friends. In college, she felt a platonic partnership with a man who set her on the back of his motorcycle and took her away from academic life on wild adventures. Later, she formed a deep spiritual friendship with a man who matched her intellectual gifts and became like a member of her family. In her forties, she befriended another man with whom she lived, as brother and sister, for several years. For her, the soul brother carried the imago.

In whatever image it appears, the romantic beloved brings a meeting with the Other. And because of its autonomy, it often brings suffering, lack of control, and lack of certainty. The very safety that we may have sought in a relationship remains elusive. But the inner marriage awaits.

∾ THE INNER MARRIAGE ❧

A Story of Holy Longing in the Sufi Lovers Majnun and Layla

In the love-mad religion of Sufism, there is a famous tale recalled even to this day in the poems and songs of many peoples. In it we can glimpse the possibility that love brings self-transcendence, even union with the divine—the inner marriage.

As told by twelfth-century Persian poet Nizami, a Bedouin nobleman had satisfied all of his desires but one: he had no son in whose memory he would live on. As he grew older, his yearning for a son grew greater. Yet for many years his prayers and alms were in vain.

Then, late in life, the man's wife gave birth to a boy, whose jewel shone through the veil of his body. They called him Qays, and he became as tall and slender as a cypress.

When he was a young boy, a girl named Layla joined his class at school, and Qays's heart filled with longing at the sight of her. Layla's face was a lamp beneath the dark shadow of her hair. Her eyes were like a gazelle's, her lips like roses. She, too, drank the potion and became drunk on the sight of her beloved.

Intoxicated with one another, they turned away from the world, but the world turned toward them, taunting them with judgment and jealousy. Qays's mind urged him to avoid Layla, but his heart was torn with desire for her. Togetherness was dangerous; separation was torture.

Layla's tribe tried to protect her honor: they guarded her at home, where she hid the sorrow in her heart.

Unable to see her, Qays roamed about like a sleepwalker, stumbling and falling. He wandered aimlessly in small alleys between the tents and among the stalls in the bazaar, where merchants sold food and spices. He sang melancholy songs, lamenting his lost love, as tears flowed down his cheeks. He lost not only his beloved; he lost himself.

The people said, "He is a majnun, *a madman." And the more they called him that, the more he became Majnun, until his vain hopes chased him out into the desert, barefoot and bareheaded. All at once, under a blue tent of sky, verses poured out of his mouth—a message for Layla to be carried on the east wind. "Invisible candle, do not torment the moth fluttering around you. My longing is my heart's consolation, its wound and its healing balm."*

At night, when others slept, he snuck back to the tribe and kissed the threshold of Layla's tent. He crawled away again before the first light, escaping her in order to find her.

Empty-handed, his coarse robe torn to shreds from top to bottom, his hair matted about his face, he roamed the deserts aimlessly. As he wandered, he composed verses and called out her name—Layla, Layla—again and again, like chanting the name of god. All other desires burned away but the desire for union with her. All other images dissolved but the image of her lovely face, the face of his beloved. She was a rosebush; he watered it with his tears.

Majnun's father made the pilgrimage to Mecca to pray for his son, to no avail. He traveled into the mountains to find him and pleaded with him to come home and find pleasure there. But the son replied that he did not choose his fate; it chose him, and he was caught in its noose.

In the meantime, Layla became lovelier to those who saw her. But she saw only Majnun; her eyes formed only the image of him.

One afternoon in the bazaar, a child was singing the verses of Majnun, like a nightingale in spring. Soon, every wanderer was singing his songs and bringing them to the people. Layla could hear the voice of her lover in their voices. She wrote down the verses on scraps of paper and entrusted them to the wind. When someone found one of them, he carried it to Majnun with the hope of hearing a response. The beloved answered at once; the messenger memorized the verse and, upon returning, delivered it to Layla.

Troubled by the madman's raving and the attention he drew to their daughter, Layla's parents made plans to marry her to another. Sitting in a litter carried by camels, bedecked like a princess, she made the journey from her tribe's tents to her husband's. But that night, when he tried to enter her garden, Layla told him that she was sworn to another man and would never share his bed. While the husband's eyes searched for Layla, hers looked only for Majnun.

Majnun's life became nothing but longing for Layla—for Her. All other desires burned away in the flame that was desire for Her. He became detached from the things of this world—the pleasures, the sorrows, the comforts, the pains. As the Sufis say, he ate the eater in himself.

In the dark of night, Majnun cried out his prayers to the glittering stars. When a deep calm arrived, he slept and dreamed of a tree growing out of the ground to great heights in front of him. When he looked up, he saw a bird fluttering through the leaves toward him. Something glittered in its beak. The bird let it drop onto the crown of Majnun's head. It was a jewel.

Upon awakening, Majnun was flooded with happiness. His body felt as if it could fly. His soul had wings. He leapt into the air, turning.

The next day, several people observed scraps of paper flying about with the

two names, Majnun and Layla, written upon them. Passing a tent, Majnun
reached out and caught a bit of paper with "Layla" in his fist, then tore it to bits.

"Why did you tear up the paper?" a woman veiled in black asked the boy.

"Because one name is enough for us. You have only to scratch me, and out
falls Layla."

"But why did you throw away her name and keep your own?" the woman
persisted.

"You can see the shell but not the kernel," said the boy, as he spread his
arms and looked down upon his rags. "The name is the outer shell, me. But
the face beneath is Hers."

Majnun vanished, becoming nothing but the beloved.

⌘

With the collapse of projections onto our romantic beloveds, the real
work begins. He is not the ideal father; she is not the feminine goddess.
Our partners, so idealized and divine in one moment, so flawed and
human the next, cannot carry the weight of our imagoes. We cannot
return to the garden through them. And we must not blame them for
this failure.

Rather, we can see through our projections to the authentic
Otherness of our partners—their distinct needs, wounds, preferences,
and sensibilities. We can bear witness to their light and to their shadows. At first, the discrepancy between who they actually are and who
we thought they were may be startling and painful. All we can see is
what the Other is *not:* not nurturing, not available, not creative, not
heroic. Definitely not unconditional.

At this stage, some relationships break down and divorce ensues. We
cannot tolerate the inherent separateness of the Other, so we repudiate
it and literalize separateness. For other couples, psychic and emotional
separation occurs, which may speed one or both partners' development
out of symbiotic union or magical thinking and toward autonomy.

Slowly, we come to see that our beloved partner is not responsible
for carrying our ideal imago. She cannot be the all-nurturing mother

or the divine goddess indefinitely. He cannot be the all-giving father or the daring hero without human flaws. Eventually, we can recognize that what they carried for us was inside of us all along. What we see in the beloved is an aspect of ourselves, whether it is the ideal parent or the ideal Self. As we begin to reclaim it, we enlarge our own souls.

For example, the longing partner can begin to cultivate more autonomy and learn to provide for his or her own needs; the independent partner can begin to cultivate more dependency and learn to feel safe with intimacy. As the two extend into their disowned patterns, they can open to feeling a deep empathic bond for the other.

When we carry our own wounds and our own greatness, we need our loved ones in a different way. Instead of requiring them to parent us or to mirror a disowned part of ourselves, we can love them more as they are, with conscious devotion rather than unconscious need. In this way, we give up our demands on our partners to provide us with an ideal Self. And instead we can choose consciously to meet each other's needs, rather than feel unconsciously driven to meet them out of fear.

As we struggle to reclaim projections and maintain responsibility for fulfilling our own needs, a deeper purpose of a loving relationship becomes more clear: it's a container in which to cultivate interdependence, the dance between love and freedom, union and autonomy.

Eventually, our holy longing for a higher union arises again. The end point of psychological development, a consolidated ego, is not enough. Our yearning for the imago in a human beloved can guide us on, transforming Eros from its conventional association with erotic union toward a desire for spiritual union.

To return to Ken Wilber's levels of consciousness: the first stage of love beyond the ego is psychic, in which we transcend the otherness of the beloved and perceive the same Self in him or her as we witness in ourselves. This taste of spiritual union is a taste of transpersonal love.

Today lovers may catch a glimpse of the Self in the Other when they meditate together, staring into one another's eyes. Or they may tune in to it if they take psychedelics together, especially MDMA or Ecstasy, which appears to melt individual boundaries and open us to this level of union. However, many seekers report that this experience, while profound, is not the basis for a functioning relationship. A glimpse of the Other's deeper nature does not imply compatible personalities, values, or lifestyles.

At the subtle level, we yearn to transcend even that distinction of the Self, like the butterfly being extinguished in the flame. Like practitioners of Tantra, we use the image of the beloved as the image of the divine, a doorway beyond form, beyond attachment, to a higher transcendence.

Finally, at the causal level, a rare attainment in human beings, the imago disappears altogether, and the soul dies to any sense of separateness, in unity with the divine.

Our yearning for the romantic beloved, then, is not merely rooted in the search for approval or the desire for sex. It is a part of Eros, a larger cosmic longing with which the whole of life pulses. Its intention is to awaken us to a prior connection with all life via the connection to one human being. In this way, the beloved serves again as a window onto the divine.

Whoever travels without a guide needs two hundred years for a two-day journey.

RUMI

You must long for the guru like a flower opening to receive the rain, flock to the guru for refuge like birds seeking shelter from a storm. You should pray to accompany the guru through all your lives like a body and its shadow, not separate for even an instant.

STEPHEN BUTTERFIELD

One repays a teacher badly if one always remains only a pupil. . . . Now I bid you lose me and find yourselves; and only when you have denied me will I return to you.

NIETZSCHE'S ZARATHUSTRA

FOUR

Longing for the Divine Human

The Search for Spiritual Communion

When we find a spiritual teacher or guide who evokes our soul's longing, the imago dei leaps out of our inner world onto an ideal human being. Like mythic Hindu *gopis* worshipping Krishna, contemporary siddha yoga devotees adoring Gurumayi, Hasidic students studying with their revered rebbe, or Sufi dervishes whirling around their sheikh, we are filled with exalted feelings of devotion in the presence of our ideal. The fires of our longing burn brighter when the revered one is near.

The teacher—priest, guru, tzaddik, roshi, lama, sheikh—has realized in human form the ideal Other living within the student, the imago of the complete or self-realized human being. They meet as two individuals, with all of their gifts and limitations, their wisdom and ignorance. But in the inner world, the teacher carries the student's own highest authority—the parent who won't fail him, the godlike human whose attributes she strives to emulate. For the student to recognize the teacher as such, there must be some match between the inner image and the outer person, some subtle symmetry that enables the inward "yes."

A friend, Jennifer, wrote of such a life-altering meeting with an Indian meditation master:

If there are words in the English language that precisely describe my feelings for Swami, I don't know them. They resembled the way I felt when I saw Elvis as a twelve-year-old on The Ed Sullivan Show, *as he shook and twisted and I screamed and cried at the television set. They also resembled an ancient, virgin love for my father that had long since disappeared with alcohol, mistakes, and just plain time. They resembled the way I felt when I was five and heard a Christmas carol for the first time—"Away in a manger no crib for a bed, the little lord Jesus lay down his sweet head." I cried for several days, and no one had been able to explain the feeling to me, not for forty-two years.*

The closest thing to an explanation seems to be one of those ecstatic experiences that you hear of nuns having, who were considered either saintly or insane. But why would the sensible daughter of two atheists spontaneously combust like that? Where does this longing come from?

I have no answer to these questions. But Swami's presence made the feelings seem rooted in my own particular sanity. I had no shame when my heart raced as he entered the meditation hall; I felt alive with joy as I burst into spontaneous tears when I caught a glimpse of him close-up, strolling through the dining hall. I would stand on the darshan line for an hour if need be, waiting to greet him. I'd bring an apple or a flower and wait. If he dismissed me, I had been false or self-effacing or needy or too sure of myself. If he welcomed me, I blushed and floated off in heaven, stumbling over the others sitting around me. Or I'd diminish my happiness, telling myself he must be having an expansive day and smiling at everyone like that. Or I thought he must not be so very wise if he smiled at me, black soul that I was.

Swami was beautiful, even at seventy-two. He had brown skin with gray shadows. His voice had little bells in it as he sat cross-legged and told us about god dwelling inside of us. Sometimes, when he lectured, I would drift away, so full of this feeling I have no words for that I heard nothing. The conventional wisdom was that Swami generated so much spiritual energy that people could absorb his words in this half-asleep state. The waves of it were thick enough to drink and digest.

One evening I waited on the darshan line, weeping spontaneously, and decided to speak with him. I had seen people pour out their troubles, and I'd never done more than say hello or tell him of my gratitude. The time had come to take what was mine. I trembled so that I could hardly hang on to myself. The music from the visiting sitar player filled the hall. At last, I stepped forward and knelt before Baba. The words tumbled out. The tears, too. He looked right at me, his eyes just drinking me in, it seemed.

"My husband doesn't understand about you, Swami. I love you more than I love him."

I don't know what I thought he would do, maybe tell me that I should leave such a man, or tell me to bring my husband to him, or tell me it was a stupid complaint. Instead, he began to giggle, his little mouth crinkling up. He ruffled my hair and said, in a conspiratorial way, "Don't tell him about us. Just keep it a secret."

I nodded and bowed like I was supposed to. "Your feelings for me cannot hurt anyone. You must never be ashamed, never feel guilty. Now don't cry, you're too serious," he said. I looked up and he was peering at the person behind me. Our meeting was over.

I glided through the next few months. I kept the mantra alive in me at all times, internally bowing to god, as I stood in the kitchen peeling tomatoes, as my husband lectured me on the evils of his lead guitar player, as my tiny son spoke about his trials in nursery school. I loved going to bed because I could lie in the dark and think about Swami and god and light and warmth in a garden of unearthly pleasures—and the garden was all mine.

Once activated, this teacher-student archetype holds a promise and a duty, an inspiration and a burden. It summons us to the greater life; it calls for the death of all that stands in the way. It offers ultimate hope, even salvation; it requires an everlasting commitment to consciousness, kindness, and a higher ethical standard. And in most cases, at some point, it demands a meeting with the shadow.

Priest or Teacher as Parent
The Psychology of Spirituality

Truly I tell you, anyone who will not receive the kingdom of God like a little child will never enter it.

MARK 10:15 (NIV)

What would lead us to endow another human being with so much power and authority that we feel a blind faith in him or her? Our tender yearnings for the divine activate vulnerable feelings of childlike devotion. One client, a married woman, told me that she trusted and adored her rabbi, who seemed to her like the ideal man: handsome but not vain, smart but not patronizing, caring but not intrusive. When he told her that a sexual relationship with him would heal her childhood injuries, she didn't question him. Although both were married, she consented to an affair. A year later, devastated and ashamed, she called me for help. She loved the teachings and practice of Judaism but felt rage at her rabbi and needed to reconcile her feelings and beliefs.

A student of kundalini yoga told me that upon meeting his Sikh teacher, he was mesmerized. He wanted the spiritual power of that man. So, he joined his community, practiced intensively, and eventually wore white robes and a turban, although this caused him great distress at his workplace. Several years later, when the teacher arranged the student's marriage to a stranger, he wanted to prove his commitment to the teacher, so he agreed. Then, when the teacher sent the young son of that union off to India alone, the student gave his permission again. A decade later, he felt confusion and regret about his decisions but was too anxious to leave the teacher and face life without his community. He came to see me to do spiritual shadow-work.

As Freud pointed out, each of us carries unmet childhood needs into adulthood, such as an unconscious longing to merge with a powerful figure for protection against frightening feelings of powerlessness. Therefore, each of us is susceptible to the vagaries of human authorities, who appear to be benign and legitimate. Because Freudians believe only in our personal history and only in individual ego, for them our longing for an almighty Other can refer only to a parent. Therefore, a projection onto a teacher or priest involves a parent imago, and religion is a replay of childhood.

Although I don't see this as the complete explanation, I do see it as a partial truth. From this perspective, we can understand how a fifty-year-old woman, an independent entrepreneur, suddenly acts childlike in relation to a spiritual teacher, unconsciously activating the parent/child archetype while trying to satisfy her early unmet needs. If she fuses internally with her teacher in order to derive strength from a parent *imago,* she is reliving the symbiotic level of relationship. If she projects godlike qualities onto her teacher, she is returning to the magic level, imagining that she is protected by thinking and behaving like this god. If her sense of self is more differentiated, she may return to the mythic level and call on her teacher to intervene in her life or in the world through prayer, meditation, or devotional rituals.

This regression in service of the ego enables the woman to locate an image of god in the Other, providing a connection to something greater than her individuality, even to something eternal. If the relationship is benevolent, it may help her repair certain wounds, solidify her own ego, and fill unmet childhood needs. For instance, in loving service to her teacher, she may come to feel worthy, even special. In the best-case scenario, if the teacher holds the projection temporarily but eventually guides her back to her own higher wisdom, the regression will have served its purpose.

But if the projection remains unconscious indefinitely, and the teacher perpetuates it, she may come to worship this person as god. She may become trapped in a position of submission. Her feelings of being special and being somebody may merely mask deeper feelings of being empty and being nobody. She may work to build the teacher's church instead of building her own. In order to avoid excommunication and to increase her sense of belonging, she may conform to totalitarian group dynamics. And, in an effort to avoid abandonment and maintain the precious relationship, she may comply with abusive, humiliating requests.

This woman's longing to be seen and feel special may be enhanced by the possession of a secret, which ties her to the teacher and to the group. Initiated into a sacred mystery, she may vow to keep a spiritual practice confidential. Or she may become aware of the teacher's shadow, which binds her to the teacher. Like the secret of sexual abuse in families that are bound together in a conspiracy of silence, the secret of spiritual abuse in religious communities acts like glue, reinforcing submission and compliance.

Heinz Kohut's self-psychology has extended our understanding of the emotional needs underlying our holy longing. According to Kohut, our individuality is shaped only in relation to others; it is embedded in their responses and cannot be understood apart from this human context. Therefore, Kohut does not use the dualistic language of self and other. He does not see one individual projecting her subjectivity onto another, such as a student/child unconsciously attributing power to a teacher/parent. Instead, Kohut and his followers use the term *selfobject,* which includes the subjectivity of both people and implies their inherent connection. Each is a selfobject to the other.

For Kohut, the relationship of a believer to god—in which the figure of a perfect and omnipotent deity with whom the imperfect and powerless believer wants to merge—corresponds to the early selfobject of a baby and an idealized parent imago. The believer longs to regain her original state of (pre-personal) union and attempts to do so by turning away from imperfection and constructing a religious relationship that protects her vulnerable ego.

With this emerging relationship, the aspirant longs for mirroring. If she becomes a valuable follower of a priest or teacher, she experiences an omniscient, omnipresent god as completely attuned to her every need. She does not, of course, see the other person in actuality, with all of the human flaws and shortcomings, but uses the teacher to foster her own sense of self-esteem and specialness.

Similarly, the teacher enjoys the admiration and devotion of the student. In this kind of relationship, each may come to overvalue or undervalue the other, depending on their unconscious needs. This may help explain why some teachers exact such exclusive devotion from their followers.

In addition, the aspirant longs for an encounter with an ideal and therefore attributes qualities of perfection to the teacher. Ideal-hungry people, Kohut wrote, are always in search of others whom they can revere for their prestige, power, beauty, intelligence, or moral stature. Then, through a process of fusion, the student unconsciously identifies with the teacher's attainments and feels soothed. In fact, in some traditions of guru yoga, this is the goal.

These satisfying experiences serve to intensify the believer's commitment to the religious relationship and motivate him to ensure an ongoing connection. He may rely on dogma and a literal interpretation of text to reinforce the relationship, as we can observe in fundamentalists of any tradition. But, paradoxically, this closed system prevents him from further developing his own separate sense of self.

If the student's self-worth develops via mirroring and her capacity for self-soothing develops via idealizing the teacher, then the relationship will have served healthy aims. Even if the connection to the idealized teacher is broken through a disappointment, the student may be able to reclaim projections and perceive the teacher more accurately, more humanly.

This was Jennifer's experience, as the story above unfolded:

When Swami went back to India with his lucky entourage, he left behind a small group of followers who were supposed to keep his love alive for me. But it wasn't like that. When I thought of him, I cried and cried. Eventually, I lost touch with the intensity of the feeling and just drifted away from it, as I had after my father left.

Meanwhile, my husband's unhappiness grew like a fast-spreading tumor. It took all of my guts to get out of that house, but I did it in a week. I went from room to room in the new house and filled them with pictures of Swami as I chanted the mantra. I even put a picture in my son's room. But I didn't feel like Swami knew how much pain I suffered. I wasn't sure he was really still there at all.

One day my girlfriend Jill called. She and her husband had met Swami when I brought them to him. Her husband had fallen like a ton of bricks, and she had resisted. She felt excluded and suspicious since her husband had begun chanting and eating tofu and reading books on Eastern religion. She worshipped Henry James and Proust and filled herself up with them at night as I had with Swami.

"I'm so fed up with David," she announced. "Now he's all upset about the Swami scandal. It's even more annoying than Swami himself."

"What scandal?" I asked after a small hesitation.

"You don't know? Oh, Jenny, you shouldn't hear this from me."

"What scandal, Jill?" Adrenaline rushed through my body.

"Oh, I don't know, it's probably a rumor. But people said that several of Swami's followers claim that he sexually molested their daughters. He said he wanted to check to see if they were virgins. David said there are always scandals around holy men, especially when they're about to die. They have to test their followers."

"About to die?" I whispered.

"He's sick, Jenny, a heart condition. This is the last year before he leaves his body." She used that phrase with a certain contempt.

"I didn't know . . ." My words faded away. I felt dizzy.

In some way, this information was simply unbearable. This was no time to lose my Swami. These scandals meant nothing. He would be my guru dead or alive. So, I created a mask, the mask of the devotee, and I became a more articulate devotee than I had been before. I had more trappings in my house. I set up an altar and burned incense. I read Swami's books, even though they bored me. I no longer felt the rapture and protection of his love as I drifted off to sleep. But I no longer remembered it, so it didn't matter.

Six months later, David called. "I thought I should let you know before you heard it from Jill," he said. "Swami died. Heart attack."

"Okay, thanks." I hung up. Something unstoppable came over me. A thunderstorm. I wailed, I raged. The world had looked so sweet for that one year. Now it seemed like a moment. I was sure I would understand one day what happened with those girls. But now he was gone. Vanished. He had left me—stolen my heart and disappeared. There was no magic. I'd been a sucker.

I didn't cry after that day. I never allowed myself to tell anyone how I really felt. I never betrayed the memory of Swami out loud. I hid my disillusionment *and loss, and the slender thread of faith snapped. It had been so delicate, and that was part of its beauty. It had been so silvery and had given me my life back. Now it wasn't just out of reach; it was gone.*

In retrospect, Jennifer told me, she learned to coexist with different truths about her teacher:

He radiated an inner beauty that I'd never seen before. And it was intoxicating, almost sexual, like the rush of a drug. So, I couldn't believe those rumors. They didn't mesh with my experience. I didn't want him to be that—cruel and deceptive.

On the other hand, I became cynical and didn't want to admit it. But it was revealed in my actions, not my words. I didn't meditate anymore. I didn't do the practices, even though I thought I believed in them. The chanting tapes had helped to calm and center me. But they also stopped my thoughts. These two realities sat side by side.

During that time, another devotee, a friend of Jennifer's, wrote a novel and received an offer to publish it from an excellent New York house. When the friend informed her teacher about it, he told her not to make the agreement. The ashram would publish it. The devotee agreed.

Jennifer was outraged. "How could you consent to this?" she asked.

"I've moved to a place where I don't make my own decisions. And I like it that way," the friend stated.

Jennifer looked into the mirror of her friend's behavior, and the reflection startled her. She recalled a hymn from a childhood church: "I'll go where you want me to go, Dear Lord, O'er mountain or plain or sea. I'll say what you want me to say, Dear Lord, I'll be what you want me to be." Understandably, that kind of obedience and dependency seemed to her to be regressive and dysfunctional. For Jennifer, the withdrawal of the projection opened the doorway to the Self.

But for other people, identification with the projection may be a valid spiritual path, assuming it is not exploitative. Within the context of the Catholic tradition or a guru lineage, for example, we may reexperience unmet dependency needs in a positive way through a relationship with Christ via a priest or through devotion to a spiritual teacher. Just as an intimate partnership can serve as a container in which we develop, a spiritual partnership also can contain and stimulate our growth, helping us reclaim lost parts of the self and move toward higher levels of development.

However, there is great danger here: believers may lose their autonomy, their voice, and their will if they surrender them to the wrong person. They may risk not living their own lives.

Today, Jennifer is grateful for the love that opened her heart. But she also lives with a feeling of loss. When I asked her where her holy longing goes now, she replied, "I visit a Catholic church. I was raised as an atheist, but I used to cry for the baby Jesus. Now the organ, the incense, the Mass give me joy. I won't convert, but I'm most happy in a church."

In some cases when the teacher, priest, or rabbi fails to carry the imago indefinitely, whether through revealing a human limitation or acting out a shadow, a wrenching separation ensues. The student may need to turn the teacher into an adversary (or adversarial selfobject) in order to push against and separate from the teacher, thereby confirming her own autonomy, much like an adolescent who finds identity by pushing against a parent.

However, the aspirant may lose the soothing relationship without internalizing his own self-worth or sense of authority. Left on his own, he may come to believe in the omnipotence of his own mind and rigidly adhere to his own dogmatic, concrete thinking in an effort to replace the presence of the idealized Other. Rather than addressing his own thwarted longings, the believer masks the trauma of disappointment by retrenching in a belief system.

One such man, who felt abandoned by his priest, sought out like-minded believers in a militant cult to reinforce his own conclusions and protect his fragile sense of identity. When he entered therapy, he insisted that I agree completely with his worldview, or he could not trust me.

Another client came to see me after a series of disappointing relationships with Buddhist meditation teachers. Each separation from a teacher was a heartbreaking rite of passage in which her sense of self fragmented as each projection snapped. She was left each time with angry negative feelings and continued to hope that the next great figure would not disappoint her but would become the all-loving father she never had and, even more, the all-wise god figure.

She could not break this ideal-seeking pattern until she internalized her own spiritual ideal. Many years later, she was able to approach spiritual mentors and learn from them because she no longer set them on pedestals from which, inevitably, they would fall.

Eventually, I, too, came to see how my first meditation teacher, more than fifty years ago, had been a substitute father or, more accurately, a shadow father. The stable quality of his presence had been reassuring and calming. The compassionate quality of his message had lifted me up out of myself, beyond the narcissistic concerns. His promise that we would attain enlightenment through practice had eased my terrors of aging and death.

Finally, his values had overturned those I had internalized from my own father. My relation to him was an aid on my way to independence—that is, to choosing values that separated me from my tightly knit family. But eventually, I had to develop for myself values that were dictated neither by my spiritual father nor by my biological father.

Of course, individual psychology is formed in a cultural milieu. Our susceptibility to authoritarian personalities begins at home and is fostered by our social institutions as well. Many parents override natural feelings of vulnerability, dependency, and sadness in their children, banishing these emotions into the unconscious shadow. They teach their children that these emotions are not acceptable because *they* were taught to disown them through their parents' contempt or their teachers' punishment or their clergy's shaming words. But these feelings remain in the darkness over the years, so that no matter how independent an adult appears, an inner child's longing for a powerful, protective parent remains.

Or adults may punish a child for temper tantrums, teaching him that his anger, which may even be justified, is not acceptable. Eventually, the anger, buried in the darkness, no longer surfaces. Later, when, for example, the young man is abused by his father/priest, he cannot feel his rage; he can only continue to protect his abuser and blame himself.

Many schools and institutionalized religions add to the mix because authoritarianism is woven into the context and content of their teachings. In fact, their ideologies, as well as their means of transmitting those ideologies, often lead us to mistrust ourselves by rewarding obedience to external authority, punishing independent thinking, and seeding guilt and shame. For example, nuns repeatedly told a grade-school boy that he was "too big for his britches." Now he cannot feel his own successes forty years later. Rather than take any credit for his business achievements, he claims that he is merely god's instrument.

A Catholic client developed an irrational fear of doctors, who carried for her the voice of a godlike authority—the ability to pronounce a blessing or a curse. Because both her father and priest taught her that she was born in sin and deserved to be punished, she saw illness as her just reward. And she gave the power over it, and so over her body, to the male doctors whom she feared.

If a child associates feeling loved with feeling shamed, flawed, and worthless, then these feelings will seem familiar when they arise in religious discipleships. Several long-term meditators whom I know feel ashamed before their guru because they have not attained a certain level of practice after many years. Each of them had a father who demanded a high level of performance from them; now they seek spiritual perfection in order to gain approval from their spiritual father.

Certainly, if we can carry our vulnerable shadows more consciously, they will inoculate us against the dangers of our own power shadows. They will remind us of our humanity and protect us from superior self-righteousness. On the other hand, when we relinquish our authority to another and banish our vulnerability to the shadow, we are at risk of falling into self-righteous aggression, which we witness everywhere today.

Just as it's not sufficient to say that the parent is the final and only source of the god image, it's also not sufficient to say that the parent is the only source of the teacher imago. As mythologist Mircea Eliade pointed out, it's our need to realize archetypes, our longing for transcendent forms, that reveals something about our place in the cosmos.

Priest or Teacher as God
The Archetypes of Spirituality

The decisive question for [a human being] is: Is he related to something infinite or not?

C. G. JUNG

While Freud's exploration of the parent imago and personal transference in therapy was groundbreaking, Jung took the next step: archetypal transference. The German root of the term *transference* means "to carry something over from one place to another." In its psychological use, transference refers to overwhelming emotions that one person attributes to another, forming a tie between the two. As a special case of projection, transference is the emotional link between a patient and a therapist in which the patient clings to the promise of change and renewal via the therapist. I suggest that the same process takes place between a believer and a spiritual guide.

Archetypal transference has hidden within it not only the image of a parent; it carries the image of an archetype or divine imago, such as the Self, which brings meaning and purpose to life. When a living teacher becomes the object of a student's unconscious ideal through projection of the Self, a link is made: the student-lover longs for union with the teacher-beloved, who is typically unavailable in a personal way, thus creating an agonizing sense of separation, which fuels the fires of longing. This inherent separation (*viraha* in Sanskrit) is the basis for certain devotional practices, such as bhakti yoga, which can bring on ecstatic and erotic states of yearning.

In a classical spiritual apprenticeship, the student is encouraged to meditate on the teacher as the image of god, deliberately merge with him or her, and even give over the sense of individual authority and control. This process relieves the terrible anxiety that accompanies our existential uncertainty: Suddenly, we are in the presence of someone who knows the truth. If we behave properly, if we maintain our faith, we, too, will know the truth.

In traditional guru yoga, the devotee worships the teacher's image, bows before the guru, touches the guru's feet, and bathes, dresses, and meditates according to the guru's dictates. These presentations of devotion are observed by others, rewarded with social capital, or punished if the guru is displeased.

But this dynamic leads to a questionable assumption: a human being can have divine authority. If the teacher knows the truth, he must be morally superior, even infallible. If so, he must be immune to the corruptions of the shadow, immune to the abuse of power, and immune to self-interest. If we follow this line of reasoning to its end, the teacher also must be immune to making mistakes. So, any behavior that seems questionable to believers cannot be questioned; given the teacher's level of consciousness, it *must* stem from pure motives and right action.

The same principle holds in any tradition. If the priest is a representative of the Pope, and the Pope is the elect of Christ, then he must know more, and we must follow his edicts without question. If the head Hasidic rabbi, known as the Lubavitcher Rebbe, is seen by his disciples as the Messiah, then whatever he says must be the truth and must be obeyed completely.

But there are inherent dangers for the ardent believer who projects the divine Self onto a living human being:

- We risk giving our own spiritual radiance to another and thereby losing contact with our own divinity. When we attribute the superior light of the Self to another, we fail to know our own essence within. I have found in my work with many clients that it is not only our darkness that we disown; it is our spiritual light, our natural radiance, which we hide. When we give it away to a "higher" teacher, we see it only outside ourselves.

- We risk giving our powers of discrimination and independent thinking to another and thereby losing trust in our own minds. When we attribute greater wisdom to another, we gradually fail to believe our own instincts and intuition. If we join a church group or spiritual community even though something doesn't feel quite right, if we commit to a doctrine even though we have grave doubts, if we use practices or dogma to ward off uncertainty, we are slowly being trained to obey external authority, rather than our own intuition or discrimination. Eventually, we will come to think that doubt is a sin, and that disbelieving the teacher is disbelieving god.

- We risk giving our emotional authority to another and thereby losing trust in our own authentic feelings. When we believe that another person knows what's best for our emotional well-being, we begin to turn away from our own fear, anger, shame, and depression, each of which is a cue about the spiritual relationship and its environment. Eventually, we will have ceded control of our inner landscape to another, and our vital emotional truths will be silenced.

- Finally, our holy longing makes us susceptible to spiritual authority and authoritarianism, to both authentic spiritual power and to power shadow. We risk giving our loving obedience to a teacher who may abuse us, re-creating a pattern of wounding, instead of healing. When the arrow of projection carries spirit and lands on a human being, that person potentially controls our soul.

Jung told the story of a patient whose persistent transference to him revealed collective religious qualities that appeared to be larger and deeper than her personal unconscious material. That is, he could not attribute her projections merely to her father and her family history. The woman's fantasies about Jung grew more and more fantastic as they explored them together. As she endowed him with superhuman traits, she experienced herself with daughter-like dependence.

She dreamed, for example, that she was a tiny child in the arms of her father, who was a giant. The giant stood in a wheat field. As the wind swept over the field, the giant swayed back and forth, rocking the child.

In response to this dream, Jung wondered whether the patient's unconscious was "trying to create a god out of the person of the doctor." It seemed to him that she was unconsciously trying to free a vision of god from the veils of the person. If this were the case, her unconscious only appeared to be reaching out toward Jung, the man. In a deeper sense, it was really reaching out toward a god. This led him to wonder whether the soul's longing for a god could be even stronger than its love for a person.

Although Jung could not be the god-man of the patient's fantasies, the imago dei that was fueling the transference could be. When the patient consciously realized the religious content of her transference onto Jung, she became freed of her dependence on him as a man. The transference to her analyst was resolved, so to speak, because her projections linked back to their archetypal sources. He was no longer the god whom she loved but the carrier of the god image by means of which she loved.

Like all symbols, the archetypal mother also represents the Self or god image. When Jung named a specific imago as an object of longing, he was acknowledging that the source of longing is not found in a reductive understanding of personal history alone; it is the Self longing for itself.

Eastern traditions have taught this message in a different language for millennia. In the Bhagavad Gita, the warrior Arjuna stands paralyzed on the battlefield when faced with members of his own family. He knows his duty—to fight—but his heart is in moral conflict. He prays for the assistance of something greater than himself. At that moment of spiritual crisis, the divine avatar, or incarnation of god, appears as Krishna.

Like the Self in relation to the ego (Arjuna), Krishna stands behind the warrior as a hidden transpersonal center. He does not tell him what to do or how to do it; he simply articulates one teaching: how the divine in Arjuna can live in direct relation to the divine Krishna. As one translator summed it up, "Established in yoga [or union with the divine], perform action."

Like Arjuna acting in service to Krishna, the ego can be relativized and act in service to the Self. It no longer acts for its own outcomes, with attachment to its own goals, but acts with the freedom of non-attachment, offering the fruits of its actions to the divine. Some current Advaita teachers speak about this as the absence of the doer, the one who lays claim to action and will.

Certain gurus describe this as their level of development. Jung referred to them as mana-personalities—the hero, chief, magician, medicine man, saint, friend of god. In his day, he did not imagine them as women but, rather, referred to the female counterpart as a sublime matriarchal figure, the great mother who understands and forgives everything, lives only for others, and never seeks her own interests. Jung wrote that the mana-personality evolves into a hero or godlike being whose earthly expression is the priest. Today we know that a male or female rabbi, sheikh, lama, or spiritual director can become a mana-personality as well.

When this charismatic personality is activated in the teacher, a feeling of creaturely dependence is activated in the student, as it was in Jung's patient. She can place her responsibilities at his feet. She can stop thinking for herself or acting from her own agency. And, through turning him into a god, she can become a knower of reality by association with him.

These living masters can appear via many archetypal images. For example, if we long for certainty, which brings an end to the anxiety of living with the unknown, we may be drawn to the wise old man or woman—the *senex,* to use Jung's term for the archetype. This figure offers the order of morality and the certainty of knowledge. Like the Dalai Lama as seen by some followers, he may carry the wisdom of authority like a compassionate mentor. Or, like the Pope as seen by some critics, he may appear distant and rigid, like an old king making decrees.

As James Hillman pointed out in *Puer Papers,* the senex is the opposite of the *puer aeternus,* or eternal youth. The nature of our senex qualities reflects the degree of our own connection with the puer archetype, who keeps us open to fresh possibilities and to the vital imagination. If the wise old man or woman loses contact with his or her own inner puer qualities, he or she may yearn for someone to carry them on the outside. This dynamic may help to explain why some teachers, who appear so self-sufficient, yearn for disciples to follow them, and even to complete them.

While the senex's masculinity may be one-sided, the puer's femininity may compensate. While the senex maintains rules and boundaries, the puer is fiery, inquisitive, and noncommittal.

At a mythological level, the puer aeternus is the archetype of spirit. Like Icarus, the puer aeternus flies high over the world, free and unattached, unable to live an embodied life. This divine figure can keep us connected to ideals and a genuine spirituality. But, possessed by it, a man or woman may suffer from an inability to mature, conform, or commit to life in this world. The puer (or *puella,* in the feminine form) may wander eternally, always longing for something better, unable to settle into a routine of any kind. He may appear innocent and childish, caught in fantasies of spiritual perfection. He may be unable to accept the limits of mortal life. In Jung's terms, he is trapped in spirit and unable to incarnate instinct.

In *The Wounded Woman,* Linda Leonard described female carriers of this archetype as wounded daughters trying to free themselves from a father complex. The puella woman may identify with her father and remain undeveloped or become an addict, displacing her dependency onto a substance. Or she may rebel and lose her own connection to spirit, becoming rigid and father-like herself. Or she may marry a senex and project the authority that she lacks within onto her spouse.

I would add that a puella woman may become devoted to a senex teacher and remain in a suspended childlike state as the king's daughter. In this condition, her own spiritual capacity remains projected outside of her, and she is always the special child, the princess, but not a divine person in her own right.

If we long for salvation, we may be drawn to the teacher who appears as savior, prophet, or messiah. The believer who feels sinful or flawed yearns for redemption from the one who has purified his sins or cleansed his karma. These saviors, such as Christ and Muhammad, tend to bring a message that is exclusive to their believers and focused on the next world, after the Rapture, after the jihad.

If we long for unconditional love, we may be drawn to the teacher who appears as divine mother, such as the Indian teachers Ammachi and Mother Meera. Such mother figures embrace their spiritual children in silent acceptance, and wounded hearts are healed.

If we long for faith, we may be drawn to the teacher who appears as shaman or magician because he can demonstrate special powers (or *siddhis*). The Indian teacher Sai Baba's reportedly breathtaking feats of materialization gave believers the hope of escaping human limitations (although later they were reportedly disproven).

If we long to break free of the bounds of rationality and conventionality, even the constraints of morality, we may be drawn to the teacher who appears as trickster. He or she stands outside of the social order and provokes our unasked questions about the arbitrariness of sacred customs and values. Like G. I. Gurdjieff, Bhagwan Shree Rajneesh (Osho), Chogyam Trungpa Rinpoche, and Adi Da, the trickster uses shock, clowning, physical force, nudity, alcohol, and drugs to awaken followers from the trance of consensual thinking. Rather than bringing order, the trickster brings disorder; rather than harmony, disharmony. In this way, he or she disrupts to show the limits of our rational minds and point the way toward nondual awareness, in which all opposites are reconciled.

After studying Indian and Chinese scripture and philosophy, Jung took a stand against the Eastern teacher/disciple model. He proposed, instead, that his form of analysis could bring about a conscious reunion of the ego with the Self. By reclaiming the unconscious contents that we attribute to the charismatic personality, he said, we come back to ourselves, to our own treasury, to that part of us that is so strange, yet so near—the Self.

(Of course, Jung is proposing working with the contents of consciousness, not transcending them or directly experiencing pure awareness or *rigpa,* empty mind, as Eastern contemplative practices propose. This is a huge difference between the teachings.)

I strongly agree with Jung that no god should be constructed out of the archetype of the mana-personality. In other words, he or she should be seen as having human greatness and human limitations. However, I also understand discipleship as a stage in human development that can become an appropriate step in maturation. That is, the projection of the Self can be a precursor to the awakening of the Self within—if psychological work is a part of the spiritual relationship.

In fact, Jung himself became a mana-personality in his time and remains so today for some people who call themselves "Jungian." For many, he serves well as teacher, mentor, and ancestor. But other Jungians, despite espousing individuation from the collective as the aim of human development, appear to require conformity in therapeutic principles and practice. Some have lost Jung's spirit of exploration and experimentation and insist, instead, that students subordinate their own soul's journey to one that looks like his. A few, sadly, have turned to *imitatio* Jung as their response to uncertainty. In the worst cases, they use Jung's shadow behaviors to justify their own destructive acting out.

Jungian analyst James Yandell put it poignantly when he asked: In order to be a Jungian, do I have to subordinate my individuality to communal standards? Because if I do that, then I am no longer, by definition, a Jungian.

Fortunately, there are many analysts today who feel tremendous respect, even awe, for Jung's genius but also see his shadow sides. They can admit the shortcomings in his work, attempt to build bridges with other psychologies, and remain open to dialogue.

I appreciate Yandell's paradoxical conclusion to his own relationship with Jung's mana-personality, which he described in a pamphlet titled *The Imitation of Jung*: "The only way I can emulate Jung in the deepest sense is by living out my own identity and realizing my own potential as fully as Jung lived out his. But if I were a Jungian in this sense, it's unlikely that I would submit myself to a training program, affiliate with a society of analysts, or identify with a movement. And without these things, I would not be a Jungian."

During the years of founding his first institute, Jung was prescient about this issue, saying, "Thank God I'm Jung—and not a Jungian!" Clearly, when we concretize and literalize the imago dei as a fallible human being, this relationship dynamic can evoke many dangers. But, on the other hand, to discard discipleship simply and entirely is to lose the gifts of a timeless pattern of relationship. Perhaps it would be best to say, with Ken Wilber, that ideally we should set out on a spiritual quest having done our psychological homework. That is, we should have attained to the rational level of development, in which the ego is consolidated. Then the imago has a place to reside. But this ideal sequence is rare among the awakening people I know, as I will discuss later.

Or we might follow Jung's suggestion to turn toward our own souls, which offer an inner initiation via our dreams and creativity. In this way Jung encountered the internal figure of Philemon, a wise old man with horns and wings, who acted for him much like a guide or imago dei. The Hindu saint Ramakrishna also met an inner wise man, a yogi or sannyasi, who initiated him from within.

In Jung's language, our holy longing fuels the journey from preconscious unity toward conscious reconciliation with the Self. He saw this process, which he called individuation, as the purpose of human life. He must have felt the holy longing intensely when he wrote, in *The Undiscovered Self*, "The individual who is not anchored in God can offer no resistance on his own resources to the physical and moral blandishments of the world. For this he needs the evidence of inner, transcendent experience, which alone can protect him from the otherwise inevitable submersion in the mass."

Jung intuitively followed his own longing through dusky cellars, blue seas, and black nights as he mapped the archetypal realm. Rather than reject holy longing, as Freud did, or romanticize it, as those possessed by spirit do, he lived his life in direct relationship to it, without human intermediaries.

In the end, Jung knew the danger of reducing the ineffable to words. He pointed out that psychology touches on the phenomenology of spirit but not on the essential nature of it. If its essence could be explained, it would become merely a subdivision of psychology. And its mystery would be lost.

For those of us who have experienced the enormity of the meeting with the divine in human form, the concepts of personal and archetypal projection do not suffice somehow. Although we need to beware of the risks, we also need to dwell more deeply in the mystery.

Priest or Teacher as Divine Human
The Teacher/Student Relationship

There is no deity superior to the Guru, no gain better than the Guru's grace, no state higher than meditation on the Guru.

SWAMI MUKTANANDA

From a purely scientific or psychological point of view, spiritual teachers are irrelevant; they are artifacts of our projections. But there are human beings among us who have attained the psychic, subtle, causal, and nondual levels of consciousness or stages of development, however rare. And from a spiritual point of view, these saints and sages are more evolved along the path, closer to the point of union with the divine.

Along with their other tasks as teachers—to model a way of life, instruct in spiritual practices, transmit a level of consciousness, and awaken our holy longing—they knowingly carry the Self or imago dei for others. As an embodiment of the attributes of god, a spiritual teacher represents the fulfillment of human longing.

A Sufi story tells of sheikh Jafar al-Sadiq, who is aware of his task. A man insulted him, so Jafar went to the man's house. "When you said those things, I made no reply. If the qualities you attribute to me are really in me, I give you my word that I shall repent of them. But if the qualities you ascribed to me are not in me, I pray to God that he pardon you. I forgive you for what you said and don't hold it against you." The man fell at the sheikh's feet and repented.

In many contemplative traditions, this relationship and its projection are accepted and encouraged as an essential part of the spiritual journey. In the various sects of Tibetan Buddhism, the lamas' lineages can be traced back for many generations. Among Hasidic Jews, the head rabbi has near-divine authority. Among Sufis, the pir or sheikh demands respect and obedience due to his station or level of consciousness. And among certain Hindu sects, the dependency that results from this relationship is even encouraged: the master acquires power of attorney from his disciples so that their financial dependency triggers emotional dependency, which can potentially be transformed into spiritual dependency.

So, from a Western point of view, the disciple projects the Self, and the teacher receives it. But from an Eastern point of view, the reverse occurs: the teacher radiates energy, or darshan, and the devotee internalizes (or introjects) it, like food. That is, from a higher level of consciousness, the master broadcasts god, and the student absorbs the vibrations.

As a result, the student feels expansive, even blissful. And she may come to rely on this state, even depend on it. Soon, the teacher appears to be the gatekeeper—the only gatekeeper—to the student's experience of peace of mind, open-heartedness, meaning, and purpose.

As the student projects the imago dei and the teacher absorbs it, as the teacher gives darshan and the student absorbs it, the pattern is set. Each becomes responsible in some subtle way for the inner reality of the other. Each begins to perceive the Other through the blinders of their level of consciousness and its imago.

The teacher may come to believe that she can surrender her individuality in order to sustain the projection of the Self for her devotees.

Conversely, the student may attempt to surrender his individuality prematurely to become the ideal follower. In the end, both try to do an end run around emotional issues to fulfill their roles. As a consequence, development occurs along certain lines (religious or spiritual) and not along others (emotional, cognitive, or moral). And shadows are more likely to erupt.

Slowly, insidiously, teacher and student may come to hold each other in position via a kind of field that emerges between them. And both have a lot to lose if the field is pierced.

Jeffrey Masson, who has written widely about Freud, also wrote a less well-known book, *My Father's Guru,* in which he described this reciprocal process between his father and Paul Brunton, a teacher of mysticism who lived with the Masson family: "My father clearly believed he was being singled out. . . . [He] felt himself elevated and special in the presence of this special and elevated man. Only if P.B. [Brunton] was an adept with occult powers could my father maintain his special status, so it was important that he have these qualities. . . . P.B. needed my father as much as my father needed him. . . . P.B. depended upon the constant reassurance that a fawning acolyte could give. Certainly my father wanted something no person could ever give him, and P.B. claimed to be able to give my father what no person can ever give another. One wanted, the other offered, transcendence of this world."

ᥟ THE INNER MARRIAGE ᥉

A Story of Holy Longing in the Christian Saint Catherine of Siena

In 1347, in Siena, Italy, in a tall brick house with a tile roof, Catherine Benincasa and her twin sister were born. Their mother, who already had twenty-two babies, sent the sicker infant to a wet nurse and took Catherine to her own breast. The sister died soon after, and Catherine's Catholic mother reminded her daily that she had a special obligation to be good—god had chosen her to survive.

At five, Catherine loved to visit the small stone church of St. Dominic just up the hill from her house. She gazed at colorful icons of the saints and inhaled incense like the breath of life. When she returned home, hand in hand with her mother, and climbed the stairs leading up to her room, she bowed her blond head, genuflected, and poured her heart into Hail Marys on each step.

At seven, Catherine wandered through the town square, enraptured by the pinks and oranges of sunset. As she stood at the city gates gazing up at the sky, all at once Jesus appeared in the heavens, robed in white, smiling at her. Behind him, a circle of saints in white awaited. A shaft of light fell on the small girl, who collapsed in the dirt.

From that day, the fire that Christians call the passion for Christ was lit in her. Yearning to be near him, she hid in a stone grotto to recite fervent prayers, vowing her virginity to Mary. She tied a rope into knots and flailed her tiny body in imitation of Christ's suffering until blue welts rose beneath the skin.

At fifteen, Catherine was to be married. Her mother and sister prepared her for the marriage, but then, in 1362, this older sister died. Catherine blamed herself for surviving the death of another cherished sister. She believed that her flirtation with worldliness during the preparation for marriage caused the death. As a result, she vowed that she would have no bridegroom but Christ. Her longing for him and him alone intensified.

Catherine struck a child's bargain with god: in exchange for her sacrifices, she would win salvation for her entire family. Her life of penance would give her power over the sins of her parents. On the contrary, if she yielded to desire, she would damn them forever. With defiance, she took shears and cut her blond curls to the roots.

Trying to break her will, her parents took away her private room and assigned her the chores of washing, cooking, and sewing for the large household. In her mind, she constructed a secret cell that no one could take from her, and her religiosity deepened. In her imagination, she turned her family into the holy family of Jesus, Mary, and the apostles and served them gladly.

At sixteen, she told her father decisively that she refused marriage. At first he was distraught. But one day he entered her room silently while she was at prayer. A white dove, sign of the Holy Spirit, seemed to hover above her head. Startled at his daughter's unique spiritual gifts, he finally agreed to her vocation.

Catherine put on a rough wool robe with an iron chain against her hips. She gave up meat and wine and consumed only bread, raw vegetables, and water. Her body wasted. She entered three years of silence, except for confession, and prayed incessantly to her bridegroom, Christ. She slept only thirty minutes every two days. And yet she continued to feel that she had not tamed her flesh and that she was an unworthy sinner.

Catherine cried inconsolably, begging her father to permit her to join the Sisters of Penance in the Dominican order. Eventually, she donned their long black mantle and white veil, while continuing to live among those she had vowed to save.

Continuing rigorous fasts and endless prayers, she burst into tears on occasion. At other times, she leaned against a wall motionless, her face pale, seeing and hearing nothing, lost to this world. During one period, she heard persecuting voices and saw visions of naked people. She felt tormented and abandoned by Jesus. But, eventually, she was able to create distance from her visions and observe them, rather than feel overwhelmed by them. With that, they lost their grasp.

First pious neighbors, then the Church began to take notice of her severe austerities and her single-minded devotion. When she was twenty-seven, they accused her of being fed by the devil because she had lived without eating for two years (and she would continue her strict diet for seven more). She begged god to help her eat and tried to force herself. But by this time the loss of appetite was beyond her control. Her pain upon eating was so great that she forced stalks of fennel down her throat to induce vomiting. In the end, she could not even receive the sacrament of the host but felt content simply to be near it.

Despite these physical deprivations, Catherine devoted immense energy to church causes. She wrote letters and rallied supporters to urge the Pope to leave France and return to Rome. She worked ceaselessly giving charity to the poor and assisting victims of the plague, which ravaged Siena.

At the same time, Catherine's prayers focused on a single driving desire: to love others as Christ loved them. Her prayer was answered in the form of a vision: Jesus appeared and took out her heart, replacing it with his own.

After years of yearning for him, Catherine was betrothed to her bridegroom. She described an inner experience in which Jesus placed a bridal ring on her finger, fulfilling her years of devotion.

Catherine began to dictate four petitions to god while passing in and out of ecstatic states. The result: The Dialogue, *a complex exchange between Catherine and her beloved god.*

At thirty-three, yearning to be fully united with god, she stopped drinking water in order to give her body back to Him. She died of starvation in 1380 and was canonized in 1461.

❧∽◉◉∽❧

Clearly, Catherine's yearning for her bridegroom had a dark side, rooted in medieval Christian beliefs: In exchange for her parents' sins, which condemned them to eternal punishment, she dedicated herself to self-denial. Her "holy anorexia," as coined by Rudolph Bell in a book of that name, began with terrible guilt over surviving the earlier deaths of her two sisters and the love of her sinful, worldly mother.

Experts on anorexia today point out that girls who feel forced to live for others and to meet their impossible high standards may go to extremes to try to control their own fates, such as by conquering their bodily desires. Like Catherine, they may define themselves by striving for perfection through self-denial. The pattern of conquest and reward that is set up through fasting and bingeing offers them a sense of mastery, a triumph over dependency, a saintlike victory. Like Christ, Catherine felt no desire, no pain, no hunger, and so became godlike in her own right.

Jungian analyst Marion Woodman wrote of this link between love of spirit and rejection of bodily life in anorexic girls in *Addiction to Perfection*. She suggested that when we reject food, we reject matter, or life itself. We reject incarnation—or "down"—and seek to become pure spirit—or "up." But perfection belongs only to the gods, Woodman said. And the striving for spirit without flesh, for light without darkness, is a denial of human nature.

The stories of holy longing offer stark similarities and differences. Rumi, Ramakrishna, and Catherine had early childhood spiritual experiences, which opened a window onto other worlds. Today we would call them altered states of consciousness. But because of the passage of time and the particularity of their religious languages and structures, we don't really know their nature. However, we do know that with these experiences, each of them awoke to a religious fervor and a basic dissatisfaction with the status quo.

For Catherine, that meant rejecting an arranged marriage and life in the footsteps of her mother. For Rumi, that meant rejecting a position as a scholar and life in the footsteps of his father. For Ramakrishna, that meant rejecting all convention. However, each of their sacrifices led to the gift of a spiritual marriage.

Differences appear in the objects of their longing. Rumi met a man who was for him an *insan al kamil,* a complete human being. Through intense communion with him, Rumi gave up his attachments to his earlier understandings, practices, and values, becoming a lover of music, poetry, and dance.

When separated from his beloved, first temporarily, then permanently, Rumi's yearning intensified nearly to the point of madness. Yet in the development of his poems we can see his evolution through the Sufi stations, or levels of consciousness, in a fairly orderly way.

Catherine's beloved Jesus was for her, too, a model of ideal human life. Through intense communion with him, she served others with the heart of Christ and strived to become his bride. In moments of ecstatic union with god, she wrote that her soul left her body and she attained her dream.

When we project the divine Self onto a priest or teacher, the opposites meet and marry: light and dark, divine and human, masculine and feminine, unlimited and limited, free and enslaved, purified and sinful. This process accounts for the sense of wholeness that arises from the union.

At certain levels of development, this student/teacher or lover/beloved relationship can be healing and urge evolution onward. In addition, people of a certain temperament, for example heart-centered devotional people, may require a human beloved as an object of their loving.

However, at a more developed stage, I believe this projection has to be left behind. An alchemical process, which could unfold within the soul, gets acted out on the interpersonal stage of life and can inhibit the turning within that is so needed. For example, if a saint, master, or rabbi stands in for the Messiah, we are less likely to focus on our own Messiah nature. If we depend on the unconditional love of a divine mother figure, we are less likely to cultivate that quality within our own hearts. If we place our faith on the outer performance of miracles, we are less likely to be called upon to develop a faith that is internally rooted. Finally, if an ideal Other is responsible for our sense of Self, then we may do just about anything to sustain it.

The result: rather than making a direct relationship to the divine in our own souls, we make the link through an intermediary, and a real, fallible human being is asked to stand in for the disowned qualities of the Self. He or she becomes the guardian of our imago dei. All too often, that person has the power to banish or excommunicate us from the community, denying us a felt sense of relationship to the divine.

If the student cannot see through the projection and turns the teacher into a god, coming to believe that only this unattainable Other promises transcendence, then he is enslaved by the relationship; he is caught in idolatry. The image is mistaken for the god behind it.

On the other hand, if the student can link with the divine in his own soul—via contemplation of the imago in a teacher—then the aspirant is freed by the relationship. In this case, the imago acts as a window, not a wall.

In this context, the teacher/student relationship becomes a container of Eros, the cosmic longing that leads us to higher and higher levels of transcendence, from a psychic glimpse of the Self to a subtle longing to lose the Self to a causal apperception of nondual awareness, in which the image of the teacher disappears with all duality into union with the divine.

PART 2

After the Fall

A Guide for
Disillusioned Believers

I cry out to you, God, but you do not answer;
I stand up, but you merely look at me.

JOB 30:20 (NIV)

A disciple asked a learned rabbi why god used
to speak directly to the people but never does so
today. The wise man replied, "People cannot bend
low enough now to hear what god says."

JEWISH PROVERB

The whole world is pining for light and freedom.
To meet this recurrent and poignant demand there
always arises a plentiful supply of those who claim
to meet it adequately. Most of these claimants are
impostors.

MEHER BABA

There are three powers, three powers alone, able to
conquer and to hold captive forever the conscience
of these impotent rebels for their happiness—those
forces are miracle, mystery, and authority.

DOSTOEVSKY'S GRAND INQUISITOR

FIVE

Meeting Spiritual Shadow

Darkness on the Path

Sadly, but frequently, the longing for the light evokes its opposite: a shattering encounter with spiritual darkness, an emptying out of hope, meaning, and long-held images of god. Our suffering hollows us out, tears at veils of spiritual persona, smashes religious idols, and ultimately leaves us bereft.

Before this encounter with spiritual shadow, we are, like Adam and Eve, faithful and trusting believers. We are the chosen; we will be saved; we can be enlightened; god is on our side.

We begin the journey in innocence, filled with a longing to be saved, awakened, or healed or simply to belong. We may find a cherished teacher or participate in a community and engage in religious ritual or spiritual practice. We may enjoy a sense of membership and moments of deep fulfillment, even rapture. We may experience ecstatic altered states of consciousness or simply a quieter mind and more compassionate heart.

But, at some point, we may meet the shadow of a spiritual authority, suffering blatant emotional or sexual abuse. Or we may feel the consequences of a series of small, insidious transgressions. Or we may uncover a coercive group dynamic that becomes intolerable. Regardless of the specifics, we come to see through the imago of an idealized priest or teacher to a dark shadow or human limitation, and our projection rattles. If the disappointment is deep, if the disillusionment is shattering, we enter the night sea journey, the *via negativa,* or way of darkness.

In the Christian mythos, this is the time of the cross. As we read in Mark 15:34: Jesus cried out in a loud voice, "My God, my God, why have you forsaken me?"

At first, we may try to deny what we see in others. One disciple of a swami accused of abuse explained, "If I believed such stories, I would disbelieve my whole life. I have no room for such thoughts. I might doubt my own perception. I might doubt my own eyes. But I cannot doubt that strength which has given me everything."

In a different scenario, we deny our own shadows, those unconscious feelings and beliefs that are deemed unacceptable by our teachers and communities. But at some point, those hidden thoughts and feelings—a cynical, gnawing doubt; an intractable, inexplicable depression; a persistent, destructive habit—erupt into consciousness. Then one day we admit to ourselves that, despite our faith in a church or a teacher's promises, despite our diligence in our attendance or our practices, we still struggle with our own darkness. A spiritual life can't save us from suffering.

One man told me, "The more I meditated by day, the more I drank at night. At first, I didn't think anything of it because my parents drank, my brother drank, my teacher drank too. Taking it for granted, the drinking became invisible. Then someone pointed out that I couldn't get through an evening without drinking. Slowly, I began to realize that, yes, I was an alcoholic. And my teacher and my practices colluded with my problem."

In yet another scenario, our beliefs and rituals fail to fulfill their promises. One Sufi told me that he had practiced dhikr, or chanting the names of god, for twenty-five years. But he never felt a moment of fana, or transcendence. Gradually his faith in Sufism eroded, and he felt too demoralized to practice. A Christian Science practitioner reported that, after a remarkable healing that had lit the flame of faith years before, her prayers seemed to go unanswered. Serious symptoms of diabetes and financial problems plagued her, despite her practitioner's explanation that they were not real but merely "claims" that god is not all-powerful. In the end, she turned to medicine for help and lost her faith.

When we strive for spiritual perfection, our practices inevitably fail us. All too often this striving stems from emotional needs for approval and a relentless inner critic. Spiritual theologian Matthew Fox has pointed out that believers who learn to trust creation see that beauty and imperfection go together both in nature and in the human body. Our imperfections unite us in vulnerability and lead to compassion for one another. But the ego's quest for perfection traps us in isolation and in a longing that cannot be fulfilled.

Some yoga practitioners who yearn for that unattainable perfect body—strong, sculpted, and flexible—report that their asana practices actually reinforce their negative body images. Instead of finding calm and sanctuary in the practice of hatha yoga, they strive for a standard that leaves them feeling unattractive, ashamed, and not good enough.

One woman told me that she thought she had left behind self-punishing behaviors and self-critical thoughts when she quit jogging but later discovered that she had brought them along to the yoga mat. Imposing grueling demands on her body and viewing it judgmentally from the outside, she maintained feelings of shame and failure. When she discovered that her yoga teacher was anorexic, she felt devastated and quit her practice.

I, too, suffered this kind of painful disillusionment with my practice. When meditators all around me reported psychic and subtle-level experiences, I simply sat, day after day, with a quiet mind: no lights, no visions, no voices, no rushes of energy. I began to wonder what was wrong with me. Or whether my nervous system was damaged. Or whether my psychic boundaries were impenetrable. Or whether I was doing the practice incorrectly. In the end, I wondered whether I was on the wrong path.

Meditation may, in addition, cause or exacerbate a recurrent social, psychological, or physical problem. Most of us know about the widely publicized health benefits of the practice. But the risks, though rare, are less well known. In a private communication, psychologist Aaron Kipnis offered me several examples: A college student attended an intensive weekend seminar on meditation and then began to miss school frequently due to disorientation. A man used a repetitive chant to attempt to treat his anxiety but grew increasingly anxious when he failed to chant. Another isolated himself to meditate for longer and longer periods in an effort to withdraw from using drugs but suffered withdrawal symptoms when he stopped meditating. Each of these people became dependent on a spiritual technique, experienced subsequent problems with it, and was unable to reduce its use.

Stanislav Grof studied and wrote about "spiritual emergency," which could include drastic changes to identity and meaning due to a spiritual experience, including a rising kundalini. These may include loss of coping ability, sleep disturbances, emotional volatility, even hallucinations. Psychiatrist John Nelson, in *Healing the Split,* examined spiritual emergencies in the context of kundalini experiences, distinguishing between breakdowns and breakthroughs that are both psychological and spiritual events.

More recently, researchers have sought to quantify some of the dangers of meditation. In "The Dark Side of Meditation," Jessica Downey reviews research by mindfulness practitioner Willoughby Britton of Brown University. Britton interviewed a hundred teachers and practitioners of Buddhism and found fifty types of negative experiences, from moderate anxiety to dissociation to psychotic symptoms that required hospitalization. As a result, she founded Cheetah House, an organization dedicated to helping people with meditation-related adverse effects.

Finally, the abuse of power and sex among priests and Eastern teachers has brought about widespread demoralization, leading many people to question the purpose of religion and the goal of spiritual practice, once seen as the purpose of life itself. After all, Hindu teachings say that when the mind is established in transcendence, and we act from the highest level of awareness, we can perform only right action. And Buddhist teachings say that when the mind is cleansed of defilements, behavior will be liberated from greed, anger, and ignorance. How, then, do we make sense of abusive behaviors by celibate priests or allegedly realized teachers?

For many believers, enlightenment or Self-realization has been thrown into doubt. For them, the spiritual quest today looks more like mindful awareness in everyday life. As Helen Tworkov, editor of *Tricycle: The Buddhist Review,* pointed out, after many teacher scandals in the 1980s, Buddhist concerns shifted from awakening the mind to establishing ethical norms. However, she said, "ethical behavior may or may not be born of fundamental insight into the nature of reality. It may or may not be released through the compassion inherent in our Buddha-nature." If ethics are separated from realization, she wrote, then Buddhist ethics offers nothing new to a predominantly Christian society, which prescribes behavior based on scripture, rather than rooted in consciousness.

To sum up, we may meet a teacher's shadow, we may meet our own shadow, or we may suffer disillusionment with spiritual beliefs or practices. In any case, our dreams of transcendence and communion fade. We lose faith and fall from grace. We feel forsaken, even by god.

With the fall, some believers turn away from god, becoming bitter disbelievers who feel confused and disoriented with the fellowship of community and the guidance of doctrine. Others retrench against the threat of loss and defend the fortress of belief with louder right-and-wrong thinking. They attempt to ascend again, denying the meaning hidden in the fall. They rationalize their beliefs, excuse their abusive experiences at the hands of others, or trade in their spiritual props for another set, climbing back toward the heavens of naivete. Still others grab for the brass ring of a materialistic life.

Those few who turn to face the disillusionment and loss are, like Job, angry, betrayed, and empty-handed. As one client told me:

I didn't want to hear the rumors about my minister's behavior. For the longest time, I couldn't look at the abuse, like a blind spot. After all, my whole life was in the church. And if I questioned anything, I would be seen as a doubter, no, a heretic.

Then, one day, something snapped: I needed to know. I no longer wanted to live in delusion.

But the truth was devastating. How could this revered man commit such a travesty? Suddenly, nothing made sense. I had no reason to get out of bed in the morning.

When the meeting with the Other occurs, the descent begins. It is this loss of innocence and descent to the underworld that initiates us into the mystery and complexity of the human shadow, especially as it is linked to divine life.

Encountering the Spiritual Other
The Breakdown of Communion

The true guru will never humiliate you, nor will he estrange you from yourself. He will constantly bring you back to the fact of your inherent perfection and encourage you to seek within. He knows you need nothing, not even him, and is never tired of reminding you. But the self-appointed guru is more concerned with himself than with his disciples.

SRI NISARGADATTA MAHARAJ

The Guru is a kind of irritation to his or her friends. You can't sleep with a dog barking in your ear. . . . The Guru is always annoying people with this demand to stay awake, to wake up. Therefore, he doesn't satisfy the seeker. Those who come to be satisfied are offended.

DA FREE JOHN (AKA ADI DA)

In *An Anthropologist on Mars,* Oliver Sacks tells the following story, which he calls "The Last Hippie": In Berkeley in the late 1960s, a young student disappeared. When his parents last saw him, he seemed to be healthy, thin, and wiry, with a full head of hair. As time passed without word, they grew more frightened and finally hired a private detective to help. The detective located the young man on the East Coast in a Hare Krishna commune.

Filled with hope and dread, his parents boarded a plane to visit the commune. A swami in orange robes brought their son to the door. He was unrecognizable: obese, hairless, and lethargic. The parents were confused and bereft. What had happened to their only son?

The swami explained: Their son was enlightened. He was imperturbable, living fully in the present moment and liking everyone equally.

Stunned, the parents asked if he had any health problems. He had complained recently about dimming eyesight, the swami told them. But, he added, his physical sight was weakening because his inner sight was growing.

The parents were distraught. They insisted on taking their son to a nearby hospital for a battery of tests. Doctors soon discovered that he had a pituitary tumor the size of a grapefruit, which had grown into his frontal lobes and put pressure on his optic nerve. The tumor had progressed so far that it was no longer operable.

Appalled, the man's parents called in Oliver Sacks for a consultation, and he administered a range of neuropsychological tests. The man had no memory except for a small period in the 1960s. And what he remembered most were song lyrics by the Grateful Dead.

So, Sacks arranged to take him to a Dead concert. When the music began, the man leapt out of his wheelchair, alive and kicking. He sang along with every word of every song. But when the concert ended, he slumped back into the chair, dazed and lethargic, and returned to his former state.

Two days later, when Sacks visited him and asked how he had enjoyed the concert, the man replied, "What concert?"

I tell this story to illustrate what I mean by spiritual abuse: a mistreatment in a religious setting that results in an injury to that which is central to soul—our faith. Spiritual abuse is a betrayal of trust by the people to whom we entrust our faith, those who carry a higher authority or an imago dei.

Identifying Covert Abuse

This kind of abuse may be covert, such as the misuse of spiritual understanding to rationalize events, which ends in neglect or another kind of harm. The Krishnas' spiritual frame led them to deny outside evidence of medical problems. They were blinded in the name of vision, overlooking bodily problems because they devalued them as unspiritual. They interpreted memory loss as living in the present moment and growing blindness as a gift. They did not intend harm; they simply denied or refused to see what was before them because they elevated everything to its highest common denominator—a spiritual reality.

Many traditions perpetrate covert abuse. A Hasidic teacher said he would offer me more teachings only if I kept the Sabbath and became kosher. A Christian Science practitioner told a woman that a major decision she made, which appeared to be mistaken, had to be correct because they had prayed about it. A Nichiren Shoshu Buddhist reported that when she stopped chanting, she grew depressed and was told her "low-life condition" stemmed from not chanting. A member of a small Hindu community reported that she gave her inheritance to the guru because he said that her financial advisor was not all-knowing, as he himself was. A man whose family belonged to the Jehovah's Witnesses was discouraged from any outside education because, they said, Watchtower activities of going door to door held greater value. A Zen Buddhist woman told me that she left her feelings of doubt about her roshi at the door of the Zendo in the name of right speech.

If human behavior is controlled by an external moral authority, and language is shaped by giving special meanings to words, believers internalize that control. Shame, guilt, and self-criticism, seeds planted in early childhood, are already in place to reinforce group norms.

A devout Episcopalian high school student, kneeling on wooden benches, learned to repeat these prayers: "We do not presume to come to this thy table, O merciful Lord, trusting in our own righteousness, but in thy manifold and great mercies. We are not worthy so much as to gather up the crumbs under thy table. Have mercy upon us, miserable offenders." When this same man later learned to meditate in his continuing quest for divine guidance, his teacher's shaming messages resonated with truth. He told me, "I'm not worthy of becoming enlightened. I need to meditate more, a lot more. If I question his authority, I might leave the group. Then I'll surely end up in a hell realm."

When demeaning and controlling messages are continually reinforced through lectures, pressures to conform, and punishments for aberrant thought or behavior, before long most of us submit. We lose the right relationship between self-worth and humility.

As the Self is projected onto a teacher and group identity is cemented with a secret teaching that carries the light side of life, the dark side typically is projected outside of the group. In this way, enemy-making begins. We come to believe that the world is divided into the in-group (the pure, saved, enlightened ones) and the out-group (the impure, unsaved, ignorant ones, or heretics).

As projection of the collective shadow takes on a life of its own, the in-group identifies with moral superiority, and the out-group carries their inferiority and the traits that go with it—materialism, hedonism, or greed. Those qualities that the community can't tolerate within it are unconsciously attributed to the enemy. With black-and-white thinking institutionalized, the nuances of shadow within the in-group and goodness within the out-group are lost. Self-righteousness is reinforced.

Eventually, the outsiders become foes, then scapegoats. In extremist groups, the enemy is ripe for sacrifice because it has been dehumanized, even demonized, no longer deserving of life. For that reason, those who kill them will be spiritually rewarded. Islamic fundamentalist suicide bombers believe, for example, that their violent acts assure them a place in paradise. In this way, the ultimate function of warring with an enemy becomes redemption.

In that context, the ends justify the means. We may begin by telling small lies to our families. (Transcendental Meditation is a stress-reduction technique, not a spiritual practice.) We manipulate others to seduce them into joining us. (The Hare Krishnas call this "transcendental trickery." Jehovah's Witnesses call it "theocratic strategy.") And we come to value an abstract set of principles that gives us inner coherence and direction over human life. (Certain Christian groups believe that nuclear war is not a risk because, if it happens, they will be taken up into the rapture to join Christ in heaven.)

When a conflict arises between our feelings and our ideology, we are told and may come to believe that *we* are wrong. The doctrine is more valid than our direct experience. Our doubts merely point to our own weakness, lack of faith, past transgressions, or poor character. Therefore, we must change ourselves in order to tolerate any discrepancy.

This cognitive dissonance between what we feel, know, or see and what we are told by a religious authority figure can have a surprising result: Apocalyptic groups that predicted the end of the world grew stronger after their prophecy failed. Needing to maintain meaning and reinforce their self-images as true believers, most members did not question or doubt their "truths" but defended them even more virulently.

The same phenomenon occurred within meditation groups: When practitioners did not become enlightened, as promised, many blamed themselves for being too neurotic and Western culture for being too stressful. The teacher and the practice were not responsible.

Robert Jay Lifton, who is well known for his study of thought reform in extremist groups, points out that any set of emotionally charged convictions about the human relationship to the divine can be carried to an extreme—when a community becomes a cult. From that point on, group mind takes hold, and there is little tolerance for doubt, ambiguity, or critique. Some communities prohibit contact with outsiders, prescribe rigorous training, and demand strict obedience.

Eventually, members report that they feel powerless to leave and fear retaliation if they try.

Identifying Overt Abuse

Spiritual abuse also may be overt: money, power, and sexual shadows in religious teachers may lead to outright coercion or molestation. One clear example can be seen in the international scandal of sexual abuses by Catholic clergy. Although there are clear distinctions to be made between child survivors of abuse and adult survivors, there are many commonalities as well. The child's innocent projection of greatness, even godliness, onto the priest is analogous to the adult's projection onto a spiritual teacher. The incapacity to give consent is analogous due to the power dynamic. The demand to keep the secret repeats the pattern. And the consequences for the mind-body of the survivor are the same: PTSD, anxiety, depression, and profound loss of faith.

Beginning in the 1980s and snowballing over the years into an outright bombshell by the early 2000s, the Catholic church's sexual abuse scandal involved thousands of supposedly celibate priests in the U.S., Canada, and around the world who were accused of child and teen molestation. Their cardinals stood accused of knowing that pedophilia and adult sexual abuse was taking place in their parishes, denying the accusations, transferring the culpable priests to other communities, paying hush money to silence victim-survivors, engaging in retaliatory litigation, and failing to report the crimes to law enforcement.

The fact that Catholic priests were not, in fact, celibate should not have come as a surprise. Plenty of evidence existed to document sexual improprieties among clergy, Catholic or otherwise. In his 1995 book *Sex, Priests, and Power,* Richard Sipe estimated that nearly 50 percent of Catholic priests break their vows of celibacy. A 1998 survey of evangelical ministers conducted by researchers at *Christianity Today* found that 12 percent of clergy admitted to having sex with someone other than a spouse, while 23 percent stated that they had been "sexually inappropriate" with a non-spouse. A 1991 survey of Protestant pastors by the

Center for Ethics and Social Policy at the Graduate Theological Union in Berkeley, California, found that about 10 percent had been involved with a parishioner. And in 1993, 70 percent of Southern Baptist respondents told the *Journal of Pastoral Care* that they knew of pastors who had had sexual contact with congregants.

Over time, thousands upon thousands of people came forward with accusations of sexual abuse by Catholic clergy. The 2004 John Jay Report, commissioned by the Catholic church itself, found almost eleven thousand cases accusing more than four thousand priests in the United States between 1950 and 2002. Other sources calculate much higher numbers. In his 2012 piece for the *National Catholic Reporter,* John Allen Jr. cited a Vatican summit at which experts estimated 100,000 victims just in the United States.

Many of the accused priests were forced to resign or dismissed from the priesthood. Some were charged with crimes, found guilty, and incarcerated. Several bishops and cardinals who had participated in cover-ups were forced to resign or retire. Meanwhile, the church settled on financial compensation for many victims; Allen pointed toward estimated total payouts of up to $2.2 billion by the U.S. Catholic church by 2012.

Institutional changes are under way. In 2002 the Pope summoned American cardinals to Rome and told them that those who were guilty of pedophilia had succumbed to the power of evil. He called the abuse of minors both a sin and a crime, signaling to bishops that they should cooperate with law enforcement in investigating allegations of sexual abuse by priests and employees of the church.

The bishops agreed to a one-strike policy, meaning that any priest who abused even one child, whether now or in the past, would be dismissed from the clergy. They also agreed to report allegations to civil authorities, relinquish confidentiality agreements in lawsuits against them, do background checks on clergy who work with children, and create a lay review board to examine accusations.

Some local dioceses have followed suit. After trying for years to silently settle cases of religious abuse and prevent jury trials, the Los

Angeles and Orange County dioceses finally agreed to changes in their policy, instituting the one-strike provision. Also, they agreed to monitor parishes and schools, establish toll-free phone numbers and a website for anonymous complaints, teach abuse prevention at parochial schools, and forbid priests to be alone in social settings with minors. Rhode Island passed a ground-breaking law saying that priests must report what they learn of spiritual abuse in the confessional. The church objected, saying that if bishops or priests become mandated reporters, like therapists who must tell police of crimes, parishioners will not confide in them.

In addition, several previously taboo topics emerged in public discourse, although they remain tentative fields of investigation: the risks of pedophiles among the ranks of Catholic priests, the risks of the culture of celibacy, and the risks of the absence of women in the priesthood.

One of the nation's leading Catholic magazines said that church hierarchy was incapable of investigating itself and that bishops had lost credibility. In response to that assessment, which seemed to reflect the opinion of the general population, the role of lay church members, who are seeking a greater voice in policy-making, is also under discussion.

Despite the scandals and financial losses, the Catholic church remains reluctant to disclose the full scope of the issue. ProPublica has published an interactive database that lets users search for clergy who have been listed as credibly accused of sexual abuse in reports released by Catholic dioceses and religious orders. It is, as of the publication of this book, the only nationwide database of official disclosures.

With decades of revelations, testimonies, and lawsuits against it, the church must undergo a sea change. The focus can no longer be on the misconduct of individual priests but must target the system that supported this behavior, covered it up, and forgave perpetrators without assurances that they had changed. If the church's policy toward priests who abuse their power is to shift from individual sin and redemption to dismissal and punishment, the church will need to separate spiritual questions from legal and structural questions. It will need to redefine the zone of its moral concern. It will, in effect, need to undergo a *via negativa*—an encounter with the depths of its own darkness, a meeting with the individual and collective shadow.

Responses to clergy sexual misconduct in other denominations have varied to date: the Episcopal church has detailed policies and trainings for its ministers on how to maintain personal boundaries, while the Southern Baptist Convention has none. Other Protestant denominations, especially those that ordain women, have begun to hold seminars on preventing abuse. The Central Conference of American Rabbis has guidelines on how to investigate, report, and adjudicate allegations of abuse. The Orthodox Jewish community, which was rocked by accusations in 2002 that a well-known youth official had been sexually abusing teens under his care, has begun to develop new policies.

Finally, moving beyond sexual abuse, scores of high-profile clergy have been accused of financial fraud and embezzlement. State securities regulators have warned of scams that play on religious loyalties to persuade people to mortgage homes or pull cash from retirement funds. In 2001, according to a story by Kathy Kristof of the *Los Angeles Times,* state regulators took action against individuals and companies that used religious beliefs to gain the trust of more than ninety thousand investors over a three-year period, in some cases even kneeling to pray with their victim-survivors. These investors lost roughly $1.8 billion in schemes involving organizations such as the Baptist Foundation of Arizona, Greater Ministries International Church, and IRM corporation.

Tales of Religious and Spiritual Abuse

The epidemic of abuse by teachers knows no denominational boundaries. It's not rooted in dogma or belief; it emerges from the deep recesses of the human shadow regardless of a leader's beliefs, even regardless of spiritual commitments. And meeting the shadow on the spiritual path—your own or someone else's—can be a life-changing event, a turning point from blind trust of another to a more authentic self-trust, from naivete to maturity.

The intention of adding shadow-awareness to our search for awakening is not to negate the profound, meaningful, even ecstatic gifts of our teachers and communities. We don't want to deny the light any more than we want to deny the shadow. Rather, the intention is to learn to hold both, the full reality of our spiritual lives—the dance of darkness and light on the path.

The following stories, some firsthand accounts, some alleged reports, may be disturbing, even alarming to read. If you begin to feel emotionally triggered as you read, especially if you find a disclosure about a teacher you know and perhaps respect, or even love, please take a deep breath and perhaps a break from reading for a while.

Contemplate whether this is the right time for you to meet this person's shadow. Do you want to break out of denial now or wait a while? What do you need to take care of yourself if you face this uncomfortable reality? Can you ask for support? How can this information help you to make sense of a teacher's behaviors—and your own? How can it help you to separate from the teacher, if that's what you choose? How can it expand your awareness about spiritual awakening—its gifts and limits?

I suggest that you read these tales as teaching stories, windows into the personal shadow, how it acts out in self-destructive behaviors and deeply harmful deeds, how people enable it and collude with it, and why we continue to idealize human beings, despite the evidence. Finally, I suggest that you read these stories with a wider lens, focusing not only on students' dark moments of ordeal but on the long-term outcomes. Consider the ways in which they gained, as well as lost, by finding a spiritual teacher and practice; the ways in which they gained, as well as lost, by meeting the shadow on the spiritual path; and the ways in which they may have reclaimed their own authority, their voices, intuitive knowing, independence, self-respect, and self-love.

Robert Karpinski, who was abused by a priest at the age of five and later himself became a priest, felt called to change the system. In 2021, he published his story on HuffPost.

"There must be systemic change in the structure of all-male leadership in the Roman Catholic Church. . . . Instead of running away from the Catholic Church or adopting a different religious tradition, I dove into the institution," he said.

"As a child, my siblings and I were taught to love the church. Our family life and traditions revolved around its worship and rituals. In a real sense, I bonded with the Catholic Church at a level that drew me into its life, despite the sexual abuse. When I entered the seminary at the age of eighteen, I suppose this deep level of bonding prevented me from acknowledging that the institution and one of its ordained representatives was hurting me."

Karpinski described how, over his nine years as a priest, he went to the church authorities to report his abuse and request that his abuser be removed from the ministry. "They offered thoughts and prayers, but no change." Again and again.

In 2002, when Boston dioceses were swept up in grand jury investigations and arrests of clergy, Karpinski testified, as a priest, about the abuse he'd experienced. But the priest who abused him and many others was never prosecuted. He was, as Karpinski said, "shuffled from parish to parish, assignment to assignment, because preserving the institution was more important than keeping children safe. In other words, the institutional, male-dominated church circled the wagons around the perpetrator while offering us, yes, thoughts and prayers."

This reality caused Karpinski to leave the ministry. "I needed to move beyond priesthood to save myself," he explained.

As journalist Michelle Boorstein detailed in 2021, a report commissioned by his own ministry revealed that Christian evangelist Ravi

Zacharias, whose global ministries, books, and radio shows reached fifteen countries on evangelical media, had been accused of sexual misconduct, coercion, and rape. The report, said Boorstein, quoted the woman who accused Zacharias of rape, saying, "He made her pray with him to thank God for the 'opportunity' they both received. . . . She said he called her his 'reward' for living a life of service to God. . . . He warned her not ever to speak out against him or she would be responsible for the 'millions of souls' whose salvation would be lost if his reputation was damaged."

Zacharias and his lawyers aggressively denied the allegation, slandered the accusers, and sued one for extortion. The board of his ministry later offered a written apology to those who had been punished for questioning Zacharias and hired an independent firm to investigate and make restitution. Zacharias died in 2020 at the age of seventy-four.

In 2022, a third-party investigation of the Southern Baptist Convention (SBC) released a report detailing how leaders had covered up sex abuse, ignored and even vilified survivors, and kept a secret list of abusers, while simultaneously telling followers the organization was unable to maintain such a record.

As reporter Sarah Pulliam Bailey noted for the *Washington Post,* SBC leaders had actively resisted calls for abuse prevention and reform. For two decades, survivors and their supporters reached out to the church administration to report child molesters and other abusers who were in the pulpit or on staff. But their efforts were met with "resistance, stonewalling, even outright hostility" by leaders who were more concerned with protecting the institution from liability than protecting their congregants from further abuse. The report also named three past presidents of the SBC who protected alleged abusers, and it found that a pastor and former vice president of SBC's mission arm was credibly accused of sexual assault in 2010.

Swami Rama, whose yogic powers were said to include changing his brain waves, stopping his heart at will, and moving objects with his mind alone, offered inspiration and instruction to many about the vast range of human capacities. But in 1990 journalist Katherine Webster reported in *Yoga Journal* that the swami had been having secret sexual affairs with female students for years. According to witnesses, he used his powers to discern their needs, cultivate their self-doubts, and coerce them into sexual obedience. For one, he promised a trip to India; for another, he disclosed they had been together in a past life.

In addition, female members reported that they donated their labor, sacrificed privacy, were constantly monitored, and were often subject to humiliation, such as kicking, shaming comments, and dismissive behaviors. In one case, he allegedly bragged to disciples that a woman would do whatever he told her, then put his dog's collar and leash around her neck and walked her back and forth. Because his disciples agreed that, in his enlightened state, he could cause no harm but only help others achieve liberation, they refused to hear complaints or investigate reports of abuse.

Sogyal Rinpoche gained popularity when he published *The Tibetan Book of Living and Dying*. The main altar of Sogyal's temple had a twenty-three-foot-high golden Buddha, which elicited a sense of being part of a respected ancient wisdom tradition. His students were taught to train their minds to view him as the "all-embodied jewel," an infallible human. The Dalai Lama and other lamas legitimized his work by their presence.

But in July 2017 former student Tahlia Newland reported in *Tricycle: The Buddhist Review* that eight of his longtime students accused him of decades of sexual, physical, and psychological abuse and a complex organizational coverup. When Newland learned that friends had been abused by Sogyal, she was freed of her dependency on him. "I realized that the central focus of my spiritual path was based on a lie—my lama was not who I'd thought him to be."

These accusations became more public. At the Sakyadhita International Association of Buddhist Women's sixteenth biennial conference in 2019, former Buddhist nun Damcho Dyson gave a speech that was reproduced in *Tricycle: The Buddhist Review*. She described how she had felt lost when she discovered *The Tibetan Book of Living and Dying* and slowly decided to take monastic vows and surrender her ego to the teacher. Eventually she became Sogyal's personal assistant—and the victim of his beatings and humiliation. "For many of us in the inner circle, it was not uncommon to have multiple lumps on our skulls or split scalps from beating," she said. She also witnessed him grooming young women for sex. Because he was not a monk, which would have required him to be celibate, most devotees turned a blind eye. Later, she personally heard tales of rape in the name of "consort practice."

In 2008, six years after her ordination, Dyson began to have PTSD-like flashbacks of his beatings and verbal abuse. She feared speaking up because Sogyal's public humiliation of people who questioned him was so intense. Students were told not to read allegations online because he was the victim of cyberbullying. They were told not to evaluate him with judgmental mind because it was not to be trusted.

Eventually, another teacher in whom she confided stated bluntly: "This is abuse." On hearing those three words, she saw through the training for what it was and escaped to India. In 2017, she joined other former students to discuss their experiences. They realized that the damage went beyond their personal experiences, shaping people's feelings about the dharma and Buddhist practice.

They wrote an open letter describing Sogyal's decades-long misconduct, which included sexual, physical, emotional, and financial abuse of students. It received wide coverage and led to official investigations and the disclosure of more disturbing accounts.

Tahlia Newland wrote a book about her experience, titled *Fallout: Recovering from Abuse in Tibetan Buddhism*. She noted, "Abuse in a spiritual context does not just affect those directly abused; it affects every single member of the community. . . . When your spiritual path is based on your trust in a person and that person shatters your trust, what happens to your spiritual path?"

The Ananda Church of Self-Realization, which split off from Swami Paramahansa Yogananda's community, became a well-known residential retreat in California in the 1970s. But in 1998 a jury decided that its leader, Swami Kriyananda, was guilty of fraud: he presented himself as a celibate despite having sexual relations with women. Kriyananda responded that, although he kept the title of swami, he had renounced his vows of celibacy when he married in 1985. Following the outcome of the trial, he relinquished his position in the church and moved overseas.

Sri Chinmoy was an Indian spiritual leader who taught meditation in the 1960s and eventually had students in sixty countries. A prolific author and musician, Chinmoy taught a spiritual path to God through prayer and meditation and also advocated vegetarianism and physical fitness.

In *Cartwheels in a Sari,* Jayanti Tamm described her life as Chinmoy's disciple and "divine child," as he called her. Her mother had married another devotee, and when Tamm was born despite the fact that the couple had been told to be celibate, a myth was born too: Chinmoy told his followers that she was the only soul he had selected to incarnate on earth. She was to be the Ananda to Buddha, the Peter to Jesus. He named her Jayanti, meaning "the absolute victory of highest Supreme." And he controlled her every breath.

She tells a coming-of-age story in a cultlike community, with her efforts to please and obey him as she grew, and her parents' efforts to work tirelessly for him. Tamm says the guru always had the last word in her household. TV was mostly forbidden; he disparaged education, so instead of doing her homework, she spent hours memorizing aphorisms

and songs he wrote. They also were forbidden to consume alcohol, caf-
feine, and meat; to dance, date, or have sex; and to socialize with outsiders. The guru created a caste system that allowed him to demote or
promote members at will. He encouraged members to keep tabs on one
another and turn in rule breakers. At one meditation session, he held
a contest for the ugliest girl—a young member with a boil on her face
won the distinction.

When Tamm was kicked out for dating, she felt compelled to beg
for forgiveness and return to the organization. But at the age of twenty-
five, she was so unhappy that she attempted suicide. Chinmoy banned
her permanently, without explanation.

He died in 2007 of a heart attack, but thousands of current members continue to idealize him and deny his shadow.

One man told me that after twenty-five years of meditation practice,
he was finally enjoying the kinds of spiritual experiences he had longed
for, thanks to the guidance of Dr. Frederick Lenz, aka Atmananda, aka
Zen Master Rama.

Originally a follower of Sri Chinmoy, in 1980 Lenz said he had
achieved samadhi and went out on his own, claiming yogic powers. His
quirky teaching style included intellectual rants, all-night music raves,
desert trips to observe the stars, and recommendations of "higher-
vibration" movies and products.

Unlike Eastern gurus who proclaim celibacy and anti-materialism,
Lenz was openly sexual and acquisitive. He pushed many of his students
into computer careers and, once they were earning high salaries, charged
high tuitions for his own classes. However, according to ex-devotees, he
also encouraged them to lie, cheat, and infiltrate organizations that he
disliked.

According to various reports, Lenz coerced his followers to engage
in sex with him, take drugs, and undergo fasting and sleep deprivation
to produce altered states of consciousness. In the 1990s several female

followers reported that Lenz fed them psychedelics and seduced them. One follower, a dear friend of mine, died of a drug overdose after giving Lenz a $100,000 donation.

Following the revelations, Lenz swallowed a great quantity of Valium and walked off the end of his Long Island dock with a female follower, having promised her his guidance into a higher spiritual plane. She survived to tell the story.

Although many of my Los Angeles friends delighted in the benefits of his Insight Training Seminars, John-Roger, aka J-R or the Mystical Traveler, founder of the church known as Movement of Spiritual Inner Awareness, was accused in the 1980s of sexually seducing male followers under spiritual pretense, accumulating vast wealth despite a vow of poverty, and using his spiritual powers to elicit obedience, as detailed by journalist Bob Sipchen in 1994. J-R, who denied the allegations, died in 2014.

In Zen Buddhism, a teacher is certified as enlightened by his or her teacher in an unbroken lineage, supposedly reaching back to the Buddha. But this claim results in a projection that renders students blind and mute, unable to see abuse or speak up about it.

Beginning in 1975, sexual and financial scandals rocked Zen centers throughout the United States. In 1975, 1979, and 1982, the married abbot of the Zen Studies Society of New York, Eido Roshi, was accused of seducing emotionally vulnerable women students. He denied the allegations. As both the abbot and the head of the board for the society, Eido Roshi held all the spiritual power as well as all the secular power. He was supported unconditionally by board members and senior students. However, in 2010, another affair was revealed, and he was ultimately asked to leave.

Zen priest Shinge Chayat, who took over leadership of the Zen Studies Society, was interviewed about the aftereffects of the scandal by staff from the nonprofit Lion's Roar for a 2014 article in *Buddhadharma* magazine. According to Chayat, the *sangha,* or community, consulted with the Faith Trust Institute, which made five recommendations: Eido Roshi had to step down; he had to make a full public apology acknowledging his misconduct and regret for causing harm; students who wished to continue studying with him had to leave with him; the society needed to conduct a formal financial audit; and the society had to consult with colleagues who had faced similar issues.

Sangha members then began working with a mediation organization called An Olive Branch, whose staff met with the roshi, the board of directors, and community members. They also facilitated a weekend for everyone involved to process their feelings of trauma and outrage and, it turns out, disclose more examples of misconduct. They created a visual timeline of events on the wall, and people posted their secrets.

As Chayat said, "We went from an organization plagued by secrecy and authoritarianism to one that is transparent and hewing to ethical guidelines."

This scandal at Zen Studies Society was followed by allegations of sexual misconduct, financial misconduct, and/or alcohol abuse against many other Zen spiritual leaders, including Maezumi Roshi of the Zen Center of Los Angeles, Katagiri Roshi of the Minnesota Zen Meditation Center, Seung Sahn of the Providence Zen Center in Rhode Island, Dennis Merzel of the Hosshinji Zen temple in Bar Harbor, Maine, and later the Kanzeon Zen Center in Salt Lake City, and Walter Nowick of Moonspring Hermitage in Surry, Maine.

Stuart Lachs, who writes prolifically about shadow issues in Buddhism, posted a piece, "For Whose Best Interest," in July 2015. It tells the story of Joshu Sasaki Roshi, a Rinzai Zen master in Japan who became a disciple of a famous master at the age of fourteen and rose through the hierarchy.

In 1962 he was sent from Japan to the United States, allegedly to bring an authorized Rinzai master to the West. In the United States, his star rose at the Mt. Baldy Zen Center in California, while other roshis fell from grace. But in 1975, rumors spread about Sasaki fondling women students during *sanzen,* the private study of koan with the roshi. There were reports of nonconsensual touching in tea ceremonies and sexual interference in marriages. Those who spoke up were hushed or excommunicated for decades, while the center's board remained loyal to him.

In 2012 a former monk posted online an open letter, "Everybody knows," about Sasaki's fifty years of sexual misconduct and his organization's complicity. The letter launched a slew of disclosures about Sasaki's transgressions, disdain for disciples, demands for unquestioning loyalty, and use of Zen teaching, such as nonattachment or checking a student's ego, to defend his behavior.

Firsthand allegations of abuse were officially denied. Lachs wrote that Sasaki's closest students felt that sacrificing young women to his sexual desires was a price they had to pay for his attention. Sasaki threatened to stop teaching if he were forced to change his behavior, Lachs reported. He also said that sex with young women kept him young.

As Lachs pointed out, after the scandals broke, new information became available: Sasaki had been at the center of sexual and financial scandals in the 1940s and 1950s in Japan, including the embezzlement of several million yen in temple funds. Lachs asked, speculatively, whether Sasaki was sent to the United States to exile a troublesome monk, much like abusive Catholic clergy were sent to different parishes.

In the end, Sasaki Roshi retitled himself Supreme Abbot, controlled the finances into old age, and refused to name a dharma heir, leaving the organization headless when he died, as Lachs put it. An independent council estimated that Sasaki Roshi had made sexual advances toward as many as three hundred female students. He died in 2014 at the age of 107.

The first Buddhist monastery outside of Asia, the San Francisco Zen Center was founded in 1962 by Shunryu Suzuki, who made Richard Baker his dharma heir in a ceremony that professes oneness with the teacher and the intent of the teacher. As abbot, Baker Roshi opened Greens, which became a popular Bay Area restaurant, and the Tassajara monastery and bakery, which eventually published the bestselling *Tassajara Bread Book*. The scandal that rocked the Zen Center in 1983 cast doubt in the minds of many about the validity of transplanting Eastern practices to the West.

That year, the center was torn apart when the married Baker was found to be having an affair with a student. As board members broke through their denial and began to explore their options, a net of other abuses, held together by secrecy and shunning, unraveled: fiscal irresponsibility (the abbot drove a new BMW and purchased expensive, antique meditation robes while the students, who worked long hours in the center businesses, lived on a small stipend); abuses of institutional power (the cluster of businesses that made up the Zen Center were incorporated in such a way that Baker Roshi had sole decision-making power); sexual misconduct (Baker had affairs with numerous women disciples); and breaking vows to obey the precepts of Buddhism, including "do no harm."

Though he denied the accusations, Baker resigned as abbot, leaving behind a shocked and humiliated community. The rift between him and the Zen Center has remained bitter for years, despite the work of counselors and consultants.

Years later, Baker admitted that his own insecurity and sense of self-importance lay beneath his behavior. Although he had had hundreds of students, he never claimed to be "teacher." In this way, he said, he avoided the responsibility for his position, including dealing with the projections and seeing his own flaws.

Several colleagues and clients have told me about how the teachings and practices of Bhagwan Shree Rajneesh, aka Osho, liberated them from emotional constraints and healed them of childhood wounds. Dancing wildly until they couldn't think, tasting the ecstasy of bliss, some devotees claim, even today, that their time with Rajneesh was the most valuable period of their lives. But many high-profile media reports have described how the Indian teacher allegedly coerced people into cathartic tantric sex practices with anonymous partners and absconded with devotees' money to buy Rolls Royces and property worldwide.

As his empire grew, Rajneesh apparently developed a dependence on nitrous oxide, stored guns at his ashram, and became increasingly isolated. Eventually he fell into paranoia, accusing his closest followers of murder, assault, and arson. *Wild, Wild Country,* a documentary that aired on Netflix in 2018, shows the degeneration of Osho and his community up close. It's a startling portrayal of a brilliant teacher gone awry, devotees who lose their moral compass, and a community in emotional and spiritual breakdown.

Erin Robbins, a devotee then known as Maitri, worked as therapist and group leader. She lived in Osho's home in 1978 at the age of twenty-five. One night he called her to his room, where he sat alone. He reportedly told her to take off her robe and gestured for her to kneel on the floor; a series of abusive actions followed. She didn't fight back, believing he was not a man but a god. She tried to let go and believe it was a blessing. He told her never to speak of it, and she didn't, even after his death.

More than forty years later, she began to see that she had been used and abused—that the sessions were not for her spiritual benefit but for his gratification. She realized how his position of power had been overwhelming to her. She had seen him as the most "magnificent, brilliant, conscious being" she would ever meet, and he had taken advantage. She could now see why, in the years that followed, she had been closed off to intimacy with others.

She posted online an open letter to her former community about her experience, concluding: "My heart breaks apart with all of you who were children in the commune that suffered neglect and emotional and sexual abuse. I am deeply sorry for looking the other way during these times. I remember noticing some of the men hanging out with very young girls. I do remember thinking it was odd, but I believed . . . that everything must be fine, even more than fine because it was happening in the garden of our beloved master. I am sorry. So, so sorry. . . . Thank you for inspiring me to open up about what I have been too terrified to expose, for all these forty-five years."

Like the wave of scandals in U.S. Zen communities, a tsunami of abuse allegations swept over Tibetan Buddhist communities as well. The lamas of various Vajrayana schools claim spiritual attainment, which is confirmed by those higher up in the spiritual hierarchy and leaves them in positions of unquestioning authority. Their institutional hierarchies, teacher/student vows, and cultures of secrecy create ripe conditions for the abuse of power, sex, and money.

In "Tibetan Buddhism Enters the 21st Century: Trouble in Shangri-la," Stuart Lachs explores allegations involving sex, alcohol, drugs, and money among teachers in several Tibetan lineages, beginning with that of Chogyam Trungpa Rinpoche. Trungpa told the tale that he escaped the Chinese invasion of Tibet on horseback, surviving near starvation, with the intention to transfer Vajrayana teachings to the West. In 1963, at the age of twenty, Trungpa moved to the United Kingdom, leaving behind his one-year-old son and the child's mother, a Tibetan nun, in a refugee camp in India. He abandoned the boy again in 1970, shortly after he had summoned him to the U.K. Three years later, when the boy arrived in the United States, Trungpa sent him to boarding school.

That pattern of abandonment and inability to bond or empathize with his children was repeated. Trungpa also abandoned his second son, with his British wife, at the age of four. The boy, who is reportedly autistic and epileptic, was left in the care of an untrained group of American devotees and, later, with Tibetan monastics in Sikkim, India. Trungpa's third son, likewise, was repeatedly abandoned to ad hoc caregivers.

In 1969, while driving drunk in the U.K., Trungpa was in a car crash and was paralyzed on his left side. He gave up his monastic vows and continued to drink heavily. In 1970 he married a wealthy sixteen-year-old student. They moved to the United States, where he attracted the attention of bohemian poets and began to set up Tibetan Buddhist centers, which he called Shambhala Meditation Centers, in Colorado, Vermont, and Nova Scotia. The public aim of Shambhala is built into its motto: "Making Enlightened Society Possible." In 1974 Trungpa founded Naropa University, the first accredited Buddhist university in North America. His brilliant books sold millions of copies and attracted many devotees.

Trungpa, an alcoholic, perpetuated the belief among his followers that he was immune to the effects of alcohol and turned it into an elixir. His alcoholic dementia was explained away as his being in the realm of *dakinis,* Tibetan guardians of the teachings. Later reports revealed that he had a serious cocaine habit as well and used Seconal to sleep.

In their book *The Other Side of Eden,* Shambhala students John and Nancy Steinbeck claimed that his devotees supplied him with drugs and alcohol and said that this was a sign of their devotion and an honoring of their vow to him (*samaya*). They witnessed women training to be consorts, which included caring for his bodily functions. While many praised the rinpoche for his transparency about his indulgences, these women cleaned up the mess.

Trungpa's wild parties, sexual assaults, and alcohol and drug abuse took place under the rubric of the "crazy wisdom" tradition, an ancient teaching style that challenges stereotypical holiness with contradictory behavior and messages. It aims to reduce spiritual pride in the teacher and reduce attachment to spiritual forms in the devotee. "Crazy wisdom" has been used as a spiritual rationalization of unconventional, even hurtful behavior by a number of teachers described here.

On his website Enlightened Spirituality, spiritual teacher Timothy Conway has questioned the reality of this lineage in an essay on "The Four Kinds of Spiritual Teachers." Rigorous scholarship, he reported, has shown that the crazy wisdom tradition is a literary invention of writers made long after the purported root teachers, such as those in

Chan Buddhism and the Tibetan teachers Tilopa and Marpa, were alive. In China, he said, stories of wild behavior were invented in the eleventh and twelfth centuries as a literary device to make teachers look more authoritative. In the Vajrayana tradition in India and Tibet, a similar hagiographic literature was made up in the twelfth century about *mahasiddhas* or adepts.

In August 1976, Trungpa empowered Thomas Rich from Passaic, New Jersey, to be his dharma heir and successor. The first Western student to be a title holder in Vajrayana, Rich was renamed Osel Tendzin, "Radiant Holder of the Teachings."

In 1987 Trungpa died at age forty-eight of acute alcoholism and drug addiction, despite widespread denial of these issues among his students. Upon his death, other rinpoches reconfirmed Rich as the lineage holder and leader of Shambhala.

Following in Trungpa's tradition of having multiple sexual partners among his students, Osel Tendzin reportedly slept with both men and women in his community. Tragically, he had become infected with HIV but kept it a secret—and continued his unprotected sexual escapades, ultimately infecting the very people who had placed their spiritual lives in his hands.

In 1988 Osel Tendzin's community discovered that he had been infected with HIV for nearly three years, and that several board members and his teacher, Trungpa, had known of his illness. He had transmitted it to a student who later died of AIDS. The lies and reckless behavior sent a jolt through the community. Suddenly, a tradition devoted to ending suffering looked just like a cult. Osel Tendzin died in 1990.

Trungpa's oldest son, Sakyong Mipham, became head of the global Shambhala organization. His title, Sakyong, means "earth protector" or "emperor," and he is considered a dharma king, the embodiment of enlightened awareness. Like his father and his predecessor, the Sakyong has abused alcohol and women, clearly imagining that he, too, transcends human limitations.

One woman cited in Lachs's article reported being sexually assaulted by the Sakyong in the kitchen of a meditation center. She said that the community's responses exacerbated her confusion and suffering and eroded her health. The denials keep her from moving on from the harm.

Another young woman reported, "Over many years I had several sexual encounters with the Sakyong that left me feeling ashamed, demoralized and worthless. Like many young women in the sangha, I was deeply devoted to the Sakyong and did whatever I could to serve him and be close to him. I witnessed the steady stream of attractive women that were invited into his quarters." At a party, she said, the Sakyong encouraged everyone to drink, then take off their clothes. They danced naked while he had sex in the bedroom. Then an attendant brought her into the bedroom and the Sakyong asked her to help satisfy the other woman.

Months before the #MeToo movement went viral in 2018, Andrea Winn, a devotee who grew up in the Shambhala community, published a report on the abuses through her initiative, Buddhist Project Sunshine, and the scandals grew worse. She alleged rampant sexual abuse of children by leaders of Shambhala. The news went viral.

Winn (as cited in Lachs's article) said: "I was sexually abused as a child by multiple perpetrators in our community. When I was a young adult, I spoke up about the community's sexual abuse problem and was demonized by my local Shambhala Center, ostracized and forced to leave. The shocking truth is that almost all of the young people in my age group were sexually harassed and/or sexually abused. . . . Many of us have left the community, and for those who have stayed, their voices have been unheard. Beyond child sexual abuse, women continue to be abused in relationships with community leaders."

She continued: "There has been a deep sick feeling inside of me for all these decades. Shambhala looked wonderful on the outside, and there is no doubt in my mind about the spiritual blessings in these practices. At the same time there has been this incomprehensible sickness."

Lachs emphasized that Winn was not trying to destroy Shambhala but, rather, was trying to save it by shedding light and transparency onto the organization to hold its leaders responsible and to provide support for survivors. As a result of her investigations, police opened inquiries on several people, and one was incarcerated.

In 2019 six long-term attendants of the Sakyong wrote a letter, echoing the letter written to Sogyal Rinpoche by his students. Both described individual experiences of verbal, physical, and sexual abuse in detail—kicking, biting, shaming, coercion, assault, all in a culture of exploitation and secrecy. And the Sakyong's students outlined massive financial extravagance and waste. They were told, in response, that the teacher's behavior was beyond their understanding, and it was a way to wake them up spiritually. As a result, they learned to devalue their interpretation of their own experience.

A woman cited in the Lachs article wrote, "It should be clear that the abusive situation was not between two consenting adults, as some of his apologists claim, but rather between a so-called tantric master with the title 'earth protector' . . . as the sole authority, and a disciple, with the sex act promising to give spiritual benefit."

In 2018 the Sakyong sent an open letter of apology to the Shambhala community and added that he was entering a period of self-reflection, a euphemistic way of saying he was resigning from his duties. After a reign of twenty-five years in which he knowingly caused profound harm to many, one has to wonder why he was not self-reflecting all along. One must also wonder how the highest lamas evaluated his capacity for this role as the "king of truth."

The Sakyong resumed teaching in Nepal in 2020.

In their article "'Not the Tibetan Way': The Dalai Lama's Realpolitik Concerning Abusive Teachers," Stuart Lachs and Rob Hogendoorn speculate about why the Dalai Lama did not take action to protect students in relation to his abusive rinpoches, Trungpa and Sogyal.

In 2018 Hogendoorn had joined abuse survivors in Rotterdam to hold a meeting with the Dalai Lama. They had handed him a booklet, "#MeTooGuru: Abuse Survivors' Testimonies for the Dalai Lama's Eyes Only," along with a petition full of signatures asking for his help. They also gave him investigative reports on alleged abuses by Trungpa and Sogyal. International press covered the meeting. When asked by a television network what he learned, the Dalai Lama replied, "I already knew these things. Nothing new."

That same year, leaders of the Shambhala movement publicly admitted to major failures in how it dealt with "abhorrent sexual behavior." In an open letter published online, the leaders said, "In our complex history there have been instances of sexual harm and inappropriate relations between members and between teachers and students. We are still emerging from a time in which such cases were not always addressed with care and skill. . . . Members have at times not felt heard or have been treated as though they are a problem when they tried to bring complaints forward. We are heartbroken that such pain and injustice still occurs."

The leaders said that the #MeToo movement prompted them to go through their own collective wake-up call. They added, "Our ignorance or uncertainty as to how to address the systemic nature of these harms has made us part of the problem."

The report noted that a few men had been removed from their positions. However, many others continue as public apologists, under the rubric of "crazy wisdom," to this day.

In fact, the Dalai Lama had received a letter alleging Sogyal's abuses back in 1992. But he still wrote the foreword to Sogyal's book.

In 1993 the Dalai Lama met with Western Buddhist teachers and suggested that students speak with those acting out and, if their behavior didn't change, shame them by public pronouncements. He asked for a joint statement addressing sexual abuse between the teachers and himself.

The teachers formed the Network of Western Buddhist Teachers and issued an open letter, which began: "Our first responsibility as

Buddhists is to work towards creating a better world for all forms of life. The promotion of Buddhism as a religion is a secondary concern. Kindness and compassion, the furthering of peace and harmony, as well as tolerance and respect for other religions, should be the three guiding principles of our actions."

They advised that teachers from all schools would benefit from studying other traditions. They should be open to the insights of psychotherapy to reduce suffering in their students. They suggested that a teacher's position rises on the request of students, not simply on appointment by higher authority. The students need to exercise care and take time in selecting a teacher and should be warned against the dangers of falling prey to charlatans. They should be encouraged to confront a teacher who behaves in unethical ways, regardless of the beneficial work of that teacher. Buddhist organizations should make clear that unethical conduct does not conform with Buddhist teachings. "Although the principles of the Dharma are timeless," the writers of the letter noted, "we need to exercise careful discrimination in distinguishing between essential teachings and cultural trappings." Finally, they proposed equality between women and men.

It's unclear whether the Dalai Lama endorsed this letter in the end. It's also unclear whether it had any widespread effect.

In their book, John and Nancy Steinbeck claim that the Dalai Lama told them, "I would say that if you are going to follow a teacher, you must examine his behavior very carefully. In your case, with Trungpa Rinpoche, you had a lama who was drinking alcohol. We say, in our tradition, that a lama is never supposed to drink. Now, occasionally there have been some teachers who drink alcohol and claim to turn it into elixir. If I were considering following a teacher who drinks alcohol and claims to turn it into elixir, or excrement to gold, I would insist on seeing this happen. If I saw it happen, I may follow this teacher. Unless I see that happen, I would never follow him. The student has to take the responsibility of examining the behavior of the teacher very carefully, over a long period."

Stuart Lachs, in his post "Tibetan Buddhism Enters the 21st Century," commented, "Like Zen Buddhism that imputed unquestioning authority and enlightenment to its masters/roshis which led to scandal after scandal for the past 50 years or so, Tibetan lamas and Rinpoches are surrounded by an imputed aura of moral perfection and enlightenment, making the case of an abusive lama, at least until recently, almost inconceivable and rarely taken seriously. . . . The prevalent view is that everything the Vajrayana teacher does or says is compassionate and enlightened activity."

Lachs and Hogendoorn note that the Dalai Lama's continued dealings with Chogyam Trungpa, Sogyal Rinpoche, and Keith Raniere (of the NXIVM cult) are revealing: he did not distance himself from these repeat offenders until his own image was at risk of being tarnished in media reports. At the same time, this critique does not erase the tremendous value of his moral standing for Tibet and his books full of wisdom.

After entering a Tibetan monastery at five years old, Lama Norlha Rinpoche moved to the West in 1976 and founded a Tibetan monastery in New York, known as KTC, in the tradition of Kalu Rinpoche. He offered Vajrayana practice retreats and charity work. He claimed celibacy but had at least six secret affairs with female students over the years.

In 2017, after two women came forward as victim-survivors of his sexual misconduct, the lama's staff disclosed the affairs and played a recorded apology from Lama Norlha. Eventually, four more women disclosed their affairs with him. Most felt that these relationships had harmed their well-being.

Lama Norlha was removed from his position as head lama of the monastery. He died in 2018 in disgrace at the age of seventy-nine. However, the day before he passed away, the Karmapa, renowned spiritual leader of the Kagyu lineage, came to bless him.

In "Tibetan Buddhism Enters the 21st Century," Stuart Lachs wonders how the Tibetan system of taking young boys away from their families into an all-male monastic world affects their emotional well-being and need for human contact. He asks: How could he have had multiple secret intimate relationships in a small, closed environment? Did his students' vows of *samaya,* their bond of loyalty, keep the secret? Did other high lamas know or care about his behavior? If not, how did this elude them? Finally, if he realized his true nature, how was Lama Norlha able to live a double life and cause harm to others?

Swami Muktananda, a meditation master known as Baba, who founded Siddha Yoga, claimed to be an adept at transmitting *shaktipat,* or spiritual energy, to his devotees. Many followers reported that as a result of his look or touch, their kundalini was awakened and their spiritual lives quickened. However, as detailed in "The Secret Life of Swami Muktananda" by William Rodarmor, late in his life Muktananda was accused of molesting teenage girls. Though he claimed lifelong celibacy, there were reports of frequent seductions under the pretext of tantric practice.

When a young woman complained about the guru's behavior to Gurumayi Chidvilasananda, an Indian woman who had studied with Baba since the age of eighteen and eventually took over for him as the head of Siddha Yoga, the latter replied that people had told her about this behavior for years. But she did nothing. Other followers rationalized the news by telling themselves that he was not fully penetrating the girls, or not ejaculating, or offering them a privileged initiation.

As the charges continued to mount, a Siddha Yoga swami wrote an open letter to Baba to make the accusations public. Baba denied the charges, while some devotees gave them spiritual explanations, and others left the fold.

Other witnesses reported that Baba beat people, permitted guns into the ashram, and used strong-arm tactics to bring errant followers into line. One young man was allegedly stripped, put under a cold shower, and beaten with a rubber hose. Devotees rationalized these behaviors as ego reductions, much like Zen masters who hit their students with a stick to stop their busy minds.

Robert G. Schneider, who lived and worked in Muktananda's ashrams in India and the United States for four years, published *The Guru's Touch* in 2017. Although it was published as a novel, not a memoir, it seemingly reflects the details of a devotee's life with Muktananda, including his appearance, practices, and the accusations against him, cited in other sources, in detail. The story builds from a follower's curious, innocent devotion to a life of practice and service and on to a shocking scene of sexual indulgence and a devotee's despair. Perhaps, as fiction, this book draws from other sources. Either way, it's a graphic telling of spiritual abuse and disillusionment.

Muktananda died in 1982 and left his empire to Gurumayi and her brother, Nityananda. A bitter family feud ensued, as detailed by journalist Lis Harris in the *New Yorker.* In 1985 Gurumayi told devotees to destroy photos and videos of Nityananda. He was accused of breaking his vow of celibacy, and he admitted his transgressions. Later that year, Nityananda told Harris, his sister locked him up, stripped him of his status and his name, forced him to cede access to funds left to him by Baba, and installed herself as sole successor. Days later, she had him beaten with bamboo canes. When asked, Gurumayi confirmed the isolation and caning of her brother. Rumors of her own affair with a close official have been unsubstantiated. But anyone who visits Nityananda for spiritual teaching to this day faces potential threats and certain banishment from Siddha Yoga.

In *The Guru Looked Good,* Marta Szabo, personal assistant to Gurumayi for many years, tells the disturbing story of her time with the teacher. Finding her way to the community with a heart full of hope and longing, she slowly moved into the inner circle. As the guru gave her flowers and clothing, she felt special and seen.

Eventually, Szabo observed a split between the image projected by the teacher—order, quiet, beauty, calm—and the reality behind the curtain. Gurumayi criticized and blamed her and others for "big egos," showed no remorse for hurting her followers, told lies, lived with armed guards, and extracted confessional letters from her lonely, overworked staff. It was all done "for their own liberation."

Yogi Bhajan, a Sikh customs inspector from India, brought his version of kundalini yoga to Los Angeles in 1969. He opened Golden Temple, one of the first vegetarian restaurants in Los Angeles, founded Yogi Tea, and built an empire of some three hundred kundalini yoga centers, including Golden Bridge, which became the largest studio in the world due to its celebrity clientele.

In an extensive article by Be Scofield, "Master of Deceit: How Yogi Bhajan Used Yoga for Sex, Money, and Power," in *Guru Magazine,* based on interviews with former directors and teachers of Yogi Bhajan's Healthy, Happy, Holy Organization (3HO), members describe years of severe physical abuse (beating, kicking, punching), as well as sexual, financial, emotional, and verbal abuse of adults and children, such as public shaming. A long-term staff member got involved with the organization at the age of thirteen and saw the guru as "a messenger of God." At eighteen, her marriage was arranged. But when Bhajan's secretary left, he broke off the arranged marriage and groomed her to be his new secretary. When she was twenty, she said, Bhajan had brutally raped her and kept her hostage with armed guards. This alleged assault, subsequent beatings, and death threats are described in detail in her lawsuit. So is her own sister's knowing complicity.

Another woman, Pamela Sarah Dyson, known as Premka, served as Yogi Bhajan's secretary for fifteen years. In her book, *Premka: White Bird in a Golden Cage,* she alleges that Bhajan coerced her into sex and, when she became pregnant, forced her to have an abortion. She describes how he told her that karma from past lives required them to have sex. "I am just fulfilling an obligation to you because of past karma. I have no need of any sexual relationship. I am beyond all that," he said.

Several other firsthand survivor accounts in *Guru Magazine* reinforce the pattern of grooming, indoctrination, manipulation, assault, humiliation, and spiritual rationalization, as well as profound misogyny and objectification of girls and women.

The article alleges that Bhajan coerced his followers to send their children away for years to his schools in India, where they were allegedly indoctrinated, beaten, and emotionally abused. He arranged more than five hundred marriages, intervened in relationships, and shamed LGBTQ+ people. He reportedly groomed young girls to be married off to his elite, wealthy friends.

In addition, according to the reporting, Bhajan was allegedly involved in smuggling marijuana and weapons from Thailand to the United States. Bhajan's "defense minister," the head of a Virginia ashram, was arrested for drug smuggling. Another teacher was sentenced to years in prison for financial fraud.

The report is that Bhajan hoarded millions of dollars in precious jewels and gems, as well as ivory and furs, although he advocated for vegetarianism. His organization also runs a multibillion-dollar private military and security company that works with the U.S. military and ICE. That is, a nonprofit, tax-exempt church oversees a for-profit security contractor tasked with enforcing immigration policies.

Finally, according to the magazine article, the organization is allegedly linked to several unsolved murders: one at a school in India for 3HO children; another, a staff member at an ashram in Eugene, Oregon; and the son of a 3HO member who was allegedly smuggling drugs was also killed.

In sum, according to this report, Yogi Bhajan was married and had kids while claiming to be celibate and sexually abusing his followers; he organized "drug-free America" campaigns while importing marijuana; and he preached a spiritual life while hoarding jewels and luxury cars. And his practices, like breathing techniques, fasts, and rites, induced trancelike states in his devotees, which made them susceptible to his demands for obedience in every aspect of their lives.

In his book *Practice and All Is Coming,* Matthew Remski states that these reports on Bhajan do not address the totality of his fraudulent spiritual claims, criminal enterprises, beneficiaries, or groomers. And it doesn't speak to the generation of children who were separated from their parents when they were sent to India on the guru's orders.

Remski warns, "One of the biggest obstructions to justice in yoga abuse crises is the false belief that reform can come within an abusive organization. Anyone who remains faithful to the internal logic and emotional affect of the group, who wants it to be perpetuated, will be allergic to the very questions that disturb logic and affect."

Yogi Bhajan died in 2004 of diabetes and heart failure. One of his student teachers is cited in the *Guru Magazine* piece, "The Yogi Bhajan cult of personality needs to end, and a restorative justice program must be implemented as a way to compensate victims and mitigate the incredible amount of damage he did."

As reported by journalist Adrian Horton, the 2019 Netflix documentary *Bikram: Yogi, Guru, Predator* paints a dark picture of the founder of "hot yoga," Bikram Choudhury. Wearing nothing but a black Speedo and ponytail, he is seen prancing among his yoga students, touching, criticizing, even shaming them. The film shows decades of archival footage with first-person testimony and court depositions that accuse him of sexual harassment and rape, as well as racism and financial abuse. When Choudhury lost a civil case for sexual harassment and wrongful termination by a former legal adviser, he fled the United States to Mexico to avoid paying damages.

As one of the whistleblowers said in the film, "This is a pre-#MeToo story that's being told in a post-#METoo world, and he got away with it, which is chilling."

Born in Kolkata, India, Choudhury came to Los Angeles and gathered a celebrity crowd. Devotees streamed in, with many sharing highly positive results. He charged high fees for his teacher trainings and built a multimillion-dollar empire. But devotion turned to dependence, and professional success relied on his approval. Those who spoke of the abuse were ostracized, so many maintained their denial.

Bikram continues to teach today.

On an island in Thailand, Swami Vivekananda Saraswati (aka Narcis Tarcau of Romania) has drawn thousands of students from around the world to learn tantric yoga. Some thirty-one women have accused him of grooming and rape, all in the name of the sacred practice of tantric sex. Several videos on YouTube offer firsthand accounts, with survivors telling stories of sexual harassment and coercion. An exposé led several women to file legal complaints, leading to a police raid and his loss of membership in the international Yoga Alliance.

The story of the teacher who was born Tony in Jamaica but goes by the Hindu name Mooji echoes the other stories here. A former street artist, then chai shop owner in London, who spent some time with Advaita teacher Papaji, he has no lineage and is a self-appointed guru. He also eats meat, which is taboo in Hinduism, and was married to two women at the same time. But he now sits at the top of a spiritual empire.

As reported in the story "Becoming God: Inside Mooji's Portugal Cult," by Be Scofield in *Guru Magazine,* former members accused Mooji of running an abusive cult in an isolated ashram in Portugal, which involved sex, money, and abuse of power. They said that he screamed, shouted, shamed, and controlled his followers through mind control techniques, pairing up and breaking up couples, and demanded that everyone bow and kiss his feet, calling him "My Lord, My Master." He cut women's hair against their will. Those who disobeyed were sent to an isolation building, with one meal a day and the mission to "know the self."

Mooji, his accusers said, enforced a code of silence that led to isolation and distress. Most members paid to work for free, doing *seva,* or service. If they had objections, they were told that the mind is poison.

In addition, Mooji allegedly slept with multiple female disciples, who competed for his attention. He told them that sex with him would quicken their spiritual awakening. When he was finished with one, followers say, she would be tossed aside, humiliated, and expelled. As of this 2019 article, Mooji, at the age of sixty-five and married, was having an intimate relationship with a woman aged twenty-seven.

One commentator in the story likened him to disgraced Hollywood producer Harvey Weinstein: "Everyone knew but they all wanted the starring role, so they played along. Harvey was sharing Hollywood stardust. Tony is selling the mystical allure of enlightenment."

Allegedly, Mooji and his team smuggled hundreds of thousands of euros from London to Portugal to purchase the ashram. He stashed the cash until they had attained charity status, then built the ashram without permits. The group then began to sell miscellaneous products, such as "earth Mooji may have walked on," beads blessed by him, and blankets used by him.

In 2017 two Mooji devotees committed suicide.

Former followers and staff members came forward, calling him cruel, narcissistic, abusive, a bully, a dangerous fraud, and a demon. One explained to *Guru Magazine,* "I know a lot of people there who are afraid to leave him and afraid to tell what is really happening there. I have begged them to leave, but they are deeply afraid of him."

When I watched *The Vow,* a 2019 HBO documentary series about NXIVM and Keith Raniere, I was shocked—but not surprised. Raniere led a group of young, attractive, wealthy seekers who became his devoted acolytes, grateful for his divine wisdom, and surrendered to his orders. They gave up their power and authority over their own decisions, over their sexuality, and over their relationships with family to be with him. Some of them were coerced to brand his name onto their bellies with a hot torch.

Unlike so many of these teachers who act out their power, sex, and money shadows, Raniere was ultimately arrested in 2018 on charges of sexual exploitation of a child, sex trafficking, and conspiracy to commit forced labor. He was sentenced to 120 years in prison.

Of course, Jewish rabbis are not immune to the shadow. And in Orthodox and Hasidic communities, a believer's relationship to the rebbe is much like a disciple's relationship to a guru.

Rabbi Barry Freundel, renowned for his expertise about conversion in Jewish law, plunged from prominence in a Georgetown Orthodox Jewish community after twenty-five years as a respected leader. As reported by Michelle Boorstein and Keith Alexander, in 2014 Freundel was arrested for voyeurism, having been caught spying on women in the mikvah, or ritual bath. Freundel had secretly videotaped dozens of women, including many who were studying with him as part of their conversion. He had been a trusted leader—until an attendant in the ritual bath discovered a clock that turned out to be a camera. Many women in his community were outraged that their rabbi, whom they trusted, had betrayed them. In 2015 he was sentenced to more than six years in prison. However, he was released early and not required to register as a sex offender, even after a guilty plea.

E. J. Dickson's 2022 article in *Rolling Stone* describes Bentinho Massaro as a blond, sprightly self-proclaimed teacher with a fondness for cigars and a gift for social media. Known as "tech bro guru," he has nearly a million Facebook followers, tens of millions of views on YouTube, and calls himself the "spiritual leader for the next generation."

Born in the Netherlands, Massaro spent his teenage years in India, where he picked up Eastern philosophy and later packaged it into a curious blend of messages about the nature of everything and nothing, the value of deconstructing monogamy, and his own superpowers, such as levitation, teleportation, and controlling the weather. He appears to rely heavily on the new age teaching of the law of attraction. A 2019 episode of *The Believers,* a documentary series available on YouTube, titled "The Controversial Guru That Wants to Upgrade Civilization," explores Massaro's Trinfinity Academy, whose stated goal is to enlighten the world by 2030. As an "upper-density being," Massaro claimed that he would be able to lead his followers to a higher plane of enlightenment.

Each time there was a controversy or mutiny in the ranks of his organization, Massaro fled, first to Boulder, then to Sedona, then to the Netherlands. The *Rolling Stone* article includes interviews with three former female followers. They described an environment in which sex with multiple partners was encouraged, regardless of people's comfort. As one woman put it, "You are being brainwashed to think that your boundaries are wrong."

He allegedly tested women's allegiance by demanding that they remove their clothes in public. He required that they get his approval for their reading material and social media posts. The women also reported that he encouraged followers to detach from relationships with family and friends, saying, "They mean nothing." Everyday attachments are mere projections, he told them.

The effects were subtle, one woman said. "[The teachings] were almost a kind of drug to me. The combination of 'nothing is real' . . . and 'this is all a game' is a really tricky one. You can start to experience life more like it is a computer game. And you start to neglect intuitions like 'I don't know if that's a good idea.'"

When he chose one of them to be his girlfriend, she was elated, the woman said. "Whoever is in Ben's favor becomes like the queen, and everyone treats the queen like you walk on air. The danger is, if you fall from that position, then you're fresh meat."

Another reported that he said he wanted to marry her but proposed that merging their bank accounts would be more powerful than signing a marriage license. After she transferred large sums of money to him, he told her, "All of a sudden I'm not feeling very attracted to you."

Those who attended Massaro's retreats had to sign nondisclosure agreements after, as he put it, "someone infiltrated his team." He promoted long fasts and polyphasic sleep, in which people sleep for only a few hours at a time. Both practices leave people weak and tired, which gave him control over his followers' bodies, especially over women's weight, which he tended to fixate on. He used sex as a reward or punishment for women's weight, shaming them for having "stored toxins in [their] fat cells."

The impetus for Massaro's rapid departure from Sedona was a follower's suicide in 2018. A longtime acolyte, the thirty-four-year-old man was found at the bottom of a ravine. According to the *Rolling Stone* whistleblowers, he had been struggling with depression. However, investigators found that a lecture by Massaro appeared to encourage nonbelievers to end their own lives. "Wake up to something important," he said. "Otherwise, kill yourself." Although Massaro never faced charges, the parents of the young man blame him for their son's suicide.

The former followers told the reporter that Massaro expressed no remorse about his student's death and seemed to lack any compassion. He displayed no patience for those grieving the loss.

In retrospect, they said, they could see the "red flags" signaling abuse, but in the midst of it, they could not. They were speaking out, they said, to ensure that those searching for answers would not be drawn into Massaro's web. As one put it, "He'd erased who I was. He made me doubt every powerful thought I'd ever had."

Swami Paramahamsa Vishwananda, a charismatic, self-proclaimed guru, was born on the island of Mauritius. He traveled to Europe in 2000, at the age of twenty-three, and began to attract a following. Eventually he was accused of coercing young men into sex against their will; sixteen cases of rape were reported to the police in Germany, where he lives, though he has never been charged. As documented in an Oct. 4, 2019, post on the blog Medium (from an anonymous source under the name "Unicorn in the attic") and in a documentary film by Marlene Halser called *Bhakti Marga: Just Love Documentary,* his followers give first-hand reports of sexual grooming, coercion, and rape.

The pattern is a familiar one: Vishwananda calls them into his private quarters, demands a foot massage, demands that they then masturbate him and, in some cases, proceeds to penetration. He tells them that this is a blessing; they are fulfilling their dharma. He demands that they keep the experience a secret. And he uses the sacred text of the Guru Gita to reinforce total surrender to the master in body and soul.

To one survivor (as reported on the Medium blog), Vishwananda said: "I am above everything."

The writer on Medium quotes Amnesty International in citing a distinction in international human rights law between "absence of consent" and "coercion" in such cases: "A shift from 'absence of consent' to 'coercion' represents a shift in focus from the subjective state of mind of the victim to the imbalance of power between the parties. . . . Coercion constitutes more than physical force or threat but may also include other forms of exercise of power over another person: emotional, psychological, economical, social, or organizational power."

This distinction also was made by psychiatrist Peter Rutter in *Sex in the Forbidden Zone,* which predated the #MeToo movement. Rutter takes the position that men in positions of power—whether clergy, doctors, teachers, or therapists—betray the trust of others by acting out sexually with those under their authority. He asserts that, in this context, given the projection and the risk of terrible loss, these people cannot consent.

In the Medium post, the survivors of Vishwananda described the feelings that led to their inability to reject the guru: their desires to be good devotees to their godlike teacher, in full surrender; the terror of losing him and the spiritual benefits they felt he gave them; and their fears of being ostracized and shamed. They reported feeling shock, betrayal, and trauma once the numbness wore off. In addition, they reported that other members of the community made comments implying their knowledge of these events.

As Vishwananda's grandiosity grew, he reportedly began to say he was god, or Krishna, or above maya, the world of illusion. He also claimed to be an incarnation of Yogananda and of Jesus, which (allegedly) he used to justify stealing relics from twenty-three Catholic churches. In 2007, he and two supporters were convicted of property damage and disturbance of freedom of religion in a Swiss court, fined, and sentenced to four months in prison. He continues to teach as a guru in Germany. And he is no renunciate; he lives a luxurious lifestyle, funded by his followers.

The Hale Clinic in Regent's Park, London, which is run by a devotee, promotes Vishwananda and sends people to his ashram. Another guru, Paramahamsa Nithyananda (see below), is closely affiliated with him, and these gurus promote each other.

Sarah Landry, a former follower of the guru Nithyananda, has posted firsthand reports and interviews with former followers on YouTube detailing this teacher's narcissistic/sociopathic behavior and crimes. She reports that he raped her and others, including the children of disciples. Another whistleblower, she says, eventually committed suicide.

Nithyananda, whose stated goal is to enlighten the world with a hundred thousand enlightened followers, had to flee India after rape charges were filed. As a result, his followers are now required to sign a series of NDAs, including a "sex contract." As posted by an anonymous whistleblower on the website Nithyananda Facts, it reads: "Volunteer understands that the program may involve the learning and practice of ancient tantric secrets associated with male and female ecstasy. . . .These activities could be physically and mentally challenging, may involve nudity, access to visual images . . . close proximity and intimacy. . . ."

According to Landry, Nithyananda reportedly has a group of children in India whom he refers to as "the direct voice of a form of God." They do "akashic readings" for devotees and give advice that must be obeyed. However, these children in the Indian ashram are allegedly physically abused, directed what to say to the followers, and forced to live in terrible conditions. One rumor states that the Indian girls are sent to wealthy businessmen to perform sexual favors in exchange for land and money.

Landry describes the familiar pattern: recruit people, gain their trust, teach them to ignore their own intuition, urge them to sell their homes, cut off their families, pay the guru money, and remain captive, fearing that, without him, they will lose everything valuable and never find another guru or become enlightened.

In *Holy Hell: A Memoir of Faith, Devotion, and Pure Madness,* Gail Tredwell offers a deeply disturbing firsthand account of the shadow side of the "Hugging Saint" known as Amma. As Tredwell describes it, her ideal image of a devotee had been herself, on her knees, pressed against a female guru, eyes locked into her distant gaze with spiritual longing. When she found Amma, this inner image was activated.

We read how she slowly changed her name, clothing, beliefs, and personality to become a special devotee worthy of an intimate relationship with the guru. As she was taught that all the good that happened to her was due to the guru, and all the bad was due to her karma, she grew increasingly dependent and distrusted her own instinct more and more. Eventually, she believed that only in this guru's ashram could she live a truly spiritual life. If she left, her life would be cursed.

In her early days with the guru, Tredwell reports, the ashram atmosphere was relaxed and open. As she entered the inner circle, the schedule became more rigid, and the demands for obedience increased. During two decades of witnessing lies, hypocrisy, and verbal and physical abuse, she learned to lie to herself to rationalize Amma's behavior.

She writes, "All I wanted was to know God. I believed through devotion and surrender as Amma's personal attendant, I could achieve it. To maintain my position . . . I was willing to do anything and make any sacrifice."

So, she carried the lies: Amma was pure, having no menstruation or sexuality. (But she had sex regularly with a senior devotee over many years—and Tredwell was raped by this same man.) Amma was kind, the embodiment of compassion. (But she hit, kicked, slapped, shamed, and shunned people who disobeyed her whims.) As Amma's rages grew darker, Tredwell's mental health declined. She was in a double bind: she was living in hell, yet she could not leave. She could not face the world with no family, no money, no career, no identity. She felt a terror of being found and punished. In her dreams, she was being hunted.

She writes, "I began to sense that I was on a sinking ship. I had to choose whether to go down with it or grab a life jacket and swim to safety. . . . My heart knew the truth, but my mind just wasn't ready to face the facts. . . . I became engaged in mighty inner battles, panic attacks, and many nights howling into my pillow, not wanting to leave, but somehow knowing I needed to get out. . . . I still wasn't ready to put my own health and happiness before others."

Slowly, with the encouragement of a friend, she prepared to escape. The recovery process was slow. Her physical and mental health had dangerously deteriorated. She reviewed her vulnerabilities that led her to this cultlike community. Her projections and rationalizations slowly dissolved. She saw through the guru trap: devotion and power can lead to narcissistic grandiosity in a teacher, who believes she is immune to consequences. She saw through the disciple trap: adoration of the idealized parent, to gain unconditional love, depends on giving up oneself. In the end, both people are caught in delusion.

As she concludes, "I did not find God, but I did find myself. And I thank God for that."

Noah Levine, a punk-rock, tattooed Buddhist teacher and author, who refers to himself as a "rogue outlaw dharma rebel," brought countless young seekers into the dharma with his organization Against the Stream. He also launched Refuge Recovery, a program for drug and alcohol addicts.

But, as reported by Sean Elder in *Los Angeles Magazine,* in 2017 Levine was accused of sexual assault, and the organization initiated a third-party investigation of its founder. In 2018 he admitted to having sex with a married woman, which violated the code of ethics for the Against the Stream organization.

Although his victim-survivors did not press charges, his group closed its centers in Los Angeles and San Francisco and dissolved the sangha. Levine had been authorized to teach in the lineage of Spirit Rock Meditation Center; the center revoked this authorization following the investigation.

His rebuttal: "They [the traditional teachers] didn't like the irreverence, the swearing, the smoking, the motorcycles."

Levine denied other allegations, too, and blamed the #MeToo movement for the demise of his empire. No women came forward publicly. No investigation, by any organization or person, resulted in a clear conclusion that Levine had engaged in sexual assault or harassment. Instead, leaders of ATS and Spirit Rock concluded that he had caused harm through his sexual conduct. Though *harm* is a relatively vague term that could mean anything from offending to attacking, Buddhism asks students to examine the intention of their actions. Levine admitted to and repeatedly apologized for unintentionally causing harm, while maintaining that his conscious intentions were not hurtful.

Following the scandal, he is once again working with Refuge Recovery.

Many decades after the death of Transcendental Meditation founder Maharishi Mahesh Yogi, I read *Robes of Silk, Feet of Clay* by Judith Bourque. She was one of perhaps a dozen women who allegedly had sexual relations with the "celibate monk" whose movement brought meditation to millions in the West.

The rumors about his sexual escapades began in the 1960s and continued into later decades. Many followers dismissed them, rationalized them, and attempted to separate the technique from the teacher. But Bourque confirmed, in firsthand reports, Maharishi's hypocrisy around sexuality, despite the profound gifts of spiritual knowledge and transcendental experience he gave to many.

While Maharishi was telling his closest students to maintain celibacy for their spiritual development, he was grooming Bourque to be his sexual playmate. He gave her special attention, dressed her in silk saris, and eventually enforced a strict secrecy around their liaisons. She lived in a "prison of silence," much like abused children in a family full of secrets.

While she believed they were falling in love, she was, rather, falling into an archetypal transference, projecting her image of god onto a fallible man. During the early stages of the affair, she was elated, felt chosen, and assumed that their bond would endure. But Maharishi did not have the same intent. His eyes began to wander, and he seduced other women followers.

Judith was devastated but could not act on her own behalf for a long time. "The prospect of throwing myself out into the real world without a job, home, purpose, friends, without Maharishi as an anchor, frightened me into indecision and passivity," she wrote.

Eventually, the betrayal and confusion were too painful, and Judith woke up out of her trance, determined to leave both him and the Transcendental Meditation movement. As she put it, "I had to leave my lover, teacher, and connection to divine knowledge."

Her experience is the essence of an archetypal transference that broke down in a traumatic way, without the opportunity to work it through with the teacher.

In his book *How Krishna Transformed,* E. Burke Rochford Jr. reviews the Society for Krishna Consciousness (ISKCON) or Hare Krishna movement and its shadow side. Founded in the United States in 1967, it attracted many young seekers who wished to leave mainstream culture. Many were forced to beg for donations, while they chanted "Hare Krishna," to support the organization. Led by A. C. Bhaktivedanta, aka Swami Prabhupada, the movement established temples around the world but lost momentum with his death in 1977.

According to Rochford, internal conflicts arose around women's roles in leadership, as they were marginalized and mistreated. Arranged marriages often led to discontent. Children were separated from parents at the age of four and sent to Krishna boarding schools from the early 1970s to mid-1980s. Accounts of physical and sexual abuse of children were rampant. (In 2005 a settlement was reached that paid financial compensation to 535 people who had been abused as children.) At the same time, scandals plagued those who were empowered by Prabhupada as gurus.

At the age of fourteen, an Indian boy was stung by a scorpion, then claimed that he was the reincarnation of Indian holy man Shirdi Sai Baba and left his home to find devotees. Years later, having taken the name Sathya Sai Baba, and now claiming he was god incarnate, he had millions of followers around the world and a multibillion-dollar empire. Today, decades after his death, dozens of products are sold in his name online.

Sathya Sai Baba's followers claimed to witness miracles such as materializations of *vibhuti* (holy ash), rings, necklaces, and watches, and miraculous healings, resurrections, clairvoyance, and bilocation. But investigations concluded that his acts were based on sleight of hand. Further accusations against Sathya Sai Baba have included sexual abuse of boys and men, money laundering, and fraud in the performance of service projects.

In 2011, Douglas Todd reported in the *Vancouver Sun* that Sathya Sai Baba sexually molested young men at his ashram for decades and included interviews with several accusers. Swedish therapist and film star Conny Larsson, for example, said that the guru regularly performed oral sex on him and asked for it in return. Sathya Sai Baba told Larsson he was correcting his kundalini energy.

A 2002 documentary film, *Seduced by Sai Baba,* produced by Denmark's national broadcast company, Denmark Radio (DR), analyzed videos of materializations of objects by Sai Baba and suggested they could be explained as sleight of hand. The documentary also presented interviews with a former devotee who alleged abuse by Sathya Sai Baba.

In 2004 the BBC produced a documentary, *The Secret Swami,* that explored the sexual abuse allegations against Sathya Sai Baba. He denied them. He died in 2011 at the age of eighty-four.

Adi Da, aka Da Free John, aka Bubba Free John, aka Franklin Jones, was an American guru who claimed to be the first, last, and only perfectly enlightened spiritual adept who had ever lived. He claimed a stature beyond that of Jesus and Buddha.

As detailed by Timothy Conway in "Adi Da and His Voracious, Abusive Personality Cult," Adi Da emerged in 1972 after studying with Swami Muktananda and working with Scientology. He self-published hundreds of books based on his study of Hinduism, but his practices were more about guru worship than the nondual perspective. He moved a group to Fiji and created an isolated community with all the signs of a cult, including an inner circle of loyalists who were charged with covering up his personal indulgences.

Adi Da faced persistent accusations of having sex with large numbers of people, alcohol and drug abuse, violence against women, financial exploitation, and extravagant materialism. He explained it all away as "crazy wisdom," whose purpose was to wake up his followers.

In 1985 ex-devotees filed lawsuits against him, which revealed his abusive behavior and the lies of his inner circle. He withdrew into seclusion and reportedly experienced some kind of mental breakdown. As the years passed, his ego inflation grew into greater and greater grandiosity, with everything he said interpreted by his acolytes as the word of god. In this way, he mythologized himself and undermined rational, critical thinking in his followers.

He died of a heart attack at the age of sixty-nine in 2008.

———

Andrew Cohen, born in New York, spent a few weeks in 1986 in India with Advaita teacher H. W. L. Poonja and then returned to the United States claiming that his enlightenment had been validated by the teacher. In 1988, at the age of thirty, Cohen founded EnlightenNext, a community of students, which included his mother and wife, whose purpose was to "redefine pre-modern notions of enlightenment for the modern world."

He told his students to be celibate, though he was not. He told them to shave their heads, though he did not. He forbid them to do outside reading. If he disliked his followers' choices or behavior, they had to bring him fruit and flowers and beg for forgiveness. As his grandiosity grew, he told them to bow to a picture of him while saying internally, "To know nothing, to have nothing, to be no one is to be free."

When Cohen's authority began to be questioned, the group fell apart. His followers started to recognize the cultlike qualities of the group and began to leave. As detailed in *Holy Shit, We're in a Cult,* a 2016 documentary piece by *The Atlantic,* Cohen eventually spoke of his emotional breakdown and his responsibility for his ego inflation and for hurting his students. At that time, he was traveling to make amends with students he had harmed. Now he has written a memoir about his experience as a guru falling from grace. It includes his own encounter with spiritual shadow and his resulting shadow-work to understand how his psychology led to the demise of his community.

Many Eastern teachers establish little fiefdoms with their own subcultures, often shaped by the leader's country of origin, whether India, Thailand, Sri Lanka, Japan, Tibet, or another country. They believe in the timelessness and universality of their teachings, regardless of the challenges of transplanting them into another time and place. However, if they bring unexamined assumptions, such as celibacy, secrecy, or unquestioned authority, into the West, they may find that they are transmitting multigenerational shadow issues.

If, for example, hypothetically, sexual abuse is widespread in Eastern monasteries, as it is among "celibate" Catholic clergy, then survivors who become teachers are carrying this untreated shadow issue into their own communities. Their personal experiences of trauma and resulting confusion around sexuality may be acted out in the West.

In a startling recent example of someone speaking out about this, the young Kalu Rinpoche, born in India in 1990 and believed to be the reincarnation of a previous, highly honored Tibetan teacher with the same name, posted on YouTube that he had been molested at an early age in a monastery. When the young Kalu, at age eighteen, was put in charge of his lineage's meditation centers around the world, he wanted to break the pattern of abuse. He asked Buddhist nuns to speak with him one by one about any exploitation they had experienced, in an effort to understand and disrupt the pattern. As reported by Pamela Rubin in an article in *Buddhadharma,* he told

Tibetan teacher Lama Palden that it took two days, and he cried the whole time.

∾ତ∽

Now, let's attempt to understand more deeply how these painful, troubling events could happen again and again . . . and continue to happen.

The light of perfection brings imperfection to the surface.

SUFI PROVERB

When we first approach a guru, we should carefully examine his qualities and his actions. He should have conquered desire and anger and banished infatuation from his heart.

SWAMI MUKTANANDA

Spiritual growth is about surrender, not about understanding. Whenever that part of you that wants to figure out, or know why, or what for, or so on or so forth, kicks in, kick it out. Kick it out.

SWAMI CHETANANANDA

SIX

Understanding Spiritual Abuse

Detecting the Patterns across Denominations

This spectacle of corrupt priests and teachers in authoritarian communities of all denominations has cast a pall over religion and spirituality. Centuries-old teachings that were meant to end suffering have, instead, perpetuated it. And clergy and gurus who were meant to transmit wisdom have, instead, acted out their sex, money, and power shadows and transmitted pain.

But when examined together, these disturbing incidents of spiritual abuse reveal patterns that, I hope, can be helpful in several ways. First, when aspirants know what to look for, they can be more discerning at an earlier stage of seeking a teacher and practice. As would be the case with any abusive relationship, if they can detect a warning sign, such as emotional coercion or physical intimidation, they can more consciously choose to stay or leave, to speak up or stay silent. This awareness can loosen the grip of the transference and make it possible to learn from a teacher without idealizing him or her. In rare cases, it can make it possible to change a personal or institutional dynamic.

If you are seeing a warning sign, please ask yourself: If I didn't believe this teacher to be awake or enlightened, would this behavior be called abusive?

Second, this quality of awareness may allow us to lose our spiritual naivete and acknowledge that the human shadow is present even in our religious and spiritual settings. Rather than lead us to cynicism or despair, this awareness can lead to a new stage of spiritual maturity that embraces shadow awareness along with the evolution of consciousness.

The priest/parishioner or teacher/student relationship can be the most sacred of a lifetime. We invest it with the vision of our highest human potential; we entrust it with soul. Yet we are reluctant to find fault and to admit violations of trust because of that very investment. If the relationship fails, it invalidates not only our own judgment, but the very vision to which we have devoted our lives. For this reason, denial is epidemic.

As Satya Bharti Franklin wrote in *The Promise of Paradise,* a book about her life at Bhagwan Shree Rajneesh's Oregon community, "Before Rajneeshpuram, I could never understand how so many Jews stayed put during Hitler's ascent. But now I was witness to my own astonishing ability to rationalize away what I didn't want to face."

When survivors finally acknowledge their own experiences of religious abuse, their communities often refuse to validate them. The Catholic priesthood has behaved for decades like a tribal brotherhood, protecting its own from charges of abuse by the laity. Suffering students' complaints are devalued in Hindu groups as "purification" (the elimination of toxic feelings or energies due to practice), in Buddhist sanghas as "deluded mind," and in Christian Science as "mortal mind" (the limited human mind that believes it's separate from god). Few religious or spiritual groups provide procedures to voice unacceptable thoughts and feelings in a nonjudgmental setting.

Other members often may blame the victim for being seductive, destabilizing the community, or endangering the higher good to humanity that the teacher offers. When a client's closest friends in her sangha refused to hear her doubts and turned their backs, she experienced a secondary trauma, the loss of precious friendships, cultivated over many years, which she had expected to endure beyond her relationship to the teacher. When a Jehovah's Witness client began to express doubt, he was told that non-Witnesses are "bad association," and if he spoke with them, he would be "disfellowshipped," or expelled.

Although a group's teachings may be valuable and rituals or practices life-enhancing, an organization's structures may be authoritarian and its members' behavior patterns compulsive and cultlike. In fact, the coping strategies that are epidemic in alcoholic homes are prevalent in abusive churches and spiritual communities:

- A priest or teacher, like a parent, exploits others for his or her own narcissistic needs. ("Thinking I had some extraordinary means of protection, I went ahead with my business as if something would take care of it for me," Vajrayana Buddhist teacher Osel Tendzin admitted after he had infected several followers with the HIV virus.)
- The teacher's transgressions are often boundary violations, whether psychic, emotional, sexual, or financial. (A follower of Chetanananda feared him because she believed that he could read her mind after staring into her eyes during meditation for years.)
- Like a child, the member chosen for abuse is made to feel special. (A follower of Frederick Lenz said, "I worked as his housekeeper for a year, cleaning and doing secretarial stuff for no pay. He had other girls over all the time. It made me jealous, but at the end of the day, I was the one who was in the same house.")
- Students and staff, like children, enable the teacher's dysfunctional behavior. ("We were all co-alcoholics," said a follower of Maezumi Roshi. "We in subtle ways encouraged his alcoholism because when he was drunk he would become piercingly honest.")
- Members deny their own feelings of doubt, danger, and common sense. ("That's hearsay. It's destructive to feed negative thoughts," said one Zen student on hearing about Richard Baker Roshi's affairs.)

- Members project their ideal onto a priest or teacher, leading to psychological dependency. They maintain that image at all costs, like a child protecting an abusive parent. (A Catholic told me, "Because [the priest] represents the church, he could not have abused her. She must have seduced him.")
- Members rationalize destructive behavior as sanctioned by god or the lineage holder, or as a sacred teaching, or as "crazy wisdom," designed to startle the mind out of its conventional trance. (A Hindu meditator said, "When our teacher was late or failed to meditate or behaved rudely, we called it grist for the mill.")
- Shameful secrets hold the system together. (When Trungpa Rinpoche suffered dementia due to alcoholism, some devotees suggested that he was communicating with spiritual beings called *dakinis*. When he died at forty-eight, only a few followers knew it was from the effects of alcoholism. The rest were not told or denied that his body could succumb to drink like that of an ordinary man.)
- Members are threatened with retaliation when they try to disclose secrets or wish to leave. ("My priest told me that if I revealed our secret, I would go straight to hell.")

Like many adult children of alcoholics, spiritual believers learn that their feelings don't matter because an authority figure knows them better than they know themselves. Therefore, self-knowledge originating from feelings or intuition is stigmatized, and we give up our capacity to discriminate based on our gut or our conscience. In effect, we give up self-trust.

Episcopal priest Leo Booth, author of *When God Becomes a Drug*, believes that religious addiction is akin to alcoholism. In the early stages, he wrote, we use the Bible, prayer, or church attendance for their calming effects. Gradually, we begin to use them to avoid facing problems and to deal with uncertainty. As black-and-white thinking increases ("Sex is dirty, women are evil, nonbelievers are doomed"), we lose the capacity to think critically or question clerical authority. We begin to think compulsively about god, to quote scripture in every situation. Slowly, rationalization begins as we defend our church attendance over all other duties, feel guilty if we miss it, and proselytize friends and family members.

As we lose other interests, Booth continues, we tithe more and more money to the church. We may undergo excessive fasting and develop an eating disorder. Eventually, we become isolated from people who think differently, avoiding nonreligious friends. In extreme cases, we may go on a crusade or mission to save the world.

Booth tells the story of one man who had a mystical experience during prayer at a Pentecostal church. He began to fast weekly, read the Bible daily, and stopped all of his recreational activities. He continued fasting for longer periods because he felt he wasn't spiritual enough. He lived in a car so that he could donate his rent money to the church. The pastor, who required his members to sign a form agreeing to abide by his "holiness standard," urged them to go out and win souls. This man bought a billboard to advertise the church.

Booth referred this man to me for psychotherapy. Slowly and gradually, he realized that he could never do enough for the demanding god of his pastor. Rather than feeling at peace, he felt nagging guilt and shame. He began to question church policies, and as a result, the pastor spread rumors about him. His girlfriend abandoned him, and he plunged into depression, the scapegoat of his community.

With spiritual shadow-work, this man came to realize that the pastor's abusive behavior repeated the pattern of abuse he had experienced with his father, who, during alcoholic binges, criticized and humiliated him. As a boy, he internalized his father's name-calling and shaming messages, hoping against hope that one day, if he submitted, he would win his father's approval. In his relationship to the pastor, then, he was that young boy again, unconsciously seeking his father's approval, which rendered him powerless against the abuse. His next step: to create a conscious relationship to the holy as an adult with an internal sense of authority.

It seems to me that we can substitute the language of any tradition or practice for Booth's Christian terminology to discover whether we are using it compulsively and, therefore, have lost our ability to think critically and to choose it or not. For example, when I began meditation, I found its calming effect refreshing and rejuvenating. I looked forward each morning and evening to quieting my mind and relaxing my body. Gradually, I began to avoid stressful or challenging situations in order to enhance my practice. I meditated for longer periods and worked, played, and exercised for shorter ones. If I missed a session, I felt terrible guilt.

The meditation philosophy seemed to answer all of my philosophical questions. I felt sorry for those who hadn't found it. I began to use meditation and my beliefs to screen out potential love interests and friends. (To this day, my oldest friend tells me that I nearly lost her with my self-righteous proselytizing.) Practice became more important than relationship and career—no contest. I spent nearly ten years teaching meditation around the country with the certain knowledge that the more meditators there were, the greater the chance for world peace. Today that naivete astounds me.

I have found Margaret T. Singer's spectrum of influence and persuasion to be helpful in identifying these psychological patterns in disciples because it does not promote black-and-white anti-cult thinking. Rather, as described in her book *Cults in Our Midst,* it illustrates the range a believer undergoes from education to propaganda to indoctrination to thought reform.

On the other hand, the patterns among teachers need to be detected as well. When the stories are told, sex tends to grab the headlines, especially when married or supposedly celibate teachers are involved. But the abuse of power is always present in sexual harassment and seduction. And it is acted out in other ways as well, such as physical abuse, verbal humiliation, and threat of exile. Financial coercion, theft, and fraud also hide deeper meanings around money, greed, and power.

The transgressions by individual clergy and spiritual teachers, even those deemed "perfect masters," reveal that they are not immune to neurotic traits or shadowy behaviors. The attainment of mystical states or psychic and subtle levels of consciousness among saints and sages clearly does not mean that they fully transcend the ego. It does not do away with the personal history, personality, or temperament of the individual. However, in some cases, it may mean that they no longer identify with the ego. They no longer try to fulfill its needs.

And, just as clearly, it does not mean that they fully transcend the shadow or become aware of all of their disowned unconscious material. Although some teachers have suggested that a sudden moment of awakening illuminates all residue in the personal shadow, I no longer believe this possibility. Even if emotional and cultural shadow-work is an intentional, ongoing part of an individual's practice, aspects of the shadow still remain outside of conscious awareness when one attains higher stages. In the end, I believe, we continue to banish material into the personal unconscious and to form shadow content at each moment because we are by nature unable to be aware of everything at once.

Hindus have a term for this phenomenon: *leshavidya,* or the remains of ignorance. Others have called it a phantom ego. In an article in my anthology *Meeting the Shadow,* Georg Feuerstein suggested that a phantom shadow may coexist with the phantom ego, permitting people at higher levels of consciousness to operate in conditional reality even after awakening to universal reality.

There is a Jewish teaching about this circumstance: Each human being has an evil inclination, or *yetzer harah.* This inclination does not disappear as a person evolves but, instead, grows stronger. The more light, the more darkness.

Feuerstein pointed out that the authoritarian style of most religious teachers does not permit them to use their followers as mirrors for their own development, which would enable them to do their own shadow-work or consciously wrestle with their *yetzer harah.* Instead, their vertical image of transcendence—their emphasis on the "up" path only—leads them to ignore concerns about integrating personality and shadow. Therefore, they tend to remain authoritarian, idiosyncratic, and even abusive.

But individual explanations do not suffice to explain the epidemic of religious spiritual abuse. Vast cultural differences lie hidden beneath spiritual abuses as well. Ancient practices that evolved in specific contexts have been introduced to us with no supporting cultural contexts and very different unconscious organizations of reality. And if waking up includes becoming aware of our invisible social and cultural conditioning, then we need to recognize those values, both conscious and unconscious, that we bring to our practices and those that we receive from them.

For example, our great emphasis on the value of the individual in the West does not exist in the East. In Japanese, there is not even a word for "individual." So, the pressing needs of Americans for attention, self-expression, and privacy may go unnoticed by Asian teachers who emphasize group mind or collective interests. As a result, when students articulate these needs, they may be devalued.

At the same time, our conscious stress on individuality has a shadow side: unconsciously we may be drawn to groups that encourage participation mystique, or the loss of self, in the collective. In this way, the burden of heroic individualism—emotional, financial, and intellectual autonomy and creative achievement—can be lightened, which is what many members of spiritual communities report. ("When I surrender to the guru's grace, I don't have to strive so hard. When I feel belonging in the sangha, I don't have to face my isolation," a woman told me.)

The striving for success also can be relieved by teachings concerning the nature of the self. If the ego or self is an illusion, why try so hard to develop it or defend it? Why struggle to have a voice or protect one's boundaries? I can recall the great relief I felt when I believed that I needed to do nothing but meditate in order to feel worthy and to contribute to the well-being of others.

On the other hand, I have observed how the striving for material success can be displaced onto the striving for higher consciousness. That is, in some communities success comes to be equated with the acquisition of flashy experiences. And, conversely, failure is equated with prayer or meditation without results. As one Zen student told me, when asked why he no longer meditates, "Because my only association with zazen is of personal failure."

Our Western emphasis on individual empowerment and its anti-authoritarian bias also does not exist in the East. Instead, many Eastern spiritual communities are hierarchical, patriarchal, and feudal in their design. But an unconscious or shadow part of us longs to surrender to authority, so that part of us fits with those institutional structures.

In addition, our emphasis on individual freedom and license collides with the East's emphasis on obedience and celibacy. Most Eastern methods of meditation evolved in monastic settings, which included abstinence from drugs, alcohol, and sex. Transplanted to America, which is obsessed with sex while condemning it as unspiritual, even sinful, these practices have been used to avoid intimacy and deny sexual problems.

Uprooted from their cultural foundations, some Eastern teachers acted out newfound freedoms with sex, money, and power in destructive ways. For instance, Trungpa Rinpoche was granted power in his teens, but his freedom was proscribed by collective medieval mores (such as concepts of communal pollution and purification) and cultural duties. Freed of restraints, he ran amok. Rooted in the same feudal Tibetan culture, Sogyal Rinpoche learned as a boy that a girl who became his sexual partner was blessed (in part because she left behind a life of poverty), and her family was blessed (because they were freed from supporting her and might receive gifts from the lama).

Conversely, some Western practitioners have tried to adopt celibacy, abstinence, and gestures of subservience, such as prostrations. It's as if both teachers and disciples are mirroring and acting out each other's cultural shadows.

While Western culture is primarily guilt-based, the East is shame-based. In Asia, the need to save face overrides any ideas about open exchange or communication. For instance, the late lama Kalu Rinpoche, a wise and compassionate teacher, forbade his students from commenting on the behavior of Tibetan Buddhist teacher Osel Tendzin, who infected students with HIV. The appearance of harmony was more important to him than the expression of personal feelings or the enforcement of ethics.

The lack of ritual in post-modern Western society also leads many of us to crave it. The slow, orderly, elegant rhythm of ceremony is an antidote to the rushed, chaotic arbitrariness of our lives. But the risk of overvaluing ritual is that we lose ourselves in ancient, esoteric forms. As Katy Butler reported in "Events Are the Teacher," the atmosphere at San Francisco Zen Center was like that of a medieval palace, where rules for how to stand, bow, and sit were carefully prescribed.

One day, as Butler bowed repeatedly with other Zen students while the roshi's car departed, she suddenly saw herself—and felt stunned at her own behavior. "The day I stood there in front of that car, I was doing something I didn't understand, taking on a piece of Japanese behavior, simply because I had been asked to." Butler realized later that the Japanese rituals at Zen Center had become a way of avoiding human contact.

The most obvious cultural gap is the gender gap. In Catholicism, Orthodox Judaism, and Islam, in which women cannot be ordained, patriarchal and authoritarian institutions remain calcified. In some Protestant denominations and Reform Judaism, which now ordain women, services and scriptures have been reimagined as less biased and more inclusive.

Historically, in the East, men and women have done spiritual practices separately, and women could not be ordained. Some traditions also teach that women cannot become enlightened. Zen priest Yvonne Rand told a story about visiting Japan while she was president of San Francisco Zen Center. With every meeting, she was introduced as wife of the president. Her Japanese peers could not even imagine a woman in her position.

Around the world, women have strived to throw off patriarchal forms of disempowerment and to find our voices, especially our valid anger. Therefore, these ancient beliefs and practices seem like a throwback. However, researchers found that many women still suffer a double-bind when trying to claim our own authority. Women who are authoritative are perceived as unfeminine. But more traditionally feminine women are perceived as childlike. This partially explains our ease with projecting our spiritual authority onto men; our difficulty with carrying it for ourselves has a cultural foundation in patriarchal institutions.

The Consequences of Spiritual Abuse

To cynics, this parade of abuses and betrayals is a soap opera of charlatans and fools, villains and victims. Their holy longing is buried beneath more socially acceptable desires, so they cannot understand why anyone would place their highest value on a church, teacher, or practice that claims a connection with the divine.

But I suggest that the situation is much more complex. While media sensationalism reinforces widespread suspicion of our religious desires, men and women in every tradition continue to have authentic spiritual breakthroughs. When they taste transcendence or stabilize higher levels of consciousness, they may come to believe that they are then prepared to preach or teach. However, a seminary training or a glimpse of awakening—kensho, samadhi, or satori—does not prepare a person to teach. It does not mean he or she can handle the complexities of guiding others, especially others with diverse psychologies from diverse cultures. If a teacher is charismatic or develops special powers but has not completed ego-work and shadow-work, his or her effects will be mixed: transmission of knowledge with resulting gratitude among students, alongside transmission of shadow with resulting devastation.

In addition, a religious or spiritual leader may have high development along the spiritual line, including deity mysticism or union with spirit, but low growth along the moral line of development. For this reason, we have seen clearly wise people, in all denominations, act as if they are unaware of the painful consequences of their behavior on others.

Following the shock and disillusionment that believers feel after meeting the spiritual shadow, some succumb to rage, blaming the church, *satsang*, teacher, god, or themselves. Their feelings of broken trust and spiritual betrayal lead them to distrust others and to lose faith.

Others succumb to depression. All at once, they lose their community, their purpose, and the meaning that bound their lives together. They regret the time they dedicated to their practices or teachers. Many feel guilty about the lies or deceptions with which they colluded. Others feel ashamed at having been duped or used by a charismatic teacher or priest. They struggle with loneliness, sexuality, finances, and other developmental issues that were delayed by living within an authoritarian setting. And they fear retaliation for separating from the group, whether it takes the form of physical, emotional, or spiritual punishment.

If their daily lives were organized by others and their beliefs prescribed by others, they may suddenly find themselves passive or indecisive. Unable to heed the cues of their own feelings and instincts, they may be dependent on obeying an outside authority. If they habituated to hours of prayer, chanting, or meditation, they may continue to slip into trancelike states or episodes of "floating," in which it's difficult to concentrate or remain in the present moment.

When sexual violations are involved, the consequences can be severe. At the March 1998 California Psychological Association conference in Los Angeles, Nanette de Fuentes gave a talk in which she likened sexual activity between a priest and parishioner to incest. It begins in a context of closeness. The priest is protected from suspicion by his role. The victim, who has an emotional attachment to him, is disbelieved because of the priest's authority. Or she is disbelieved because of the myth of the seductive woman, whose evil nature coerces the man. Her silence is obtained through threats. And she is responsible, through her secrecy, for maintaining his public image and the image of the church.

To see the consequences of religious abuse up close, the 2021 documentary film *Procession,* which aired on Netflix, interviewed middle-aged adult male survivors of clergy abuse. They described their priests, from a child's point of view, as larger than life, their hands as instruments of the sacraments. They were told, while being groomed for sex, "This is what you do with a special friend."

These men carry decades of anger and shame, suffer nightmares, vomit on Sunday mornings, and despise the church. As we watch them walk through their memories, the film makes a remote reality a visible horror.

The loss of trust and innocence is accompanied by the loss of self. Experts suggest that the closer the relation to the offender, the greater the trauma to the child. Most suffer symptoms of post-traumatic stress disorder (PTSD), such as heightened anxiety, sleep disturbances, deep distrust, sexualized behaviors, chronic depression, eating disorders, substance abuse, and suicidal thoughts.

In an article by Anne Simpkinson in *Common Boundary* magazine, David Clohessy, a survivor of clergy abuse and former president of the Survivors Network of Those Abused by Priests (SNAP) in Chicago, described the resulting shift in perception for him: "It's like getting up one morning, walking outside, and all of a sudden the law of gravity isn't in effect anymore. It is something that is so far beyond the pale of expectation for a kid. . . . It is just a horrible, horrible betrayal."

I would make another link: Children often see their clergy as god. Developmentally, they may be unable to distinguish the human being from the imago dei. For that very reason, they are vulnerable to being told that the abusive behavior is "god's gift" or "god's punishment." And, for that same reason, they cannot discriminate between an individual's behavior and an entire tradition of faith. Because the one they turn to for safety is the one who betrays them, they often give up their spiritual desires or try to submerge their religious yearnings altogether.

But the results of spiritual membership are not all negative. Many students also report more complex consequences than the media acknowledges, especially the anti-cult press, which demonizes alternative communities. Several disillusioned believers told me that, in retrospect, they see how they needed to break away from their families, especially an authoritarian parent, and used their spiritual families to do so. They longed for a parent imago, or they longed for a home where they would be taken care of. That is, a younger part of them, perhaps a child part, needed to fulfill its unmet needs for dependency.

In *The Wrong Way Home,* Arthur Deikman called this hidden motivation covert dependency—the wish for parents and the parallel wish to be loved, admired, and sheltered by a group. This longing, he said, generates a hidden fantasy that can transform a priest or teacher into a parent and a fellowship group into a family. The result: we feel secure at last.

One client reported that the sense of belonging and kinship she felt at her church helped to heal the loneliness and alienation she felt in her family. However, her daughter, who was raised in that church, needed to separate from it and look elsewhere in search of her own identity. A man who was raised as a secular Jew in an enmeshed, controlling family became Orthodox in his twenties. His family was just as outraged at his religiosity as they would have been if he had converted to Catholicism or Islam. And, in that way, he made his separation.

Author Andrew Harvey has said that his guru/disciple relationship with Mother Meera mirrored his tie to his own mother. They both left him wanting more. So, he re-created the early dynamic in an unconscious effort to heal it. (He described his excruciating separation from Meera in his book *Sun at Midnight.*)

Carl Jung made this point many years ago when he suggested that a "secret society" could be used as an intermediary stage on the way to individuation. However, while we may use a group identity, such as a religious or spiritual community, to differentiate from another group, such as a family, we risk losing our autonomy when we belong to any collective. Therefore, for Jung, this is only a temporary solution, and our psychological task is really to differentiate ourselves from others and stand on our own feet. From that point of view, all collective identities are transitional and, at some point, interfere with individuation.

But before many members of spiritual communities are able to separate, they may fulfill early developmental needs and gain deeper meaning and purpose that had not been provided by their childhood religions, material pursuits, or political activism. Long-term meditators may learn to discipline and empty their minds. A few gain peak states, their restless yearning satiated for a time. And a select few establish a new level of consciousness.

But most also point to the emotional damage they suffered at the hands of a priest or guru or coercive group dynamic. As one woman told me, "I trusted completely, and that trust was betrayed. I was vulnerable, and that vulnerability was misused. Whatever innocence I had when I arrived, I lost. I created pain for people I loved and postponed finding real solutions for how to build an adult life, trading away precious time for a solution that wasn't a solution. In short, I paid dearly for the riches I gained."

Again, the patterns of abuse are non-denominational. In her book *Leaving the Fold,* and various articles, Marlene Winell describes the physical, emotional, and cognitive consequences of indoctrination by fundamentalist Christian communities, which she calls religious trauma syndrome (RTS). RTS, she says on her website, Journey Free, is "experienced by people who are struggling with leaving an authoritarian, dogmatic religion and coping with the damage of indoctrination. . . . RTS is a function of both the chronic abuses of harmful religion and the impact of severing one's connection with one's faith."

Winell suggests that the doctrines of original sin and eternal damnation, reinforced at church, school, and home, cause the most psychological distress by creating a double bind: "You are guilty and responsible, and face eternal punishment. Yet you have no ability to do anything about it."

Winell compares RTS with PTSD. The latter is caused by a traumatic event in which a person experiences or witnesses actual or threatened death or serious injury, or a threat to the physical integrity of self or others. "Losing one's faith, or leaving one's religion, is analogous because it essentially means the death of one's previous life—the end of reality as it was understood," she says.

Winell outlines the symptoms of religious trauma syndrome:

Cognitive: Confusion, poor critical thinking ability, negative beliefs about self-ability & self-worth, black & white thinking, perfectionism, difficulty with decision-making

Emotional: Depression, anxiety, anger, grief, loneliness, difficulty with pleasure, loss of meaning

Social: Loss of social network, family rupture, social awkwardness, sexual difficulty, behind schedule on developmental tasks

Cultural: Unfamiliar with the secular world; "fish out of water" feelings, difficulty belonging, information gaps (e.g., evolution, modern art, music)

In terms of recovery, Winell says, "breaking out of a restrictive, mind-controlling religion is understandably a liberating experience. . . . However, the challenges of leaving are daunting. For most people, the religious environment was a one-stop shop for meeting all their major needs—social support, a coherent worldview, meaning and direction in life, structured activities, and emotional/spiritual satisfaction."

"For many people who leave their faith," she concludes, "it is like a death or divorce. Their 'relationship with God' was a central assumption, such that giving it up feels like a genuine loss to be grieved."

Who Is Susceptible to Spiritual Abuse?

Although many people wrestle with holy longing, those with certain personal and family histories may be more susceptible to spiritual abuse. In the 1970s, when many Westerners turned East, the social and political aspirations of the 1960s had begun to fade. Like me, many seekers looked inward with the hope of transforming ourselves rather than our world—or transforming ourselves on the way to transforming our world. When we felt a gap between our actuality and our potential, our holy longing was stirred.

In 1991 researchers Mario Mikulincer and Ilana Peer-Goldin found that we feel happiness when we live our ideal images of ourselves. That is, when we experience our ideal self, as we do during heightened states of awareness or communal spiritual experience, we find the deepest satisfaction. The gap is closed between what is and what's possible. On the other hand, when there is a wide gulf between our reality and our ideal, the researchers found, we are most vulnerable to unhappiness.

Other research has shown that certain life turning points leave us susceptible to propaganda or religious conversion and to spiritual abuse: leaving home for the first time, entering the workplace after college, and facing the loss or death of a loved one. In other words, during key transitions we are open to shifts in meaning and purpose, which leaves us open to conversion—that is, finding a new teacher or teaching.

I would add that certain personality styles and developmental issues make us vulnerable as well. A dependent style leaves us open to identifying with authoritarian leaders, who appear to play out our passionate but unconscious fantasies, whether they involve creating world peace or destroying America. Obsessive compulsive disorders may find a place in ritualized routine. Narcissism fits with an emphasis on self-involvement and feelings of specialness. And borderline personality disorders make believers susceptible to overidealizing others, merging with them to hide from their own shameful inferiority, and filling their sense of emptiness with dogma. Trapped in a world of projections, those with borderline traits may distort reality by disowning their own shadows and creating scapegoats to carry their darkness for them. In addition, they suffer from a deep fear of abandonment and annihilation, which keeps them obedient and submissive until they feel betrayed, when they tend to retaliate with little concern for themselves or others.

In addition, the results of early sexual molestation—feelings of shame (especially about the body), porous psychic boundaries, anxiety, depression, and a tendency toward dissociation—leave young people open to the allure of charismatic teachers. Feeling fundamentally flawed, survivors of sexual abuse may seek to become healed by association. Due to their unmet longings, their shadows lead them to project a healer or savior onto a teacher, end up in a cultlike trance, and unconsciously repeat their early abusive experiences with their spiritual guides.

Men and women who are caught in the archetype of the *puer aeternus,* or eternal youth, also are drawn to the high ideals of spirituality—and typically avoid the shadow. To others, they appear childlike and naive, and especially over-trusting. Psychologist Rollo May called this trait "pseudoinnocence" and described it as the inability to see human destructiveness, which leaves one susceptible to others' shadows.

Granted a feeling of specialness by parents, which often covers over an inner emptiness, puers may lose their connection to the body and to earth. Unconsciously identified with the Self, they may become inflated. Chosen by an admired teacher, they feel special, as they did in childhood. As a result, the shadow is split off from the Self, and they long for the light. Or they project the Self onto a teacher or savior. But in either case, the Self remains unstable, childlike, and vulnerable. It's not tempered by suffering but instead seeks to maintain its grandiosity, avoid frustration, and overcome limits through spiritual experience. In this way, they seek a religious or spiritual solution to a psychological problem.

Religious and spiritual leaders are vulnerable to becoming perpetrators of abuse for parallel reasons. As a target of these powerful arrows of projection, which idealize him, a religious guide may feel his own unfulfilled needs for admiration and mirroring being met by his followers. If he has disowned his inferiority, he may project it onto a student or a whole population and feel superior, as if he is a savior. Slowly, he may come to believe that he is the center of the universe.

After an assassination attempt on Pope John Paul II, for example, his sense of election became evident: he stated that he believed the Virgin Mary had altered the flight path of the bullet intended for him because he was put in his position and kept there by divine providence. At a feast for the Lady of Fatima, he placed the bullet on a statue of her.

If the devotion and selfless service of a teacher's followers lead her to feel invested in her position, she may unknowingly begin to enact their expectations of her. Like a romantic couple that is unconsciously living out each other's projections in order to receive love, the religious guide and her believers may unknowingly lose their individual separateness and become ensnared in a folie à deux. Instead of the freedom to shine as she is, the teacher may unconsciously feel pressure to fulfill the students' pictures of the imago dei, just as the students unknowingly attempt to fulfill the teacher's images of the dutiful follower.

If a teacher in this situation becomes isolated from peer feedback, while he is banishing into the shadow those feelings and behaviors that don't fit his idealized image, he becomes cut off from his own vulnerability and from the opportunity to learn from his mistakes. As a result, he may succumb to identifying with the imago dei, ultimately believing himself to be so special that he's immune to the consequences of his actions, even immune to the HIV virus, as in the case of Osel Tendzin.

In this way, a religious teacher's isolation can have disastrous consequences, including sexual ones. In a 1985 *Yoga Journal* article, Buddhist meditation teacher Jack Kornfield described the results of interviews with fifty-four supposedly celibate spiritual teachers of all traditions about their sexual activity. Only fifteen actually remained celibate. Thirty-four of the thirty-nine others had had sexual liaisons with students. Their motivation, Kornfield said, was not always abuse of power. They yearned to step out of the isolation of their roles and, I would add, out of the isolation of carrying their students' projections. And although this study was small, is now dated, and doesn't reflect the scale of current reports, its insights remain useful.

In a psychotherapeutic relationship, the same danger arises with the client's transference onto the therapist, who carries both parental and godlike projections. With good training, a therapist aims to carry the projection knowingly and then hand it back at the proper moment, so that, in the end, the client can reclaim the power bestowed on the cherished Other.

However, this therapeutic ideal has been violated by countless professionals who have taken emotional, financial, and sexual advantage of their patients while succumbing to their own omnipotent fantasies. In California and other states, an ongoing list of these clinicians, their violations, and their consequences is published regularly in professional journals and magazines.

Before I became a therapist, the risk of this happening seemed remote and difficult to understand. We simply know, rationally, that this is unethical and destructive behavior, so we "just say no." However, in a few brief moments when I have caught the arrow of a projected ideal and felt myself expand into it, I experienced the risk: Instantaneously, I *wanted* to be seen that way; I *wanted* to be loved that way; the power brought a heady rush. It could, for a moment, make me forget my own flaws.

As a veteran of shadow-work, I recognized that, in those moments, my power shadow colluded with a client's feeling of powerlessness or dependency. Like Peter Pan's Wendy, I began to stitch back my own shadow by recalling my wounds and limitations and embracing my basic humanity. Instead of feeling the loss of inflation, I breathed a sigh of relief.

Clergy and spiritual leaders also are at risk of perpetrating abuse if they suffer from untreated emotional problems, such as early traumas of abuse and abandonment, sexual compulsions, deep-seated narcissism, or alcohol and drug addictions, all of which tend to go unacknowledged because of their position or presumed level of consciousness. These emotional issues tend to reappear—manifesting as, for example, a need to control, a contempt for weakness, a tendency for grandiosity—and become enshrined in the group.

Osama bin Laden is a case in point. The son of a Yemeni man who moved to Saudi Arabia and a concubine who was either Palestinian or Syrian, he was an outsider from birth. In addition, he was neglected by his father, who had many wives and children, and then abandoned at the age of ten when his father was killed in the United States. In college he visited nightclubs and bars, drank alcohol, and got involved with women. Eventually, overcome with guilt about indulging his own needs and desires, he turned to fundamentalist Islam and a longing for the father/god. When the West discovered him, he lived in a cave with four wives, fifteen children, and no running water.

All of those qualities that were banished into his shadow—personal desire, materialism, freedom of expression—were projected onto the infidels, especially Americans and Jews. And those traits that remained conscious in his persona—self-denial, asceticism, single-mindedness, self-righteousness—became enshrined among his followers.

James Gordon, author of *Golden Guru,* also pointed out this correlation between a guru's shadow and the ideals of the group. For instance, in his autobiography Osho wrote that he had decided at the age of six or seven, upon his grandfather's death, not to let anyone become close to him. That is, he banished his dependency needs into the shadow. He fulfilled this vow in his later isolation, as well as in his admonition to devotees to remain emotionally unattached to others, even while being sexually intimate.

We can detect each other's shadows by noticing what we criticize in others. When a religious teacher accuses others of moral failings, then begins to fall into the same behaviors that he deems wrong, he is at risk of abuse. For example, in his last few years, Osho fell into the same traps that he criticized in priests and politicians: he grew intoxicated with power, retaliated harshly against opponents, and used women to do his bidding because of their emotional loyalty.

Ken Wilber's research into human development over many decades sheds another light on what leaves students and teachers susceptible to receiving or perpetrating abuse. People do not develop globally, with all of their traits moving forward in lockstep, Wilber noted. Rather, there are multiple lines of development or multiple intelligences—cognitive, emotional, psychosexual, aesthetic, moral, kinesthetic, spiritual—that appear to grow in independent ways. And the hierarchical levels of development, discussed above, appear in a particular developmental line.

So, a religious leader, for example, may have high spiritual development, even including deep insight and realization, but average interpersonal development and low moral development. Therefore, he may be a charismatic leader, a mediocre church manager, and a poor risk at evaluating a moment that requires moral clarity for right action. At that time, despite his other gifts, he may be unable to stop his shadow from acting out.

This insight about lines of development helps us explain the many tales of religious and spiritual abuse in this book. Many leaders from other cultures, especially in monastic traditions, have only basic education and little or no training in ethics and morals. Even if their traditions have an ethical code, it's often dismissed for those who are chosen at birth or those who have the endorsement of a lineage.

In the same way, a believer may be highly developed cognitively, thinking through religious teachings, but poorly developed emotionally, leaving her vulnerable to denial or to silence at a charged moment. As potential abuse approaches, she may not be able to identify how she feels, to know why she feels that way, or to articulate it for self-defense.

Meeting the Shadow of Addiction

For some Westerners, the unsurpassed rise of science and technology has meant a rejection of religious life. However, the holy longing stirs in us—and only spirit can properly contain it. If a religious or spiritual context is not available to channel our yearning, it will find other objects of desire, and the more concrete and mundane realms of life— our lovers, pornography, online games and social media fantasies, as well as food, drugs, and alcohol—will be forced to carry it.

Before one of the founders of Alcoholics Anonymous, known as Bill W., launched the program, Jung told him that the craving for alcohol, or spirits, was equivalent, on a low level, to the thirst for Spirit, or union with god. This profound insight may have led the founders of AA to build their organization on a spiritual foundation.

It also helped me to realize that *any* addiction masks our holy longing. A chocolate cookie, a shot of vodka, a hit of Ecstasy, a roll of the dice, a designer dress—each can carry the projection of the Self or imago dei. Each can hold out the promise of a high that alters our state of consciousness one last time. And the craving for each of these objects of desire hides our deeper craving for transcendence. These substitute highs camouflage our holy longing with a temporary solution, a quick fix, which only leaves us hungering for more.

So, the battle is joined: to drink or not to drink, to eat or not to eat, to go there or not to go there, to take that or not to take that. The forbidden object becomes dangerous and revered.

In *The Thirst for Wholeness,* Christina Grof described her feeling of holy longing since childhood: "The pit of my stomach felt empty, my heart hurt, and my entire being aspired toward something I could not identify. As I grew, the ache in my soul permeated all aspects of my life. I felt monumentally homesick for something undefined, for an unnamed entity, place, or experience. Nothing I did seemed to alleviate the yearning within me."

Then she found the "delicious oblivion" of alcohol: "My boundaries melted, the pain disappeared, and I was, I thought, free. I felt comfortable within my own skin. . . . I was at ease with people in a way that was impossible in my daily life. I felt included, accepted, and cherished—until alcohol turned against me."

In a frantic effort to fill the void, many people throw themselves into their addictive behavior. They might, for example, consume enormous amounts of alcohol, cigarettes, and drugs. Trying to beat their addictions, they feel intense relief and remorse in the first stages of withdrawal. But for most addicts, a repetitive cycle occurs: intense craving, obsessive thoughts about the forbidden desired object, then a burst of acting out, which is often accompanied by euphoria. Addicts will then try to push their longing away or, alternatively, find another way to gratify it. But, ultimately, neither denial of the craving nor compromise with it will work.

Marion Woodman wrote of this phenomenon in the context of

eating disorders in *Addiction to Perfection*. Obese and anorexic women battle for consciousness through their acceptance or rejection of food, she said. They project the imago onto the forbidden food and want to eat it, to commune with that which they have projected outward. People who binge will eat until the ego gives up and surrenders to a larger, archetypal force. On the other hand, people who starve themselves will fast or exercise until they feel light and weightless. They want to leave the mire of matter, Woodman said, to fly with the spirit.

In either case, Woodman suggested that these compulsions replace meaningful rituals that previously offered religious transcendence. In submitting to a spiritual rite, we invoke the gods, offer up the ego for sacrifice, and feel reborn in a new level of awareness. But alcohol does not replace spirit, and starving does not replace fasting. In each case, the concrete is substituted for the symbolic, and involuntary, repetitive routine replaces voluntary submission of the ego to a greater force.

Those who successfully and finally eliminate a craving for a substance or behavior discover that, beneath it, a deeper craving remains. Buddhism teaches that all emotional stress comes about because of craving or *tanha,* which translates as "thirst." This addictive yearning, which cannot be filled, is not fundamentally different from other cravings. But it reminds me of the Buddhist teaching about hungry ghosts, creatures who have swollen bellies but needle-thin necks. Even though they are surrounded by food, they cannot satisfy their hunger or thirst because they can eat or drink only one drop at a time.

In her book *Holy Hunger,* Margaret Bullitt-Jonas described her struggle with binge eating as rooted in warring desires. She wanted to make a speech that her unavailable father would listen to in silence. And she didn't want to utter a word; she was defeated before she began. She wanted to weep in her sad mother's arms and hear that her feelings were okay. And she wanted to run from such intimacy and self-exposure. She wanted to live inside every inch of her body and be at home inside her skin. And she wanted to be rid of her body and punish it for its needs. She wanted her life to be unpredictable and fresh. And she wanted to be in complete control. She wanted to be awake, vital, and alive. And she wanted to be asleep and entirely numb.

Finally, she said, she had no idea what she most deeply desired. She played out her dilemma with food. One day she could trust the desire to be open to life and eat lightly. The next day she would be gripped by the need to control and binge. Her mind became a tyrant, her body its prisoner. She became a woman who was perpetually restless, afraid of her inner emptiness, unable to listen to her longing. Instead, her longing spun out into insatiable craving. She choked off words and filled up the silence with food.

Through Overeaters Anonymous, prayer, and telling her true story, Bullitt-Jonas eventually discovered that it was not food she desired after all. When she stopped attaching her desires to food, a larger, deeper desire could flow through her, a desire for something infinite, something elusive yet present. She called it a power that welcomes her passions and her hunger, a power that does not eliminate desires but transforms them.

When we meet the spiritual Other in addiction, we no longer consciously inhabit our holy longing. We become its captive. We are pulled beneath the waves of desire, even to the point of drowning. But if we can redirect our longing toward the holy, the undertow can deliver us to the next level of awareness. And in this way addiction becomes a vehicle of evolution.

Death and Transcendence

In 1999 I was saddened and disturbed to hear of the death of Nigel Watts, author of *The Way of Love,* a short tale about the life of the Sufi poet Rumi. Watts reported that he planned to commit suicide because he could no longer bear separation from the beloved, the Sufi name for god. And he did.

His story reminded me of the members of Heaven's Gate, a small cult that committed mass suicide in 1997 because they believed that, with the passing of a comet, they would be taken by a UFO to a more evolved level of life. More recently, we were faced with the enigma of suicide bombers who attacked the Twin Towers in New York and continue to attack civilian sites in Israel and around the world, blowing themselves up as part of a holy war. Why did all of these people devoutly desire death, even long for it?

As more information has emerged about the terrorists, we in the West have been even more surprised. In a 2002 article on the topic, published in the *Journal of Psychohistory*, psychoanalyst Joan Lachkar reported that support and encouragement for suicidal killings runs deep through Muslim culture. Young children try on the clothing of suicide bombers. Pictures of those who died in this manner adorn walls and books. Teachers praise martyrs, and a popular film portrays a young Egyptian boy who blows up Israeli soldiers and himself as a hero, while the audience cheers.

Lachkar described suicide bombers as traumatized children who were emotionally abandoned, suffered severe loss and betrayal, and were raised by unavailable or violent caretakers. The result: due to their rage and shame and their inability or lack of opportunity to heal, they are overcome with a desire to retaliate.

Enter their charismatic leader, Osama bin Laden (or the next terrorist leader), who provided them with an enemy to hate and an ideology to relieve their uncertainty and to back up their dissonant feelings. Their fragmented sense of self merged with him, their ideal imago, and took on the group identity. Their sense of powerlessness dissolved; their lack of meaning and purpose dissipated. They became willing to die for the cause—even eager to die, because in death they will meet Allah and his prophet, the objects of their longing.

I would add that beyond or beneath the personal histories of those who yearn for death lie religious tenets that support that inclination. Believers who become identified with the "up" arc, the Self or spirit, tend to devalue life in the body, its creature comforts and sufferings. I suggest that their unconscious depression or psychic numbness colludes with these teachings, which devalue matter as "earthly fetters," and therefore they long for the other world.

Split off from spiritual modes of transcendence *in* life, they come to mistake death for transcendence—death as a path to god. They yearn for physical death because symbolic or ego death is unavailable or unknown.

In the end, few faithful believers can live indefinitely cut off from their own emotional vitality and intuitive wisdom. Eventually, they will want to reclaim their emotional shadows. Few can live indefinitely in a passive, dependent, childlike state. Eventually, they will feel their powerlessness mount and will want to reclaim their autonomy. Few can live indefinitely while projecting their imago dei onto a limited, mortal human being. Eventually, they will meet the spiritual shadow and suffer feelings of disillusionment and loss of faith.

At the same time, few religious leaders can carry the burden of this projection indefinitely. Jung asserted that possession by an archetype turns a person into a flat, collective figure, a mask behind which he can no longer develop as an individual. Eventually, because he carries only the light and colludes in ignoring his own dark side, it may act out impulsively in hypocritical or abusive behavior. It may act out in coercing others to die.

In "Encountering the Shadow in Buddhist America," Katy Butler wrote about her experience following the revelation of the affairs of her roshi, Richard Baker: "My black meditation robe still hangs in the back of my closet. I never lost faith in Buddhist teachings, but for some years I didn't know how to reconnect with them. Instead, I did what a friend called 'remedial work,' examining my personal history and the anger and self-righteousness I expressed when the scandal broke. I was among those who hoped to find a sanctuary within Buddhism for my personal wounds. But my culture and family history trailed me into my Buddhist community like a can tied to the tail of a dog."

For me, remedial work involved turning from the light to the dark side, from the *via positiva* to the *via negativa,* or shifting my psychic energy and attention from spirit to shadow. During that transition, I wrote the following piece.

My Longing for the Dark

A Meditation on Down

My father dreamed of becoming an astronaut, shooting up and away from our blue pearl, up until he would step out, in rarified air, onto a red world with no downward pull.

I dreamed of becoming a yogi, shooting up and away from my mortal coil, up until I would step out, in rarified air, onto a golden world with no downward pull.

Like him, I dreamed of up, while everything around me moved inexorably down, down into decay, down into dirt. Today I turn my ear toward the quiet call of the dirt. I turn my ear toward the whisper beneath the dirt, the whisper beckoning me down, down to the land of Down.

It is a large turning, from up to down. It is a change of direction as pivotal as reorienting the compass needle from north to south. It is as if my compass had been leading me away from myself, up and away from my bodily juices, up and away from my cravings for sweets, up and away from my earthly diggings for grasses and tubers and blooms.

And now the return has begun. The silver ship is plunging down from heights into depths, down from light into dark, down from heaven into hell. What is this linguistic force that, like gravity, pulls certain words together, creating allies, and separates others, creating walls? Why do *down/deep/dark/dirty* seem wed together with the familiarity of ageless mates? And why do they seem to be fit bedfellows for the making of soul? On the other hand, why do *up/high/light/pure* seem like the recipe ingredients for a life of spirit?

Is the dream of up a defense against down? Must the longing for spiritual ascent be a denial of soulful descent?

For me, down and up seem separated by an endless winding wall, forever sundered into the realms of hell and heaven, each with its own gods, each with its own demons.

I grew up with the gods of up, looking down on me and wagging their fingers of scorn. But who are the gods of down?

The dark stranger who leaps out of a crack in the earth is Hades, lord of the underworld, also known as Pluto. The myth known as "Hymn to Demeter" is the only Greek story to include Hades. It introduces him as he abducts the innocent maiden Persephone, who is gathering flowers, and carries her off to his dark home. Most of the interpretations of the Eleusinian mysteries focus on the nature of Demeter, the quintessential mother and goddess of grain, and Persephone, the mother-bound virgin who becomes queen of the underworld.

But who is Hades, this god of down? What is it about him that makes us fear his realm? Is Hades a violent rapist, or is he a sexual initiator for the maiden? Does he help her break the overly close bond with her mother and thus find her womanhood? Or does he violate their intimacy with a force that is unforgiving? Certainly, he carries her over the wall that divides up from down; he guides her from the light world of ego into the dark world of soul.

This god of down has several other names: Trophonios means the nourisher; Euboulos means the good counselor; Ploutos means the wealth giver; Zeus Chthonios means the underworld side of the all-seeing god of Olympus; and, finally, Aidoneus means the unseen one, the invisible god. Thus, Hades has many aspects that are associated with fertility, generosity, even wisdom. But, ultimately, he remains hidden, lord of a separate realm, not lord among people or houses or trees.

Even the everyday vernacular reveals biases against the realm of Hades, prejudices that are deeply built into our ways of seeing and feeling. When we have the blues, for example, we say, "I am feeling down." So *down* means unhappy, dejected, downhearted.

When we have a bad habit, we say, "It's my downfall." When we are down on our luck, we are downtrodden. If we live uptown, we are seen as more fortunate than those who live downtown.

So, down and up are habits of mind that, like all habits, cause the seeing to be blind. For if we view down as a falling to be avoided, and if we view up as a rising to be strived for, then we cannot see the gifts of every small downward move. And we cannot feel movement unless it is felt as forward and up.

Down is more than a figure of speech. It holds a whole archetypal world, a realm that has come to be associated in depth psychology with a movement toward soul, an orientation toward feeling, toward body, toward the unconscious shadow. One does therapy to uncover depths in the self, to go down into the pain, down into the psyche, the promised land.

A few years ago I noticed that I had silently, unknowingly begun to associate going down, feeling deeply, with feeling sad. I had associated down with an emotional state, or array of states (sorrow, melancholy, depression, grief), limited to sadness. This, I had come to feel, was the only appropriate response to the state of human suffering when it is viewed honestly—that is, with depth. So, people who seemed happy, complacent, upbeat, and optimistic also seemed shallow to me, to have no depth and no appropriateness in their response to human suffering.

In other words, up, which had carried light in the first half of my life, began to carry shadow. And down, which had been disowned, began to carry light.

If the larger world, the Judeo-Christian framework, favors up, the move away from the Fall and toward the Resurrection, then the alternative world, the framework of critique, which questions cultural assumptions, might naturally favor down. This compensatory move helps us stay conscious—until we fall, once again, into the unquestioning gravitational fields of words.

I notice my use of the word *falling* here, and it makes me wonder why we can't fall up. I realize it just may be our gravitational world that divides the pie of reality into up and down, generating the fantasy of flight as freedom from gravitation and the fantasy of ascent as liberation from suffering.

For me, certainly, Hades was an abductor; he stole me away from the upper world, where I was gathering flowers of innocence. He pierced my spiritual persona and forced me to face all that I had sought to avoid, all that I had hoped to escape by dedication to the light. And he initiated me in the darkness of my own cave, where, like Persephone, I left dreams and ideals, family and friends, far behind.

Like Persephone, who becomes the bride of Hades and resides with him in darkness for half the year, then returns to her mother in the upper world during the other half, I, too, can now hold the darkness and the light. When I arise from the underworld, I carry its darkness with me now; I carry its stillness and loss. And if I move too far up and begin to float away, I can hear Hades whisper beneath the dirt, beckoning me down, down to the fertile land of Down.

From suffering I have learned this: that whoever is sore wounded by love will never be made whole unless she embrace the very same love that wounded her.

MECHTILD OF MAGDEBURG

What we have to be is what we are.

THOMAS MERTON

When Zusya, a Hasidic rabbi, was criticized for unorthodox behavior, he replied, "In the next world I will not be asked why in this life I was not Moses, but rather why I was not Zusya."

HASIDIC TALE

Do not seek to follow in the footsteps of the wise; seek the things they sought.

BASHO

SEVEN

Rekindling the Flame

*Shadow-Work for Spiritual Abuse
and Disillusionment*

A fortunate few find the narrow path through the darkness and undergo an authentic initiation. We travel from spiritual innocence through the dark descent toward a new level of consciousness—spiritual maturity. We evolve from dependency on a spiritual parent through meeting the shadow toward spiritual adulthood.

Having been emptied out of old ideas and images, having been left fallow for a dark season, we become fertile soil for new life—open but not naive, eager but not impatient, and ripe for blossoming.

With practice, we learn to meet the darkness in ourselves and in our priests or teachers, gradually coming to accept it as a part of being human. No longer susceptible to being true believers and perpetrating fundamentalism, we may be able to see our own shadows, accept the limitations of our teachers, and empathize more deeply with others who hold diverse views.

We learn to trace some of the roots of our religious longings to early family issues (feelings of isolation, emptiness, or low self-worth, patterns of victimization and caretaking, a need to feel special, an inability to face limits, an inability to deal with negative emotions or conflict, and a driving perfectionism). And we learn to acknowledge the dark sides of our spiritual beliefs, working through overly simplistic black-and-white ideas until we can eventually hold greater paradox and ambiguity, until we can witness the dance of darkness and light.

For some, this inner work requires separation from an esteemed teacher, which can evoke powerful feelings of loss, guilt, anxiety, and shame. It may require separation from an institutionalized community or an informal group, which also leads to intense feelings of grief and isolation. And it may require separation from a set of teachings or a philosophy, which triggers strong feelings of meaninglessness and purposelessness.

Others will leave but maintain their practices, meditating privately or creating an informal practice group.

And others will want to stay and try to rehabilitate a community, rebuild on a reformed foundation, and even ask a teacher to be accountable, make amends, and establish new ethical rules.

I don't offer a universal prescription here, suggesting that readers reject a church or teacher. Instead, I suggest that we work toward making conscious the "religious unconscious." That is, I suggest that we begin to contemplate the underside of our spiritual lives, questioning the dubious behaviors of our priests or teachers, as well as the dogmatic and authoritative assumptions we have taken for granted. In this way, we can begin to see through those beliefs that maintain our suffering and our shame. We can begin to see through those imagoes that block our transcendence.

In the end, whether we leave or stay, shadow-work for spiritual abuse and disillusionment requires that we reclaim lost parts of ourselves—self-worth, independent thinking, emotional shadows, bodily awareness, the capacity to initiate action, and images of god—that did not fit our spiritual persona and that we now permit entirely new feelings and images to emerge. And it requires that we reclaim those parts—power, wisdom, compassion—that were sacrificed in a projection onto an idealized teacher because our capacity to carry our own greatness was so diminished.

Communal Shadow-Work

In a 1990 *Common Boundary* article, Katy Butler described a ceremony used by Buddhist monks in the first few centuries after the Buddha's death. On the eve of every full and new moon, they gathered in the forest for "confession before the community." There they publicly recited the Buddhist precepts and admitted their shortcomings, their violations, and any damage they had done to their community.

Butler suggested that if we reinstated such a quiet ritual, a brave, disgraced teacher or priest might safely acknowledge his or her misconduct. He or she might gain insight into and disclose the wounds that brought him or her to perpetrate it. Perhaps the sangha or congregation could confess its deep disappointment and feelings of betrayal. Its members could acknowledge their participation in denial and rationalization. And the whole group could apologize to those members who had been mistreated and compensate them in some way. After full acknowledgment and restitution, healing and a new beginning might be possible.

In a few cases, communities have attempted to make amends in this way. Some individual members of the clergy who perpetrated abuse and received treatment have acknowledged the harmful effects of their behavior and attempted to make restitution. For example, Episcopal priest Father Leo Booth wrote openly in his books about his own recovery from alcoholism and religious addiction, which he defined as using god, a church, or a belief system to escape reality and elevate self-worth. However, Booth insisted that individual treatment is not enough. He urged both clergy and parishioners to examine how the church perpetuates destructive, shaming beliefs and enables religious abuse.

He pointed out that many churchgoers are raised to have a childlike fear of displeasing god, which leaves them vulnerable to exploitation. In the church's sexist, patriarchal system, Booth said, god is father, Christ is son, and women are left out. The resulting imbalance of power is reinforced by liturgy and doctrine. Covert messages—"God is the judge who punishes or rewards us"; "God will provide if we obey"; "If we truly trust in Him, we won't have doubts"; "Clergy have power over us because they are superior"; "God wants selflessness and self-love is a sin"—lead us to abandon large parts of ourselves in the shadow.

These kinds of destructive messages are not the sole province of the church. They can be heard in most traditions that are patriarchal, controlling, racialized, shaming, or based on abuse of power. I recall one meditation teacher telling me that his form of practice was the only way to enlightenment, and others were a waste of time. Another told group members that if they did not meditate enough, they would be responsible for the lack of peace in the world.

To prevent religious abuse, Booth said, we must be willing to revise the institutional elements that create and maintain it. In other words, community-wide repair needs to include education, support, and methods of restitution for survivors, perpetrators, and other members. Some experts have suggested that priests, rabbis, and roshis follow the same code of ethics as doctors and therapists. That is, inappropriate contact between a leader and a member of the flock would be a breach of professional boundaries. Others argue that legally institutionalizing boundaries has not helped therapists to stop violating them. Rather, thorough and ongoing education about projection, transference, and boundaries might go further to help professionals internalize boundaries and protect those under their care.

Today Father Booth's words seem prescient. Following the many accusations of sexual abuse by priests, both believers and experts alike are calling for institutional reform in the Catholic church. Because huge, wealthy institutions are by nature conservative, built to support the status quo, such reform is unlikely. However, the church's central metaphor might help at this time: The institution itself is undergoing a crucifixion and descent. If it is allowed to die as it is, like the dying and resurrecting Christ, it may be able to be reborn to a new life.

In addition, I suggest that individual religious and spiritual teachers must learn to recognize and manage their own shadow material. If they knew their own areas of vulnerability, the ways in which they might act out under pressure, they could anticipate them, find other outlets, or even ask for support. Finally, spiritual guides need to practice self-care in such a way that they are not socially or professionally isolated and, therefore, likely to fall into self-inflation or self-deception.

In an article in *Los Angeles Psychologist,* Nanette de Fuentes proposed several stages of congregational healing from clergy abuse:

1. Shock ("I can't believe this!")
2. Denial ("I won't believe this.")
3. Bargaining ("What if he stayed part time?")
4. Anger ("Is she making up the charges?")
5. Depression ("Will anyone come here again?")
6. Holy rage ("How can we cleanse the priesthood?")
7. Finally, acceptance

However, she agreed with Booth that while individuals go through these successive stages, there can be no real healing without justice. That is, the truth must be told. The abuser must be named and condemned. The survivor must be heard and protected from further abuse. The abuser must face consequences and make tangible restitution.

A handful of spiritual teachers have publicly admitted their wrongdoing and worked toward reclaiming those parts of themselves that were sacrificed by carrying the ideal imago for others. Their openness and authenticity may one day lead the way for other teachers and clergy to come forward and acknowledge their own grandiosity and their own limitations. If so, we could reimagine religious institutions in a climate of greater openness because this openness and trust would be built on hard-won awareness and a concern for the well-being of others, rather than on a fear of external authority and punishment.

For example, as reported by Anne Cushman in *Yoga Journal* in 1994, yogi Amrit Desai, an adept in kundalini practice and founder of the Kripalu yoga ashram in Massachusetts, taught that sex would slow students' progress toward enlightenment and that celibacy would enhance kundalini or spiritual energy. In 1994, when a woman disciple told others that she had had sexual relations with Desai because he told her that it was a spiritual gift and special privilege, he denied her story. His denial was accepted by the community, even by the woman's husband and son, who remained at the ashram after she left.

Another woman then came forward with the same claim. This time, Desai admitted both affairs and confirmed a third. He resigned and offered to pay for the women's therapy. He also made a public apology to the community.

His students were outraged, heartbroken, and deeply demoralized. The man who carried their imago dei had habitually violated the moral code he imposed on them. Long-buried resentments surfaced. As one disciple told Cushman, "I feel murderous rage at having sold out my voice to [the guru]. People here are under a great hypnosis about what their value is in the world. We do not see ourselves . . . because the focus is on an exotic spokesperson of the truth who embodies beauty, and grace, and the power of the lineage that he stands in. Try standing next to someone of that stature and that degree of realization and finding your voice."

To facilitate the healing process, Kripalu staff invited a diverse group of psychotherapists to assist them in dealing with unresolved emotional and interpersonal issues that years of yoga practice had left untouched. The radical result: At Kripalu, the traditional guru/disciple relationship was recast in a more egalitarian mold. Those who used to adore their teacher uncritically learned to accept his fallibility.

As Desai told his students, "If you have a conflict with me, and if I don't live it fully—if I blame you or feel ashamed—then that experience goes under the carpet, in the basement, in the dark area. . . . It just waits there until somebody else pushes the button. Then the same fear that I had in my dealings with you comes back because it has not been lived fully. The seed didn't burn to ashes. That's why my determination in this lifetime is to face everything."

Eventually, Desai left Kripalu. Since his resignation, a council of long-term residents is helping to shape community policy and form a new vision that takes the focus off the guru. The nature of service at the ashram has changed as well: Students no longer work around the clock for a dollar each month. They now put in forty hours each week and receive stipends and insurance. Although celibacy is required for single residents, marriage is permitted.

Desai told *Yoga Journal:*

Many spiritual seekers came to live at Kripalu to explore a spiritual lifestyle. Many experienced the feeling of finally 'coming home' and the possibility of living in a conscious community with a guru, a spiritual father who would nurture their spirits, love and care for them. . . . But, in order to keep the dream alive, they suppressed a lot of their feelings. In time, these suppressed feelings were destined to shatter the dreams. We tend to believe that love ends when dreams are demolished. In reality, the shattering of dreams is the opportunity for the emergence of true love.

In the beginning, Desai thought his role was "fixing and teaching." But, as he said:

The traditional model from India . . . was not effectively addressing the issues many disciples had around childhood abuse, parental authority, and self-expression. . . .

Unfortunately, in some ways the teaching of the Eastern guru-disciple relationship of love, selfless service, and surrender reinforced codependence and suppression. Many residents transferred their feelings about parental authority to me, the spiritual authority. . . .

We are . . . dismantling the old form, which has served its purpose. . . . It calls for a profound shift in my role. . . .

I'm now exploring how to blend the most profound teaching of the yogic tradition with Western psychotherapy to create a new psycho-spiritual model that is appropriate to serve Western disciples. This model has no map.

In *Avalanche,* physician-turned-healer W. Brugh Joy also openly explored his own fall from grace. In his early life, Dr. Joy deeply identified with the Self in the imago of Christ—inspired savior, teacher, redeemer. Therefore, he longed for the light, experienced altered states, developed healing abilities, overvalued spirituality—and split off the shadow sides of his nature.

But, thirty years later, the shadow erupted in a dream: seated in a car, he looked into the rearview mirror and locked eyes with "evil incarnate." Attending to the message from his unconscious, Dr. Joy allowed this dream to penetrate him and change him. The result: the encounter "raped his innocence," as he put it, and initiated him into his own vulnerability, which he had disowned.

This shift appeared in his life in many ways. For example, as a teacher at the Findhorn community in Scotland, Dr. Joy had been loved and appreciated, even venerated, carrying an ideal imago. But on a later visit, he spoke to the community about the negative consequences of feeling special and the risks of identifying with light over darkness. Following these remarks, he was attacked by his listeners because his statements were heretical in the new age community. He suddenly became the object of a negative projection, a scapegoat.

Dr. Joy realized that the shadow of the community was erupting— and he was the mirror. He also recognized that those qualities that were attacked were parts of himself, not merely disowned parts of his attacker. He was able to view the event as an initiation into carrying a collective shadow projection, just as politicians do. But he was doing it consciously.

Finally, Dr. Joy could see that spiritual viewpoints are filters that accept and reject certain feelings, thoughts, and images. As such, they exclude whole chunks of life, including aspects of the divine itself. "If you can't give up the power that is yours through identification with the deity that is dancing you—Warrior, Saint, Healer, the Mother, the Father, or anything else, pleasant or unpleasant—you are seduced and in danger of losing your soul," he wrote.

In an effort to transcend to the next level of consciousness, he wrote, we need to surrender our attachment to the power of the archetype that is dominant. The consequences of that act may include humiliation, powerlessness, and a loss of sacred values. But it also may mean our evolution.

What if we imagine a spiritual community that added the tools of psychology to its spiritual teaching and practice? What if it included knowledge of the shadow and shadow-work in its understanding and practices? What if it deconstructed its patriarchal hierarchy and designed a horizontal-style, consensus-based organization? What if it empowered women as well as men?

Let's go further in this exercise: What if this community included service to others as a spiritual practice and antidote to narcissism? Not *seva* to the teacher or to the group's business ventures, but service to the common good, the surrounding community of people in need.

Roshi Wendy Egyoku Nakao trained with Maezumi Roshi at the Zen Center of Los Angeles (ZCLA) and with Roshi Bernie Glassman in Zen Peacemakers. When it was discovered that Maezumi Roshi was sexually involved with students and an active alcoholic, scandal rocked ZCLA, and most students left in despair. Roshi Wendy stepped up and, following a fire, decided to rebuild inside and out. She trained the remaining members in council to process their feelings about their disillusionment with their teacher and to resolve disagreements. She studied communication skills and looked directly at shadow issues in the community.

"We work now on our emotional integration and our discernment to detect potential conflict," she told me in an interview.

She singled out a shadow of Buddhism: it has been filtered through a male monastic lens. She asked: "What would practice look like if the voices of women, such as Buddha's abandoned wife and early followers, had not been written out of his life story?"

At the Zen Center, Roshi Wendy broke up the traditional hierarchy and created a peer sangha, or community, for shared stewardship, with autonomous circles of leadership. All of this built a new container for an intentional spiritual community, and as problems arose, the container remained strong. She noted:

> The old forms collapsed, but forty people came together to build a new structure, tell the truth about our history, and learn how to create another kind of community. During the past twenty years, we've woven consciously the many threads of zen center—including its light and shadows, its vertical and horizontal dimensions, its feminine and masculine energies—into a resilient fabric with a newly emerging story. Stitch by stitch we are sewing the robe of buddhas, the robe of awakened ones, which is the robe of liberation and service.

This orients us to a great vow, Roshi Wendy said. For Buddhists, the decision to take refuge means to commit to a life that is far larger than your own preoccupations. Members of the center care for local homeless people, create food baskets for local churches, offer nonviolence training to teens, do prison ministry, and plant trees. The call to serve, she said, is part of the Bodhisattva vow to liberate all beings by doing practice for all beings, not merely ourselves. "So practice occurs in the environment of service," Roshi Wendy concluded. "And service is practice." (Roshi Wendy stepped down as abbot of the Zen Center in May 2019.)

These profound efforts at communal shadow-work by teachers and groups have been rare. The few cited here are models of meeting the shadow on the spiritual path and allowing it to alchemically transform teachers' roles, students' roles, and even an institution, with its systemic dynamic. But this communal inner work must go hand-in-hand with individual shadow-work if those who were abused, traumatized, and heartbroken are to recover and find their way through the dark tunnel toward the light. The next section describes how to do this personal inner work.

Individual Shadow-Work

Separating from a Teacher and Imago Dei

When the disciple is ready, the guru disappears.

GREG BOGART

When we have to imagine an object of attraction as evil, dark, and demonic, we do so to be able to have some control over it, to help us break the power of its attraction.

W. BRUGH JOY

For students or parishioners, the required sacrifice may mean letting go of identification with being a student and moving out of a naive, childlike role. As long as we remain in an obedient, dependent position, we banish many of our own qualities into the shadow, including our inquisitiveness, financial ambitions, emotional and sexual needs, and creative longings. In this way, our own development is derailed.

Research on people in religious communities has confirmed this finding: despite radical ideological changes and initial relief from inner conflicts, many members' basic traits and unconscious conflicts remain intractable or reappear with their departure from the fold. One of my clients continued to see herself as an outsider even while she fully participated within the group for many years. A middle-aged man continued to act rebellious in his church congregation, as he had in his family. And a young woman kept trying to live up to the perfectionism of her demanding father with her spiritual father.

In each case, the re-creation of parent-child or family dynamics in a religious community may not lead to their resolution. Instead, these people need to separate from their surrogate parents and families in an effort to step into a more independent, responsible, adult position so that their internal development—their "growing up"—can continue.

Some students may be able to accomplish this task by remaining with the community as a loyally dissenting member. Others may see through their projections, move to the margins of the community, and even continue their practices. But some will need to break their ties, separating altogether from the priest or teacher and the group.

When the student is faced with an inner conflict between her devotion and her growing individuality, difficult challenges typically arise. If she has been encouraged to meditate on the teacher or merge with him in a symbiotic way, she may have difficulty finding her own separate boundaries. If she has projected an imago dei and has an idealizing transference, she may, through gradual disappointments, see the human being more clearly behind the ideal image. This recognition may enable her to leave with tender feelings. Or she may be devastated by the appearance of the teacher's shadow, unable to maintain her own self-worth without allying with another's perfection, and begin the search for a new, more perfect ideal.

If the aspirant has enjoyed service to the teacher or to the church, he may feel that without that outlet he has no direction or purpose. If he has learned to distrust his own impulses, he may wonder if his need to separate stems from his own selfishness or laziness. Typically, these self-doubts will be fueled by negative messages from the group, which may criticize his doubts and discourage his efforts toward independence.

If she has buried feelings of inferiority, envy, or resentment beneath her admiration, they may rush to the surface, leaving her with deep ambivalence toward her teacher. This process is evident in the history of psychoanalysis, in which each of Freud's disciples struggled with the guilt of differentiating from him and the fear of his rejection. In the end, most ended up by turning the "good father" into the "bad father," or symbolically killing him off in order to do their own creative work. A few, instead, killed themselves.

This, then, is the disciple's dilemma: a tension between feeling dependent, grateful, and fulfilled as a student and eventually feeling the need for more autonomy, self-expression, and fulfillment from other sources. In many cases, this tension forces the student's separation.

For all of these reasons, the onset of this passage is filled with confusion, fear, guilt, and loss. As former Zen priest Josh Baran put it, when he left his community, despite his teacher's pressure to stay, "The leaving process was the most difficult transition of my life—and during this period I gained more insight than in the previous ten years" (see "Sorting It Out," by Susan Rothbaum, in *Yoga Journal*).

Some believers can be aided during this time by images that arise spontaneously in dreams and creative works. In his article "Separating from a Spiritual Teacher," Greg Bogart reported several clients' dreams as they worked through the process of separation from spiritual teachers. One man, who spent years in an ashram with vows of celibacy and poverty, struggled with a desire to leave and marry. He dreamed that he entered a large meditation hall in which hundreds of seats were arranged facing away from the guru's seat up front. According to Bogart, the dream portrayed the man's readiness to remain in a reverential relationship with the teacher but with his attention directed away from the guru and toward the world.

Another man, who suffered from a series of painful disillusionments with several teachers, worked deeply to release his negative feelings toward them. He dreamed that he was in a lush green meadow, standing near a large, ancient, beautiful tree. He was observing a vigil for his dead teacher and father, who were buried beneath the tree. It was a solemn moment, yet he was at peace. Bogart's client felt that the burial of his dead teacher and father signified the death of the man's need for an external spiritual guide and heralded the emergence of his capacity to become his own source of wisdom. As the client said, "Now, with these men fertilizing my roots, I can become my own father."

Finally, I cannot fail to mention another reason for leaving a spiritual guide: aside from completion of a psychological journey, in which developmental needs demand more autonomy, a student's spiritual journey may demand it. After all, we submit to a teacher with the promise of a new level of consciousness, and for some, this does occur. Once we realize our own divine nature and internalize the imago dei, the teacher's purpose has been fulfilled.

Reclaiming the Light

As Marianne Williamson wrote, "Our deepest fear is not that we are inadequate, our deepest fear is that we are powerful beyond measure. It is our light, not our darkness, that most frightens us."

Perhaps that is why, when we find a beloved priest or teacher, we so easily give away our light, our spiritual authority, and permit another to carry our flame. We come to believe that he or she alone can mediate the divine for us. We are not made in god's image; the one who carries our imago dei alone is. So, we are no longer burdened with a direct relationship to our own light, our own radiance, our own Self.

As a result, we identify with a narrow range of archetypes: the student, the seeker, the believer, the child. If we become an obedient spiritual son or daughter to a surrogate parent, we cut off those qualities that adhere to the adult self. If we disown all of the light, we carry those qualities that we attribute to the darkness, such as evil sinner, doubting Thomas, or lazy meditator. If we are spiritually abused, we may become identified with being a victim, which leaves us guilty, ashamed, and disempowered.

In the end, during the separation from the teacher or teachings, spiritual shadow-work requires us to retrieve those qualities that we attributed to the teacher or priest. When we have internalized them and brought them back into our own treasury, we will carry our own light. And we will be able to live out a wider range of archetypes, providing a richer, deeper life.

In *The Direct Path,* Andrew Harvey described his own difficult journey of reclaiming the light from Indian teacher Mother Meera. As a devotee, Harvey was instructed by Meera to get married and write a book claiming that her divine force had changed him from gay to heterosexual. As a result of that painful encounter, in which she asked her devotee to tell a lie, Harvey saw through the projections that led him to exalt her as "divine mother." Angry and disappointed, he faced the dark shadow of his teacher and made a painful, difficult decision.

He went public with her request and his objection. In response, Meera denied having made it. As a result of the controversy, he lost a teaching job, became ill, and received threats against his life. During a fierce attempt at self-reflection, he stripped down his beliefs to their essentials and allowed himself to undergo a rite of passage.

Five years later, divested of trust in the traditional teacher/student system, he wrote a book about communion with god without a human mediator. "Without the radical disillusion with the guru system in all of its aspects that I have endured," he wrote, ". . . I would have continued to project, probably in more and more subtle ways, my own divine truth and essence onto Meera or Rumi or the Dalai Lama, and so have avoided the ultimate adventure—which is to claim complete responsibility, in and under God, for one's own spiritual development."

If Harvey had continued to believe that his development was an effect of the guru's grace, he said, he would never have claimed the depths of his own realization or known that he would make deeper and more honest spiritual progress outside the guru system, which, at that stage, kept him diminished.

Reclaiming Independent Thinking

Although we may need outer authority for guidance at some stages of life, at another we need to develop beyond these parental figures and cultivate our internal resources—our own ideas, beliefs, feelings, intuitions, images, and actions.

In his book *The Double Mirror*, Tibetan Buddhist student Stephen Butterfield described the process of relinquishing his doubts and queries in order to follow a Buddhist path. He had a lot of questions for his teacher, Trungpa Rinpoche. But the teacher responded, "Do not intellectualize overmuch. Just do the practices, and their cumulative wisdom will become apparent as you go along."

Butterfield tried to follow this advice, but he was never able to completely silence his questions or find satisfactory answers to them. Instead, his questions went underground, banished into the shadow, so that he could gain Trungpa's acceptance, belong in the sangha, and receive initiations.

After a long series of disappointments and betrayals, Butterfield could no longer stand the tension between the sustenance of his inner experience and the destructiveness of his organization and its teachers. He stopped practicing.

And all his questions erupted—those he had ignored because they were too threatening and those he had carefully avoided because he believed they would block his way. Some questions were too basic to ask without embarrassment. Others revealed pride and egotism or resistance to the guru, which was fatal.

Why was he doing the practices? What did they have to do with enlightenment? Is Buddhism a vehicle or a crutch or a shell, useful only until we hatch from it? Does Buddhism even exist apart from the activity of minds using it as a frame of reference? Were the robed men to whom he had bowed over and over any more awake than anyone else? If they were not, who was? And, finally, if his questions were coming back as a result of not practicing, then was his practice repressing them?

This loss of independent thinking may occur within any tradition. A former member of Herbert W. Armstrong's Worldwide Church of God told me that when the end-of-the-world predictions of the "prophet" failed to come true, he was terrified of questioning their validity. He still held out the hope that, at Armageddon, he would be saved with the rest of the faithful. So he submerged his doubts.

But, years later, when allegations of incest by Armstrong surfaced, my client's doubts forcefully erupted into consciousness: Perhaps Armstrong was not all-perfect or all-knowing. Perhaps he was flawed. Or perverted. The seismic force of those thoughts shook his belief system and broke him open. Slowly, and with support, he worked to develop a more complex and nuanced view of his religious teacher. He became able to value certain qualities in Armstrong and to reject others, to appreciate certain teachings and to disclaim others for himself.

A similar process occurred for a client who was raised in the Christian Science church. When her elderly parents, who were lifelong members, became gravely ill and had to choose between using medicine or facing death, they both went to a doctor for the first time in their lives. As a result, their church shunned them.

My client reported, "It was horrible to watch these two old people being abandoned by the very church they had supported. I had seen miraculous healings and had felt the sweetness of community. But with this act of judgment and rejection of my parents, all of my doubts came crashing in."

Our religious leaders and institutions teach us that we must choose between faith and doubt. So, to be believers, we bury our doubts and adopt the languages and beliefs of our communities. Our longing for certainty and our intolerance of ambiguity lead us to seek simple black-and-white answers. As a result, we give the power of definition over our lives to others. They circumscribe how we spend our time and money, eat, dress, have sex, marry—and what we believe. They delimit right thinking from wrong. They define who is on god's side and who is not. They proclaim who is going to heaven or becoming enlightened and who is not. As believers, we gain certainty, access to the sacred, and the promise of salvation. Therefore, our questions become taboo, forbidden thoughts that threaten to topple the system of beliefs.

Instead, I suggest that we cultivate the faith to doubt—the trust or confidence to explore more fully and honestly what we actually believe. Our forbidden thoughts can show the way; they can guide us toward the shadow, where, like hidden treasure, our disowned ideas, opinions, and doubts lie dormant.

When I was beginning to separate from my meditation community, I remember thinking that there must be some value to emotional attachment, which in my tradition was viewed as a trap in samsara, the transitory world of suffering. Until that thought snuck up on me, I deeply believed that the only way to liberation was to remain free of all attachment, whether to comfort, love, money, beauty, or another human being.

But that forbidden thought opened a tightly shut door. I could see that my attachment to nonattachment had deeply personal, emotional roots. That spiritual premise supported my terrors of intimacy, sexuality, failure, and death. I gradually came to believe that I needed to face those fears by going through them, rather than avoiding them. I needed to take a psychological journey through my fears before I reached a level of consciousness or stage of awareness in which nonattachment would emerge spontaneously.

This led me to sort out other teachings that I had absorbed without discrimination. For example, before becoming a meditation teacher I had been a political activist. But when I came to believe that meditation reached the source of problems—consciousness—and, therefore, it was pointless to struggle with symptoms, I stopped all political and social action. Today I see the narrowness of this assumption. A spiritual practice that is purely introverted and without any social engagement risks self-absorption. It also risks colluding with sexist, racist, oppressive, and corrupt political and economic systems and, therefore, furthering the suffering of other human beings.

I came to conclude that, while my practice held great value in the spiritual line of development, it had severe limits. And some of the teachings surrounding it were inadequate or even destructive as they were lived in the West. This distinction enabled me to reclaim my independent thinking and my faith to doubt. I could affirm my holy longing, while clarifying the extent to which my attitude toward meditation had hampered my emotional, cognitive, and political development.

Finally, I could begin to hold both the positive and negative sides of my experience, which enabled me to heal the internal opposites that accompany black-and-white thinking: light and dark, masculine and feminine, believer and infidel, sacred and secular.

With mature spirituality, we can hold the tension of opposites, such as immanent and transcendent, and see the beauty in paradoxes, such as a human being who is wise and has a shadow. Paradoxical thinking—both/and—frees us from the self-righteousness of either/or thinking. And it can slowly release us from the need for certainty and open us to the mystery of life.

Finally, we can learn or, in some cases, relearn how to define our own values and compose our own lives. The aim here is not, as cult deprogrammers suggest, merely to normalize those leaving spiritual communities; it's not to help disillusioned believers conform or adjust to conventional values. The result of that approach is regressive, and the student who views his or her years of engagement as "missing years" is often filled with regret. The teacher or group is then viewed as bad, and the family or society becomes good, which leads to the opposite split involved in membership.

Instead, our aim is to integrate and move beyond our individual and group experiences in spirituality in such a way that evolution continues. We include and transcend those insights, as Ken Wilber puts it. As the past spiritual persona with all of its attendant roles and values dies, a new life is born.

Reclaiming Authentic Feeling

Our spiritual personas keep us functioning in a narrow range of feeling, whether for the purpose of a practice or for the purpose of control by a spiritual authority. For instance, we may reject sexuality because of a traditional fear of hell, cut off anger because we are afraid of our own impulses, or shut down grief or fear because of the forced optimism of a new age community, whose members insist that we "create reality" through positive or negative thinking.

I can remember the moment when an old friend asked why I always had a silly smile on my face when life was so difficult. I had not known that I had adopted a contented grin. But, when she pointed it out, I began to realize how urgently I wanted to feel contentment, balance, and equilibrium. The grin masked the disowned, difficult feelings that had been banished during my many years as a meditation teacher, even from me.

It can be frightening to explore forbidden feelings and to seek out emotional authenticity after years of subtly training ourselves to feel only in limited ways. Mark Matousek wrote about reclaiming his own authentic emotions in his memoir, *Sex, Death, Enlightenment*. As a young boy, he desperately needed an image of victorious manhood and, armoring against his feelings, became obsessed with the appearance of strength and triumph. When he turned to Buddhism, his hero simply changed clothes. The fruits of self-inquiry substituted for the ideals of fame and fortune. And he fell in love with the seeker-as-hero and with the spiritual life as a glorious quest for the grail.

But in 1994 his mother suffered a terrible death. His ex-lover was diagnosed with HIV. And he panicked with the terror of his own mortality. The shock of his vulnerability and helplessness pierced his spiritual armor. His perpetual optimism failed him; he landed on his knees, and as he put it, without the ability to stand up tall he didn't know who he was.

As every doubt assailed him, so did doubt in the dharma. The results of his practice disappeared, leaving him feeling like a fraud. His spiritual life did not save him from suffering as "ignorant" people suffered. He lost the pride that protected his fictitious hero-self from humiliation.

When Matousek faced his terror of weakness, the hero crumbled. As his forbidden feelings—fear, disappointment, failure, negativity, inertia—flooded him, he felt raw and exposed. Those very shadow qualities that he most despised in others he was forced to face in himself. At last, he wrote, he joined humanity in a new way, as a fragile, wandering soul, a real person in real distress, with no ultimate solution.

Matousek grieved as he buried his mother. He grieved for his ex-lover. He grieved for his own invulnerable hero-self. And he discovered, to his surprise, that grief was the antidote to his inflation and his feelings of separateness. That long-lost feeling opened the door to another vision of spirit, which was stripped of ideals, grandiose images, superhuman power, and rapturous talk of enlightenment. He felt the pain and the relief of letting the spiritual hero die and becoming an authentic human being.

Reclaiming the Body

In many religious traditions, the primary splitting of opposites takes place between flesh and spirit. As the argument goes, the body is the container of evil forces, and the devil resides in its instinctual, animal impulses. We (our conscious egos) must strive to control them at all costs, redirecting our desires for higher purposes.

This view of the human body is sacrosanct in patriarchal cultures, especially in celibate monastic traditions (Christian, Buddhist, Muslim, or Hindu) in which priests value only the "higher" realms of spirit, mind, and rational thought, and the "lower" realms of soul, body, and nonrational feeling are banished into shadow. And it has been reinforced by the Cartesian mind/body split that we inherit from science.

In *Beyond Religion,* David Elkins said that when he was a minister, most spiritual problems among his male congregants were sexual problems. These men were not acting inappropriately but were suffering terribly with the "sin of lust." Because the church taught them that the feeling of lust was as sinful as the action of adultery, they struggled with guilt and shame, banishing any erotic thoughts or feelings into the shadow. The women in the congregation were not permitted to wear shorts or other revealing clothing that might cause a man to have impure thoughts. These Christian women got the message that they were not to look too attractive because, if a man felt lust for them, they were equally responsible for the sin.

Given this cultural milieu, which is common in conservative Jewish, Christian, and Muslim communities, many of us learn at a young age to live outside our bodies, identifying with mind or spirit, and to devalue and overcontrol them. If as adults we adopt a new tradition with this body-negative message, it resonates with this early teaching. So, we are attracted to doctrines that devalue this world and the body and to spiritual practices that may lead to dissociation. The teachings may look different at first: a change of language, a change of clothes. But the diminishment of embodied life is the same.

When I first entered my meditation community, there was no

public position about sexuality. In fact, it was purported to be a practice for "householders," or people who married and had careers. But after I became a teacher, I heard increasingly negative messages about sex: celibacy would speed enlightenment, devotees around the teacher must be celibate, and sexual energy was crude or "gross."

With my liberal upbringing and education, I had never heard this kind of overt negative attitude about sexuality before. But I can see now that it resonated with covert childhood messages from my parents, which instilled fear, guilt, and shame about bodily feelings, as opposed to the verbal messages I received, which were more liberal. As a result, the archaic Hindu teachings let me off the hook. With celibacy for a higher purpose, I no longer needed to deal with difficult bodily feelings or desires.

In a strange twist, bodily repression may cause some of the exact behavior that it is meant to keep at bay, including rape and incest. When the body hardens against feeling and emotional vitality is damped, we attempt to become obedient, even docile. But our buried impulses build charge in the shadow and may erupt unpredictably, as we saw in the many stories of priests and teachers in chapter 5.

Just as forbidden thoughts and feelings can be cues to enhance spiritual shadow-work, so can forbidden bodily sensations or symptoms. Our bodies register the subtleties of our experiences, even beneath our conscious awareness. They contain hidden information about risks and dangers, longings and desires. A woman told me that each time she had an audience with her Buddhist teacher, her mind felt calm, but her pulse raced, her hands sweated, and her body would not be still. At first she attributed the bodily response to anxiety. Of course she would be nervous under the gaze of this great meditation master.

But months later, when the teacher tried to seduce one of her friends, she was shocked. Her body had been trying to warn her of danger. She simply did not know how to listen to the wisdom of its language.

Perhaps the most surprising and disturbing insight I had, after leaving my community, was that my physical mortality had not been altered by decades of practice. Somehow, somewhere, I had come to believe that through meditation, I would attain a level of consciousness that would ward off death. This transformation of the human condition, I believed, was the inevitable end point of right practice. And yet, from the instant I left the movement, I knew it was not true.

It took a long time, however, for me to accept the new realization. The profound disappointment that accompanied it threw me into despair. Like my fears of intimacy, sexuality, and failure, I would have to face my fear of death.

I began to wonder whether my longing for the light had been, after all, a flight from death. A flight from darkness, doubt, intimacy, even responsibility, yes. But a flight from death?

Perhaps, beneath all the other fears, the fear of death lurked in me as it does in so many others. But instead of building castles of money, power, or fame to ensure my immortality, I built a castle of spirit.

Reclaiming Action on Our Own Behalf

A primary purpose of religion is to set the world of darkness or shadow against the world of light. To help ensure that its members participate in the light and avoid the dark, each tradition prescribes certain behaviors and proscribes others, slicing the possibilities for human action into good and evil. In such a black-and-white universe, right and wrong are two distinct paths, one leading to heaven, salvation, or enlightenment, the other to hell.

If we believe in this promise of salvation, project the imago dei onto a religious guide, and sacrifice our independent thinking and authentic feeling, then we will probably also sacrifice our agency, our capacity to take initiative on our own behalf, especially if that initiative involves disobeying a religious authority who exerts overt or covert control over our membership and, therefore, over our salvation.

In his twenties, a client joined a small group led by a kundalini yoga teacher whose charisma and knowledge attracted intelligent students. My client was drawn to the promise of spiritual awakening through secret practices, which quickly opened his psychic abilities, leading him to revere the teacher. When the older man forbid his students from eating meat, engaging in sexual relationships and masturbation, and wearing gems or jewels of any kind, my client acquiesced.

"It all made sense in the context of working with energies," he told me. "We sought to refine our energies and transform them from the grosser to the subtler by sending them up the spine to generate kundalini."

At a more covert level, he said, the teacher forbid the seeking of power of any kind and the expression of ego in the forms of individual desire or passion. Again, my client tried to obey. He directed his ambition toward spiritual attainments. Eventually, he felt no passion for anything but enlightenment.

But one night the teacher tested my client's ability to obey: he told the student to kneel and give him oral sex. As a kundalini adept, the teacher said, he would transform the sexual energy generated by this act into spiritual energy for both men. My client submitted.

From that moment, he was tormented by doubt and filled with shame. His teacher was a hypocrite who preached celibacy and engaged in a secret sex life. My client's obedience to the teacher's moral values suddenly seemed wrong, even sinful. His devotion, a source of such sweetness, turned sour. The meditation practices, previously so alluring, became unappealing.

Yet for weeks he could not take action. He sat, passively, unable to speak up or act on his own behalf. He walked about in a daze, unable to eat or sleep. He faced a terrible crisis: Was he more committed to this man than to his own well-being? Should he continue to obey this man rather than follow his own intuition and act to change his life?

As he lost weight and suffered from insomnia, he sought out medical advice from a trusted healer. This healer told him he needed to eat meat and deal with his sexual energy. But if my client listened to the healer's advice, he would have to disobey his teacher. Slowly and gradually, he came to the conclusion that, at this stage of his spiritual life, obedience to this spiritual authority was no longer healthy for him. Disobedience was required for his evolution. He left the group.

He began to date women, explore sexuality, and think about a career, all of which had been forbidden to him. At first he simply rebelled, eager to experiment with every taboo. But gradually he established his own internal moral compass.

Taking courses in the field of psychology, he learned about Kohlberg's stages of moral development. In the first stage, he told me, "I was obedient to avoid punishment. Then I became identified with being the good disciple, and my compliance was based on the teacher's approval. Finally, I'm learning how to act morally because it fits my own moral values. With the help of psychotherapy, I'm now internalizing my own spiritual authority." I have heard stories like this man's from members of every tradition.

For example, teachers who suggest that prayer, meditation, or scripture alone can solve practical problems cultivate passivity in their followers. When a problem remains intransient, believers blame themselves because they cannot blame god or their teacher. Reclaiming action on our own behalf, we can reverse this passivity, not merely to react or rebel in an adolescent way, but to act from adult conscious choice.

Furthermore, we can reclaim our power to act on behalf of others. In addition to believing that spirituality was only "up," many of us also came to think that it was only directed "in." That is, a movement "out" into the world was not a spiritual move but a political one. Today we need to heal the split between "in" and "out," between introverted spiritual practice and extroverted social action. We need to bring those qualities that we have developed through contemplative practice back to humanity to serve others in need and to change the institutions that perpetrate abuse and oppression. This is not a call for social action that stems from unconscious projection—"We are the people, and they are the enemy." It's not a call for action that stems from a patronizing superiority—"They are downtrodden, and we can save them." It is a call for action that stems from the awareness of our common humanity, the knowledge that each of us yearns for something greater, and the wisdom that the shadow lurks around the corner. And it is a call that is rooted in our awareness of our spiritual unity, the knowledge or the direct experience that we are one.

Reclaiming Images of the Divine

> When the human spirit has come of age, it cannot return to the image of god as a heavenly parent.
>
> BISHOP JOHN SPONG

> The ecstatic lover has burning faith in every Divine Manifestation—as formless Radiance, as various Forms or Attributes, as Divine Incarnations like Rama and Krishna, and as the Goddess of Wisdom, who is beyond form and formlessness, containing both in Her mystic Womb.
>
> RAMAKRISHNA

Creator, Redeemer, Lord, Healer, Judge, King, Lover, Master, Father, Mother, Goddess, Liberator, Allah, Buddha, Most High, Gaia, Emptiness, Divine, Spirit, Self, Consciousness. . . .

We need to reimagine the imago dei and reclaim personal images of god that lie in the shadow and form the root of so much suffering. If our images of the divine do not fit our race, gender, temperament, ethnicity, or stage of life, they may no longer serve as divine guides but act, instead, as shadow figures by sabotaging our spiritual intentions. We can learn to reimagine them so that we are, indeed, made in the image of our god. As a result, we can begin to distinguish the voice of the divine, in answer to our prayers, from the chorus of inner voices that keeps us from quietude.

In *Transformation of the God-Image,* Jungian analyst Ed Edinger described the stages of evolution of the god image in Western civilization: In animism, the individual is embedded in an environment filled with spirits. In matriarchy, the earth mother is at the center of fertility rites and death and rebirth cycles tied to the land. With the rise of cities in Mesopotamia, Egypt, and Greece, polytheism emerged with its family of deities that was headed by a father, much like the city's king. Among the Hebrews, tribal monotheism arose and with it the possibility of a personal relationship to god, who ruled by the law. A more universal monotheism emerged with Christianity, including the images of the good son, Jesus, and the bad son, Lucifer.

Finally, with Immanuel Kant, the god image leapt into the interior world. Jung pointed out that since Kant, we recognize that all of our experience is filtered through our subjectivity. We cannot experience a god or an archetype directly; we can only experience its effects via our own psyches. Jung referred to this as the reality of the psyche.

Once we see through our subjective filters, we no longer identify with a single image of god, Edinger said. We see it as a living reality in our own souls. And each experience of it—each meeting with an overwhelming archetype—is a defeat for the ego. This is the path of individuation, the current stage of evolution of the god image for Jungians.

This perceptual shift has dramatic consequences for our religious traditions. If we make this distinction between inner or subjective reality and outer factors, then we may begin to favor an internal rather than an external image of god. So, for example, in Judaism, the sacred object of longing is the Messiah, who will usher in the return of paradise and the end of the separation between the human lover and the divine beloved. Is the Messiah to be thought of as a human being who will appear, like the prophets, on the world scene? Or is it to be imagined as our own Messiah nature, which lives in all human souls?

The latter is the radical stance taken by Hasids, or mystical Jews, who believe that the secret, inner Messiah nature sleeps within all living beings—and has awakened in their illumined teachers, or tzaddiks. The eighteenth-century founder of Hasidism, the Baal Shem Tov, whose name means "master of the names of god," danced with ecstatic abandon to fuel the fires of his longing for union. The story goes that he was so filled with divine presence as he sang and danced that his individual ego dissolved in transcendence, just as whirling dervishes dissolve in fana.

The same dilemma appears in traditional versus mystical Christianity. Is Jesus the one and only Christ? Or is the Christ nature hidden beneath our human nature in every one of us?

A medieval Christian monk, Thomas à Kempis, wrote a guide for the faithful that advocates the practices of humility, charity, and obedience. He urged believers to turn toward the will of god through prayer and scripture and away from materialism, willfulness, and pride. His model for this pious life was Jesus, as evidenced in the name of his book: *The Imitation of Christ.*

The monk took Christ's words—"He who follows me will never walk in darkness, but will have the light of life"—to mean that Christians needed to imitate Jesus's life and manners. Stories abound of saints and seekers who have strived to live as Christ lived: to feed the hungry, to suffer as the crucified Christ, to be reborn as he was resurrected. The fourteenth-century anchoress Julian of Norwich asked three things of god: to experience the suffering of those who witnessed Christ's passion; to experience a severe illness at age thirty that mirrored his pain and terror of death; and to experience the wounds of contrition and compassion and the wound of longing with her will for god.

In the twentieth century in Italy, Padre Pio yearned to be purified of his sins and therefore embraced the suffering Christ. For thirty years he manifested continuously the five wounds or stigmata of Christ. During Mass, he claimed to be united with Jesus, like two candles burning into one, and to relive the Christian drama. Some observers saw a crown of thorns on his brow. After Mass, witnesses wiped blood from his head and clothes.

In the twelfth century, the Christian god looked like a king or judge, and people behaved toward him as toward their feudal lord. But when a new god image arose in human consciousness—god as beloved— a more devotional feeling spread among aspirants. As a result, spousal mysticism emerged, in which monks and nuns anointed themselves to prepare for the kiss of Christ, the experience of union with him.

Saint Clare of Assisi, whose unconsummated love for St. Francis is legendary, was bound in her soul to Christ. Living with absolute poverty, she freed herself of personal desires and worked to serve and heal those in need. She understood the inner workings of the imago dei, as evidenced by her writing: "Place your heart in the figure of the divine substance. And transform your entire being into the image of the Godhead Itself through contemplation."

A contemporary woman once described for me her passion for Christ. In the tradition of St. Teresa of Ávila, who sang, danced, and played tambourine as she ardently burned for her beloved Jesus, this woman also called herself a bride of Christ. A divorce lawyer by day, she had a secret life at night. I asked her to write the story of that part of herself:

As the darkness falls, the longing rises. As the sun sets below the horizon, and the container turns from blue to black, I turn from a woman of day to a woman of night. I become a bride of Christ.

I remove the colors that adorn me, the shades of gold that complement my hair, the shades of blue that bring out my eyes. I remove the watch that keeps me prompt and the jewels on my ears that join me to tribal women the world over. For at night I wear white, nothing more. And I stand alone, not as part of any lineage.

Slowly, I purify my body, cleansing it of ambition and fear, smoothing it of sharp edges and jagged points. The chores of the day are lifted from my muscles, and then the deeper burdens, the heavier cares, wash away. As my body lightens, it becomes an instrument for His symphony. It is tuned to His tune. It plays only His song.

I cleanse my mind, emptying it of human images, of people hungry and lost, of people wanting, wanting. I open my mind as the shore opens to the sea, by simple being there, in the way of the sea. And the waves rush in, unceasingly. Then my mind can wait, wait without hope, for Him to arrive.

As my body is washed clean as a bone dried in the desert sun, and my mind is as empty as the simple tone of a gong, I open to receive Him. I open like a new bride to her groom. And the smallest residue that remained in me of the day is pushed aside as He enters me slowly and fills me fully. And I know once again why I am a bride of Christ.

Jung, who wrote in *Psychology and Religion: West and East* about the imitation of Christ—behave like Christ and become like him—pointed out that it had not been fulfilled. Jesus, Jung wrote, has been turned into an external object of worship, a concrete icon, which prevents the imago from sinking down into the depths of the soul, as the teaching intended. That is, discipleship has become imitation; symbol has become idol.

Pious believers use Christ's image as a way to escape doing their own spiritual work. As Jung put it, Christ lived his own unique life regardless of convention and as a heretic in his own tradition. He took up his own cross, his own destiny, as we need to take up ours. But, instead, we believe that Christ and his cross can deliver us from our conflicts. Instead of bearing the tension of our own opposites and walking through our own darkness, we ask him to carry our burdens and remain as children in relation to an all-powerful Other.

This concrete rather than symbolic use of an imago can take place in any tradition. Some followers of Eastern teachers also mimic their behavior, phraseology, diet, or dress. They place the teachers outside themselves as divine mediators, rather than assimilating them internally as images of the Self. There may be stages in which it is helpful for an outer figure (guru, priest, or therapist) to carry a projection of the Self for a while, if at some point the seeker recognizes it, struggles with it, and eventually sees that it belongs in her own treasury. But if she adores the teacher indefinitely, the process is thwarted. The believer remains untouched in the deepest parts of herself and stuck in a projection of the Self.

Cultural shifts reflect shifting images of god even today. Leaders of the mythopoetic men's movement pointed out years ago that many boys in our culture suffer from a "father wound," the absence of an older man who can affirm their masculinity. Certainly, some boys and men with this unmet need yearn to find someone to fill it, such as a surrogate father or a father-god.

Certain Christians have vocally critiqued their tradition from within, calling for believers to reimagine the images of the son, the father, and the mother of god. In *Why Christianity Must Change or Die,* Anglican bishop John Spong pointed out that the hunger for god is deep and pervasive, but it's not the same as the hunger for answers that the church traditionally gives. It's the Christian task, he said, to return to the direct experience that led to church creeds.

Spong has called himself a believer in exile: he is committed to Jesus Christ, but he is exiled from literal understandings of Christianity, including archaic images of god. In a radical leap away from the church, he suggested that, given the discoveries of science and psychology, a theistic personal god with parental or supernatural qualities—a divine worker of miracles, a dispenser of rewards and punishments—has become outdated.

In particular, Spong selected the image of Jesus as rescuer for reimagining. Jesus was cast in the role because of our need to overcome the fall in the Garden of Eden and to restore the world to the perfection intended by god, Spong said. Jesus came "down," became the perfect sacrifice, and removed the consequences of sin in the crucifixion. With the resurrection, he traveled "up," and in this way god validated his offering.

Spong sees through this narrative with the aid of the theory of evolution. The fall becomes, for him, the dawn of self-consciousness. Similarly, with the aid of the cycle of consciousness described earlier, we can imagine that each of us "falls" from unconscious union and travels "down" into incarnation until we consciously begin to yearn for union once again. Jesus can become, as Spong calls him, a spirit person, a window onto the holy, and an image of what each of us might look like in a fully realized state.

A friend of mine always remembered a stained glass window in her childhood church that portrayed an image of Jesus praying in the garden before his death. Beneath the image were the words: "Not my will but thine be done."

She told me that this image set her on her path. It would reappear for years later in her prayers. And she would recall it at moments when she cried out to god.

In her fifties, she returned to her childhood church, accompanied by her mother. They found that the window had been taken down. But after some investigation they discovered it in the church basement. With help, they pulled it out and set it up so that the sun lit it from behind. My friend sobbed as she stood and reclaimed her original imago dei.

In *Avalanche,* Dr. Joy told a similar tale of a woman he met at a conference. Deeply involved in Buddhism, this woman resented her early Christian upbringing. Sitting in a morning meditation with the aim of allowing images to rise up out of her unconscious, she was shocked when an angel appeared, announcing that her name was Veronica. The woman told Dr. Joy, "I don't believe in angels. Too Christian."

A few days later, the woman was meditating—and Christ appeared. In her imagery, she ran from him, upset that a Christian figure was desecrating her sacred place. But moments later Veronica appeared and reassured her that Christ and his teachings were part of her future evolution. Her defenses dropped, and she allowed this disowned imago to return to the sacred for her.

Other women have turned toward feminine images of the divine after failing to find adequate reflection in masculine images. Whether, as children, we develop a sense of self in relation to a mother who is present, comforting, and containing, or we develop a longing for a mother with those qualities, we yearn for an image of the divine feminine that is accepting, consoling, and healing. While women have explored feminine spirituality to find a god who looks like them, some men also yearn for god as mother, declaring that only from her do they feel unconditional acceptance.

During the Paleolithic and Neolithic eras, the goddess spun the web of life. She was seen in ancient stone, rhythmic oceans, and womb-like eggs. She was honored in undulating snakes, ageless trees, and the sweet-scented rose. In ancient Greece, Gaia, mother of the gods and the earth, and her daughter Demeter, goddess of the grains, maintained a link to the Neolithic great mother, before the rise of the patriarchal age and the rule of Zeus.

In ancient Egypt, the goddess Maat, an ostrich feather on her head, personified divine harmony and balance. Isis, wife of Osiris, was worshipped for three thousand years as queen of heaven, queen of earth, and queen of the underworld. Hathor, the divine cow mother, needed only to imagine a thing for it to manifest. She was worshipped as the star Sirius, and her devotees sang and danced in her temple. In her form as Sekhmet, the lion-headed goddess with a musical rattle and healing necklace, she could bring destruction by withholding the waters of life.

A friend told me that most of the women in her family had remained invisible. They were afraid to reveal themselves. She wanted to know her own innate power; she desired to feel her anger at its root. She made a pilgrimage to the Temple of Karnak in Egypt to see the seven-foot black statue of Sekhmet, the lion-headed goddess. In a dark chamber, my friend sang and chanted to the goddess in high, intense bursts of sound that surprised even her. The goddess's eyes, a flat paint in one moment, suddenly sparkled to life and shone love on my friend. Not a soft, gentle love, but love and power, she said. Sekhmet embodied ferociousness, a raw force. But my friend called it the heart of power— strength and compassion. Following this ritual moment, she was no longer afraid of her own inner resources; she was no longer ashamed of her power. She broke the pattern of her female lineage.

A lovely client in her thirties told me that she felt unattractive, and although she loved her husband deeply, she had no interest in sex. For a long time, she insisted that her parents had given her an ideal childhood and had the kind of marriage that she wished to emulate.

Slowly, during the course of therapy, she gained a more nuanced view of them, which included their shadows and limitations. Struggling with her new dislike and shame about them, she began to explore her own womanhood. Her matronly and self-sacrificing mother had offered no model of healthy femininity. So, instead, she had identified with her charismatic, workaholic father, who, she said, never related to her femininity. As an adult, she had rejected the Christian church of her childhood and replaced it with a "rational need to understand," which she viewed as a more adult relation to god.

In her leisure time, she began to visit museums for inspiration and renewal. Sitting one day across from a painting of Aphrodite, she suddenly felt worshipful. She discovered in that moment that she faced an image of the divine that was her, yet not her.

As she sat with the image, her mind quieted, her breath slowed. She felt a deep sense of recognition in that moment, a self-recognition that had been lying just beneath the boundaries of awareness. She loved this goddess just as she was—and wanted only to remain in her presence. She felt no need to do anything or to be anywhere. She wanted only this timeless moment with her.

"This is what religion should be," she told me.

In her journal, she began a dialogue with Aphrodite, who was surprisingly talkative. And eventually the woman found clues to her own feminine beauty and passion reflected in the goddess.

The widespread need for nonwhite images of the divine arises naturally from the racial and ethnic diversity of our culture. Today there are more than thirty-seven million people of Mexican descent in the United States, and the divine mother in the form of Our Lady of Guadalupe is one of their principal images of god. When Cortez and the Spaniards invaded Mexico in the sixteenth century and slaughtered millions of Indigenous Americans in the name of Jesus, a legendary miracle occurred in Mexico City: While walking to church, a peasant heard celestial music and a heavenly lady appeared, cloaked by the sun. Calling him "the smallest and most beloved of my children," she told the man that she was the mother of god, mother of the creator. And she wanted a temple built for her on the nearby site of an Aztec shrine.

The bishop responded to the peasant's request for the temple by asking for a sign from the Lady. First, she cured the man's uncle, who was terminally ill. Next, she sent him to find out-of-season roses, which he arranged in his cloak. Standing before the bishop, he opened his cloak, and the flowers scattered on the ground. The three-dimensional image of the Lady was imprinted on the cloak in bright colors.

One of my clients, who is part Catholic Latina, part Jewish, had always hidden her ethnic identity. Her parents had kept their mixed racial and religious past a secret and asked her to do the same. As a result, she felt unseen, unknown, and fraudulent. While openly exploring her Latino lineage in therapy for the first time, she felt compelled to make a journey to the cathedral in Mexico City where the image of the Lady of Guadalupe is enshrined.

Standing before her, my client felt awe. She was moved by the sunlight emanating from her, the stars on her cloak, the moon beneath her feet, and the angel who holds her up on the moon. But, mostly, she felt stunned by the eyes, which look alive because they reflect images of other people who appear to be in front of her.

For the first time, this woman saw an image of the divine who also seemed to see her, all of her, the real her. In the Lady's mirror reflection, this woman felt less alone and more authentic than she had ever felt. As a result, she began to reclaim the neglected part of her cultural and spiritual heritage, which had been hidden in the family shadow.

Although this woman's encounter with a god image was shaped by an emotional unmet need, it cannot be explained by that alone. She beheld an imago dei, a powerful and mysterious Other that transcended her ego awareness. And it, in turn, beheld her.

Similarly, some Black Americans yearn for god images that look like them. Psychologist Rossalyn Marie Richardson told me about a study she had undertaken in which she found that white images of god and biblical characters were tied to low self-esteem in Christian Black Americans. The effort to live with a false cultural self that is rooted in idealizing an imago that doesn't mirror your own experience can lead to loss of cultural pride, she pointed out.

Richardson's study showed, for example, that Black males exposed early in life to Black biblical characters had higher self-esteem. Although several participants in the study claimed that the racial identity of the Bible's characters was irrelevant to them, one man reported that his relationship to god improved after he discovered that the historical Jesus could have been African, based on one theory of genealogy.

Recovery from spiritual abuse and disillusionment through shadow-work is not easy. For some, it takes a rude shock—the sight of a "celibate" teacher having sex—to break out of the trance of indoctrination. For others, the words of an ally—"This is abuse"—can break through denial. For yet others, the slow erosion of critical thinking and personal will, accompanied by the physical exhaustion of working in service around the clock, can lead to a creeping doubt.

If the disciple can heed the call, spiritual shadow-work can begin. She or he can finally allow forbidden feelings—grief, anger, regret, resentment—to surface. They may be welcome or frightening at first, but they can lead to authentic conversations with therapists, family, or friends. She or he can finally allow forbidden thoughts: What is awakening? Is this teacher really awake? Do these practices fit who I am? Was Jesus really the son of God? Would he agree with this teaching or approve of this behavior? They may bring relief or terror at first, but they can lead eventually to independent thinking. She or he can reconnect with the wisdom of the body and allow its messages—"I'm uncomfortable here" or "This doesn't feel right"—to surface. This can lead to inner guidance from yet another source.

One or all of these can lead to moral action, such as a student's separation from the teacher and community or the reclamation of her or his voice in efforts to reform it. That action can lead to the reclaiming of our own spiritual essence—our light, Self, Christ nature, Buddha nature. When we stand in our own light, we no longer need to project it onto others. We can learn from them, acknowledge their gifts, and remain connected to our authentic selves.

This authentic self is not the true self, as pointed out earlier. Rather, we are growing up and cleaning up on our way to waking up. We are extending each line of development: emotional development, which is often derailed in religious "purity" communities and spiritual celibate communities; cognitive development, which is often stalled by the transmission of knowledge from authorities and the taboo of outside influences; and bodily development, or gut knowledge, which is often slowed by teachings about the impurity or insignificance of the body.

And we are extending moral development, as we shift from the early stage of obedience, punishment, and unquestioned authority to seeking approval and maintaining the social order to depending on our individual judgment and individual rights and, finally, to universal principles, such as human rights, justice, and equality. These stages of moral development, as defined by Lawrence Kohlberg, become visible as we continue to do spiritual shadow-work, become increasingly accountable for our own behaviors and reactions, and open our hearts in increasing compassion.

Creativity as Practice*

I have suggested that a daily spiritual life can be more authentic when it is rooted in the yearning of the human soul. Our particular form of holy longing can offer a glimpse into the hidden object of our desire. And it, in turn, can lead us backward to self-knowledge and forward to our destiny.

Rather than training us to value only certain aspects of life and to devalue others, our spirituality can help us reclaim "down" and proclaim "up." Instead of insisting that we blindly accept received knowledge and preexisting imagoes, it can help us fertilize our imaginations and dream of new possibilities in art, culture, and even our social systems, which cry out for radical reform. To do this, religious and spiritual institutions would need to include and honor what Matthew Fox called the *via creativa.*

---

*An earlier version of "Creativity as Practice" appeared in *The Spirit of Writing,* edited by Mark Waldman (Tarcher/Putnam, 2001).

In *Original Blessing*, Fox suggested that when we allow ourselves to fully experience the *via positiva*, the way of light and blessings, as well as the *via negativa*, the way of darkness and shadow, we come to know creation and the void, fullness and emptiness. Out of their union, a third thing emerges: the word or image, signaling the birth of new creation.

In the creative moment we are, as Meister Eckhart said, generative, as god is. We are like the creator and, therefore, living in its image. That is, the imago dei is no longer outside us; it is in us, in the soul, in the imagination, creating new life. In the Christian mythos, this is the resurrection.

Of course, it may not mean that we have attained higher levels of union, such as psychic, subtle, or causal levels, which may have been attained by Rumi, St. Catherine, and Ramakrishna, among others. But it can mean that the internalized imago fuels creative work, directing our longing toward new images and new work.

On the other hand, when the holy longing is twisted or denied, the forces of creation turn destructive. Misplaced creativity can lead to a drive for power in which the human energies of innovation and ingenuity are harnessed for destruction, as we long to vanquish an enemy or prove that god is on our side.

In effect, the life of the imagination *is* the spiritual life. We must, as Rainer Maria Rilke put it, give birth to our images: "They are the future waiting to be born."

Many years ago, as a new meditator, I believed that sitting practice alone was a spiritual act; meditation alone constituted a spiritual life. My reasoning: only meditation sent my energy and attention up.

Therefore, a clear line was drawn for me between sacred and profane activities. But my sacred wound of disillusionment also led to the discovery of writing as a spiritual practice, which opened my imagination in magical, unexpected ways.

I never dreamed of becoming an author. I didn't fantasize about writing the great American novel or winning a Pulitzer for investigative journalism. But in 1981, after leaving my spiritual community, I met a writer who had just published a groundbreaking bestseller. We felt an immediate kinship. Although I had no writing experience, she hired me to be the editor of her publications, which explored innovations in consciousness research.

I vividly recall the first day on the job: I sat at the terminal, blank mind facing blank screen, paralyzed. But as I began to take assignments, become engaged with research, and articulate exciting ideas, I found that journalism fit my temperament. I fully enjoyed gathering information, seemed to have a gift for synthesizing it, and thrilled to the thought of transmitting it to others.

Then I submitted my work to my editor. She took a red pencil and deleted or altered every word. The text returned to me unrecognizable. My heart sank. She demanded a dense and telegraphed style in order to jam data into a small space. But it could not remain abstract and remote; the verbs needed to carry it off the page. And it could not show a trace of me; in the objective voice, the subject disappears.

As a novice, I was eager to learn. So, I submitted and rewrote . . . and rewrote . . . and rewrote. Finally, an article was accepted. And the process began again on the next piece. I heavily researched a topic, synthesized various sources, quoted a range of points of view, uncovered a key conclusion. And she marked it up in bright red.

One evening, at the terminal for a typical ten-hour day, tears running down my cheeks, I was about to give up. I felt hopeless; I would never become a journalist and certainly would never please this woman. And yet . . . I had felt such joy in finding just the right word to make a sentence fly. I had felt such gratification in hearing from satisfied readers.

Suddenly, I remembered a story from the Tibetan Buddhist tradition: A solitary monk named Milarepa lived in the woods, practicing meditation day and night and eating only nettle soup. For many years he tried to attain realization, but his fasting and prayers were not enough. One day another man, Marpa, emerged from the woods. Their eyes met, and Milarepa felt an instant bond, recognizing Marpa as his teacher.

Marpa asked him to build a small stone house in a certain corner of the woods, "over there," then disappeared among the trees. For the next year, Milarepa gathered stones, one by one, lifted them slowly, and carried them to the site. Then with painstaking attention he fit them together until they formed a sturdy structure.

Marpa emerged from the woods, glanced at the stone house, turned his back on it, and, pointing in another direction, said, "Oh, no, over there!" Then he wandered off into the forest.

Milarepa's heart sank. But he set about his task as if he had no choice. He began to take apart the house stone by stone, carry each one to the other site, lift it, and fit it into place. A year later, he stood back and viewed the house with a sense of satisfaction at completing the task.

Just then, Marpa returned, approached the house, shook his head, and proclaimed, "Oh, no, over there!" as he pointed in a third direction.

Again, Milarepa submitted. Again, he took apart what he had built and carried the stones to the new area. Again he fit them together until the house stood once more. And again Marpa appeared, shook his head, and pointed. "No, over there."

After Milarepa rebuilt the house that time, the story goes, he became enlightened.

I stared at the terminal, tears dried, smiling. I had believed that only my meditation was spiritual practice. But clearly the work of writing and rewriting could also teach me about discipline, nonattachment, impermanence, and discrimination.

I began to write as if setting words in a sentence were setting stones in a house. I wrote as if my awareness of the writing process were more important than the content of the writing. To my surprise, I saw fewer red marks; the writing got better!

Soon I discovered another key: I would do intensive research, then sit down to meditate for an hour, emptying my mind, relaxing my body, letting go completely of the writing project. When I returned to the empty screen, words flowed from me in an easy river, with no struggle.

Slowly, I learned to trust this process: fill the mind, empty the mind, get out of the way. And the red marks disappeared.

The cycle of mentoring was over. But the writing life had just begun. And my spiritual journey continued, as it included wider and wider orbits of life.

A spiritually authentic life is an ongoing creative act in which the creature and the creator long to be united. If we choose to live it within an existing tradition, a finished work of art, we can decorate it with our own detail. If we choose to live it outside of tradition, we can design it with images from our own soul.

Finding Our Spiritual Myths

> Myth is the secret opening through which the inexhaustible energies of the cosmos pour into human cultural manifestation.
>
> JOSEPH CAMPBELL

As I wrote in the book's opening, a psychological lens that includes the shadow is necessary in order to extend our vision and understanding of spirituality, and it's necessary in order to recover from spiritual abuse and disillusionment. But it's not sufficient. At this point, we can lift off the lens of psychology and view our spiritual journeys through the lens of myth.

In this way, we can see beyond our personal, local histories to the universal patterns that lie beneath them or behind them. In these timeless larger stories, we are the heroes and the princesses, the wanderers and the warriors, the healers and the saints.

Like us, the protagonists of myth begin life in innocence, their awareness limited to their immediate environment. Unexpectedly, they hear a call to adventure, an invitation to leave home to find Home. Reluctant to change or risk danger, a few refuse the call.

But if they meet a key person, such as a potential partner or beloved teacher, they overcome their reluctance and cross a threshold: they leave the familiar, conventional world of family, friends, childhood beliefs and values. They follow their holy longing and find that it leads them away from the known toward something more, something mysterious or transcendent. This departure signifies the first stage of any rite of passage: separation. This may mean separation from biological family or from spiritual family.

In the new life, the hero undergoes tests, such as those exacted by a new romantic relationship or a religious teacher. These trials may test the hero's loyalty, obedience, compassion, or level of awareness. The hero may find allies while meeting these challenges and may encounter enemies, who attempt to get him or her to resist change or alter direction.

Eventually, the mythic hero faces a primary ordeal: the encounter with the shadow in the form of a beast, a whale, a minotaur, a dragon. Similarly, during the ordeal of a loving partnership, the hero meets the shadow of his or her idealized beloved—a cold, cruel, or unconscious aspect of the beloved's nature. Likewise, in a spiritual discipleship, he or she meets an idealized teacher's dark side, such as greed, self-centeredness, or hunger for power.

In myth, the dark side of the gods is evident: Hermes, the trickster, lies and steals. Hades abducts and violates Persephone. Theseus abandons Ariadne. Even in the Bible, Abraham exiles his son Ishmael, Judas betrays Jesus, and Joseph is banished by his father and brothers. Those who are wounded suffer in profound ways.

In another context, the ordeal may take the form of an illness, an accident, or a loss that shocks the hero into mortality awareness. But in every case, the hero's innocence is lost. This encounter signifies the second stage of a rite of passage: descent and initiation.

In facing the ordeal, we may at first succumb to denial and attempt to hide from the new awareness. We cannot bear to see our ideal tarnished or mortal. Instead of consciously following the descent, we stop—and fall helplessly into depression, going down without undergoing initiation.

At this time, we may feel forsaken by loved ones, allies, even god. Just as one who struggles with addiction may need to reach bottom before feeling the touch of a higher power, we may need to feel that all is lost before a connection to Spirit or higher Self is found.

But if the hero is to complete the journey, this setback is only temporary. A renewed attempt to deal with the shadow arises.

And beneath the concrete violation a hidden alchemical process takes place. When we follow each of the mythic stories above to its conclusion, the moment of descent is also a moment of awakening. Persephone, once an innocent mother's girl, becomes queen of the underworld, able to hold both darkness and light. The abandoned Ariadne is led to marry a god, Dionysus, becoming immortal. Joseph becomes counselor to the pharaoh and a wise interpreter of dreams. Jesus, betrayed, is led to his crucifixion and, ultimately, to his resurrection.

So, if this rite is sacralized, and the concrete process becomes alchemical, disillusionment becomes dissolution. We surrender the ego's control, and that which appeared to be solid and unchanging—our beliefs, opinions, attachments, fears—liquefies. Suddenly, we see through it.

The idealized teacher, whom we thought was infallible, becomes another vulnerable human being, no matter how spiritually adept. The dogma we gripped to ward off uncertainty and meaninglessness becomes another series of words, perhaps of value, perhaps not. The fear of loss of community, or religious loneliness, becomes the doorway to courage and a more authentic life.

This has been my experience again and again. At the bottom of a descent, my mind's precious concepts, its need to be right, its denial of shadow—all dissolve, and my sense of self explodes. Inevitably, my heart opens to include more and more.

And the ascent begins again. I transcend to the next level of awareness, all the while including everything that has come before. And I step onto the other shore.

From there the hero looks back and sees how innocent she was, how blind, how narrow-minded. And, with this new level of awareness, she can never go back again. She can honor both the concrete violation that stems from meeting the shadow, including the excruciating feelings that it evokes, and its mythic meaning, which sets the suffering in the larger story. And she can see how evolution itself is at work in her life.

Transformed, the hero enters the third stage: the return. He or she follows the road back to the world with a boon: the sword, the stone, the new level of consciousness. For Rumi, the gift of ecstatic poems of union with the Beloved. For Ramakrishna, the teachings of the great Advaita Vedanta. For Catherine of Siena, the modeling of a life joined to Christ. For me, this book.

Through the Shadow to the Light

Soon after the first edition of this book, in which I disclosed my deep disillusionment with the dream of awakening and my grief about not having met ordinary people who had fulfilled that dream, my life took a sharp right turn, and there they were: a few dozen men and women who, like me, had been dedicated to meditation for decades but who, unlike me, had passed through the advanced stages of awakening and now live full-time in nonduality or unitive consciousness. They would not call themselves heroes, but they have completed the hero's journey, the great return of consciousness to its source.

During the past decades, I have come to know them well. Sitting in weekly *satsangs,* where members speak about their internal experiences in meditation and give one another reflection and mirroring, I have listened to the details of their original awakenings and of their ongoing moment-to-moment spiritual experiences. And I have been startled to discover the lived reality of enlightenment in all its splendor—and all its ordinariness.

My awakened friends appear in various shapes and sizes, with distinct temperaments and styles, and work as artists, businesspeople, musicians, and office workers, but they have no interest in being spiritual teachers. However, as friends, they have taught me much and reignited my aspiration and holy longing for enlightenment, which no longer seems like an unattainable dream. Let me begin to give you a flavor of what I have learned.

The evolution of stages of awareness or levels of consciousness (as described in this book) does not take place in the neat, orderly way I had imagined. For some individuals, a particular stage may last for only a brief time. For instance, the witness, pure awareness, or mind essence in one friend passed quickly, while for another it has endured for many years. In the latter's case, it has been a liberating but not so pleasant experience, accompanied by the freedom of less attachment to thoughts, feelings, and actions but the absence of bliss, love, or new knowledge.

Also, the stages may appear to be overlapping or simultaneous. For one friend, glimpses of deities or celestial realms (the divine mother, in his case) overlapped with glimpses of identification with Spirit. Although neither one has stabilized, he experiences both regularly.

A female friend evolved in a few months from the witness of pure awareness to experiences of deity mysticism or celestial perception to experiences of identification with Spirit to experiences of union with Spirit (*nirvikalpa* samadhi) to experiences of returning to the world of form and identifying with all form as Spirit (*sahaj* samadhi). This level of nonduality is not conceptual for her; it's a direct experience. As she put it, the whole cosmos, far and near, is in her body. There is no more far and near, no self/other, no subject/object, no separation of any kind.

One startling finding: many of these people have not completed their ego's homework and shadow-work. One woman, clearly awake, still struggles with very difficult, traumatic relationship issues. Another, an abuse survivor, still dissociates at odd moments, although she maintains awareness during her dissociative states. And one man still suffers compulsions, although he witnesses them.

So, I must conclude that they did not travel the linear path from pre-personal to personal (ego) to transpersonal work. Rather, they woke up in the spiritual line of development, and traces of their ignorance remained in their emotional and cognitive development. Each of them urged me to resolve emotional and shadow issues as much as possible before awakening so that the bliss and clarity of the higher levels of consciousness can be fully lived.

In addition, they make a distinction between pain and suffering. One man, who was living at the level of *sahaj* samadhi, had a near-fatal car accident and lives with chronic back pain. However, he insists that he does not suffer. The pain *is;* the suffering is a choice.

About a decade ago, I was sitting with these friends. Each time I would speak, someone retorted, "That's a concept." I would speak up again, and I would hear, "That's a concept." I would try to say something else, and I would hear, "That's a concept."

This went on for some time until, in an instant, my mind stopped and emptied out onto the floor. The contents of consciousness were unloaded—and I sat, open-eyed, with a hollow head, grinning.

I had experienced this state many, many times in meditation, but never in the waking state with others. This was pure awareness plus waking awareness—satori, kensho, and other names. It was expansive, free, and liberating.

Hours later, the first thought arose: I am not my mind.

As time passed and more thoughts returned, I could see through them, as if they were thin veils, not the concrete realities they had appeared to be. I could see through my ego's constructed separate self-sense, and how hard I had worked to build it, defend it, and use it to my advantage. And I came to see that we all use these constructions of mind to cover our wounds and our existential fears of what lies beneath.

Since that shift in awareness, I no longer live in or through my mind. I enjoy it fully, even as I write this sentence. But my mind is no longer the central mediator of my experience or the primary source of my identity.

A few years later, another shift occurred: As I was speaking with several awake friends, my body became transparent. It expanded to contain all of life flowing through it, rising and falling away through my body. All life forms were created, maintained for an instant, and destroyed inside this body.

I'm aware that this first state of empty mind is unchanging; this next state of empty body is unchanging. But my own stabilization of these states does change. And my interpretation of them does change.

I continue the practice of shadow-work to avoid traps like my ego's attempts to identify with or reify these states. I continue to move my attention in search of blind spots. I also continue to practice extending my various lines of development through writing, exercise, music, and play with my grandchildren.

Today, sitting among the satsang members, my dreams of transcendence and greater union continue. I see that the evolution of consciousness is ongoing; it has no end point. And my faith is rekindled in holy longing, the impulse of evolution itself.

Having undergone the meeting with spiritual shadow and suffered the loss of innocence, which initiated me into the complexity of human life, I have found the narrow path through the darkness and feel myself traveling again toward the light, toward a conscious reunion with the source, the Self, pure awareness, which already always is who I am.

Acknowledgments

Writing a book is essentially a solitary task. But I wish to honor my psychological ancestors, whose work is my inspiration, especially Sigmund Freud, Carl Jung, James Hillman, and Ken Wilber. And I wish to thank the community of Pacifica Graduate Institute, especially my dissertation committee: Dr. Aaron Kipnis, Dr. Dianne Skafte, and Dr. Claire Douglas. That research formed the seed of this book. I wish to acknowledge depth psychology as one of my spiritual lineages, and to thank my first Jungian analyst, Suzanne Wagner, for introducing me to the shadow in dreams.

My thanks also to the following:

To Maharishi Mahesh Yogi, who lit the fire more than fifty years ago and led me to my lineage, Vedanta. And thank you to all my teachers since, who have helped keep it burning by transmitting their wisdom and practices to me.

To Swamiji and Joan Harrigan, whose profound insight and steadfast guidance reoriented my path.

To my satsang: No words can suffice. You welcomed me home.

To H.A.: for demonstrating, once again, that enlightenment is not what we think it is.

To A.H. Almaas: for the practice of Inquiry.

To the many people who have shared their tales of spiritual longing and disillusionment with me, as well as to those who have written their stories with honesty and authenticity, which I retell here.

To Candice Fuhrman, agent and friend, who shepherded this work into the world. To Barbara Moulton, who carried it further into the future.

To friend and mentor Jeremy Tarcher, who is alive in my writing, as well as Joel Fotinos and Mitch Horowitz, at Tarcher/Putnam, who published the original edition of this book.

To my writing teacher, Marilyn Ferguson. Without her, I may never have written a word.

To Rabbi Zalman Schacter-Shalomi, whose community of Sage-ing International initiated me into Elderhood.

To the staff at Inner Traditions: Ehud Sperling, Jon Graham, Jeanie Levitan, Erica Robinson, Aaron Davis, Jamaica Burns Griffin, Nancy Ringer, Eliza Homick, and Priscilla Baker. And to the two best publicists any author could want: Ashley Kolesnik and Gail Torr.

To Steve Reicher, my first imago amore. I carry you in my heart.

To Rick Archer, for founding *Buddha at the Gas Pump*, cofounding the Association for Spiritual Integrity, and advising me on this book.

To my beloved giggle group: Neil, Steve Wolf, Malcolm Schultz, Paula Perlman, Rhoda Pregerson, and Janet Bachelor, and as well as to Linda Novack, Riley Smith, and Bruce Langhorn, all now deceased, for the best belly laughs during the decades of our friendship.

To my grandchildren, Kaleb and Eli, Jayden and Sienna: may your longing carry you to the Great Return.

To Neil, whose unwavering devotion healed me and showed me the Way of marriage and whose profound awakening to a vast non-duality brought us fulfillment.

The Association for Spiritual Integrity (ASI) Code of Ethics and Good Practice

As spiritual teachers, we commit to:

Holding ourselves to the highest standards of ethics, right behavior, and professional competency, as commonly recognized by our peers.

Performing our roles as teachers in a caring and compassionate manner, in both one-to-one interactions and groups.

Respecting the rights, dignity, and safety of all students and fellow practitioners.

Fostering autonomy, empowerment, self-sufficiency, and emotional maturity in our students.

Treating students' questions, concerns, doubts, and experiences with respect, and never trivializing or dismissing their inquiries.

Being self-aware, open, and humble about the limitations of our knowledge and experience.

Making only honest, realistic statements regarding the benefits of our teachings, practices, courses, and other offerings.

Refraining from giving counsel in matters outside of our areas of training and expertise, and making appropriate referrals as needed.

Being honest and transparent regarding our professional business and financial matters.

Honoring the sanctity of privacy and maintaining the confidentiality of everything conveyed to us in confidence.

Abiding by local laws with respect to the disclosure of information in cases of sexual abuse, child endangerment, and the intention to harm oneself or others.

Using only with proper care and caution any techniques that can potentially cause harmful side effects.

Acknowledging that, regardless of our spiritual attainment, we are human beings with human personalities, limitations, drives, and needs.

Not seeking or presuming exalted privileges or glorified status because of our role as spiritual teachers.

Never manipulating, exploiting, or deceiving a student to satisfy our personal aspirations, needs, or desires.

Establishing and maintaining clear professional boundaries with all students, employees, and associates.

Never abusing the trust of students to obtain sexual gratification, money, free labor, or other personal benefits.

Being particularly mindful of sexual boundaries with students and honoring them at all times.

Cultivating and practicing honesty, integrity, compassion, humility, and empathy.

Engaging in continuous self-reflection, learning, and holistic personal growth.

Regularly reviewing our motivations for serving as teachers and monitoring the integrity of our words and actions.

Encouraging feedback about our own methods and behavior and taking feedback seriously. This includes complaints submitted to ASI.

Addressing promptly any personal issues, concerns, or challenges that might affect our professional competency.

Offering support to our colleagues and fellow ASI members to the extent that we are able and available.

The Code of Ethics for Insight Meditation Society (IMS) Teachers

We agree to uphold the five training precepts:

We undertake the precept of refraining from killing.

We undertake the precept of refraining from stealing.

We undertake the precept of refraining from sexual misconduct.

We undertake the precept of refraining from false speech.

We undertake the precept of refraining from intoxicants that cause heedlessness or loss of awareness.

In addition, IMS has adopted an unlawful harassment prevention policy as part of the teacher code of ethics.

For more details on the code of ethics, visit the IMS website.

Bibliography

Allen, John L. Jr. "Vatican Abuse Summit: $2.2 Billion and 100,000 Victims in U.S. Alone." *National Catholic Reporter,* February 8, 2012. Available online.

Anthony, Richard, Bruce Ecker, and Ken Wilber, eds. *Spiritual Choices: The Problem of Recognizing Authentic Paths to Inner Transformation.* New York: Paragon House, 1987.

The Atlantic. Holy Shit, We're in a Cult. Documentary, September 26, 2016, available on *The Atlantic* website.

Bailey, Sarah Pulliam. "Southern Baptist Leaders Covered Up Sex Abuse, Lied about Secret Database, Report Says." *Washington Post,* May 22, 2022.

Baker, Connie A. *Traumatized by Religious Abuse.* Eugene, Ore.: Luminaire Press, 2019.

Bell, Rudolph M. *Holy Anorexia.* Chicago: University of Chicago Press, 1985.

Berzin, Alexander. *Wise Teacher, Wise Student: Tibetan Approaches to a Healthy Relationship.* Ithaca, N.Y.: Snow Lion Publications, 2010.

Blachly, Peter Macdonald. *The Inner Circle: 17 Years in the Cult of the American Sikhs.* Sheep Island, Maine: Sheep Island Press, 2021.

Bly, Robert. *Kabir: Ecstatic Poems.* Boston: Beacon Press, 1976.

———, ed. *News of the Universe: Poems of Two-Fold Consciousness.* San Francisco, Calif.: Sierra Club Books, 1980.

Bogart, Gregory. "Separating from a Spiritual Teacher." *Journal of Transpersonal Psychology* 24, no. 1 (1992).

Boorstein, Michelle. "Evangelist Ravi Zacharias Engaged in Sexual Misconduct, Report Says." *Washington Post,* February 11, 2021.

Boorstein, Michelle, and Keith L. Alexander. "D.C. Rabbi Who Secretly Video-Recorded Dozens of Women Is Released from Jail." *Washington Post,* April 1, 2020.

Booth, Leo. *When God Becomes a Drug.* Los Angeles, Calif.: Jeremy P. Tarcher Publishing, 1974.

Bourque, Judith. *Robes of Silk, Feet of Clay.* Cardiff, Calif.: Waterside Press, 2018.

Buddhadharma. "Ask the Teachers." Column in *Buddhadharma,* Winter 2014.

Bullitt-Jonas, Margaret. *Holy Hunger.* New York: Vintage Books, 2000.

Butler, Katy. "Encountering the Shadow in Buddhist America." *Common Boundary,* May/June 1990.

———. "Events Are the Teacher: Working through the Crisis at San Francisco Zen Center." *CoEvolution Quarterly,* Winter 1983.

Butterfield, Stephen T. *The Double Mirror: A Skeptical Journey into Buddhist Tantra.* Berkeley, Calif.: North Atlantic Books, 1994.

Campbell, June. *Traveller in Space: In Search of Female Identity in Tibetan Buddhism.* London: Continuum Books, 1996.

Caplan, Mariana. *Eyes Wide Open: Cultivating Discernment on the Spiritual Path.* Boulder, Colo.: Sounds True, 2009.

———. *The Guru Question: The Perils and Rewards of Choosing a Spiritual Teacher.* Boulder, Colo.: Sounds True, 2011.

———. *Halfway Up the Mountain: The Error of Premature Claims to Enlightenment,* Chino Valley, Ariz.: Hohm Press, 1999.

Capps, Donald. "Sex in the Parish." *Journal of Pastoral Care,* Winter 1993.

Cohen, Andrew. *When Shadow Meets the Bodhisattva: The Challenging Transformation of a Modern Guru.* Rochester, Vt.: Inner Traditions, 2023.

Conway, Timothy. "Adi Da and His Voracious, Abusive Personality Cult." Enlightened Spirituality (webpage), 2007.

———. "The Four Kinds of Spiritual Teachers." Enlightened Spirituality (webpage), February 27, 2005.

Corbett, Lionel. *The God Image.* Asheville, N.C.: Chiron Publications, 2021.

Cushman, Anne. "Shrinking the Guru." *Yoga Journal,* November 1994.

Dalai Lama. *The Path to Enlightenment.* Ithaca, N.Y.: Snow Lion Publications, 1994.

De Fuentes, Nanette. "Unholy Crisis: Sexually Abusive Catholic Priests and their Victims." *The Los Angeles Psychologist,* July/August, 2002.

Deikman, Arthur. *The Wrong Way Home: Uncovering the Patterns of Cult Behavior in American Society.* Boston: Beacon Press, 1994.

Diaz, Johnny. "New Mexico Archdiocese to Settle Sex Abuse Claims for $121.5 Million." *New York Times,* May 18, 2022.

Dickson, E. J. "The Instagram Guru 'F–king' His Female Followers 'to Freedom.'" *Rolling Stone,* April 18, 2022.

Downey, Jessica. "The Dark Side of Meditation." *Yoga Journal,* April 18, 2018.

Downing, Christine. *Myths and Mysteries of Same-Sex Love.* Lincoln, Neb.: iUniverse, 1986.

Downing, Michael. *Shoes Outside the Door: Desire, Devotion, and Excess at San Francisco Zen Center.* Berkeley, Calif.: Counterpoint Press, 2001.

Dyson, Damcho. "This Is Abuse." *Tricycle: The Buddhist Review.* July 15, 2019.

Dyson, Pamela Saharah. *Premka: White Bird in a Golden Cage: My Life with Yogi Bhajan.* Maui, Hawaii: Eyes Wide Publishing, 2020.

Eckhart, Meister. "The Nobleman." In *Meister Eckhart, from Whom God Hid Nothing: Sermons, Writings, and Sayings.* Edited by David O'Neal. Boston: New Seeds, 2005.

Edelstein, Scott. *Sex and the Spiritual Teacher.* Boston: Wisdom Publications, 2011.

Edinger, Edward. *Transformation of the God-Image.* Toronto: Inner City Books, 1992.

Elder, Sean. "Noah Levine Blames the #MeToo Movement for the Demise of His Punk Rock Buddhism Empire." *Los Angeles Magazine,* July 10, 2019.

Eliade, Mircea. *The Sacred and the Profane.* New York: Harcourt Press, 1959.

Elkins, David. *Beyond Religion: A Personal Program for Building a Spiritual Life outside the Walls of Traditional Religion.* Wheaton, Ill.: Quest Books, 1998.

Falk, Geoffrey. *Stripping the Gurus: Sex, Violence, Abuse, and Enlightenment.* N.p.: Million Monkeys Press, 2017.

Feuerstein, Georg. "The Shadow of the Enlightened Guru." In *Meeting the Shadow,* ed. Connie Zweig and Jeremiah Abrams. Los Angeles: Jeremy P. Tarcher Publications, 1991.

Finnigan, Mary. *Sexual Violence in Tibetan Buddhism: The Rise and Fall of Sogyal Rinpoche.* Portland, Ore.: Jorvick Press, 2019.

Fox, Matthew. *Original Blessing.* New York: Tarcher/Putnam, 2000.

Franklin, Satya Bharti. *The Promise of Paradise: A Woman's Intimate Story of the Perils of Life with Rajneesh.* Barrytown, N.Y.: Station Hill Press, 2010.

Friedman, Lenore. *Meetings with Remarkable Women: Buddhist Teachers in America.* Boston: Shambhala, 2000.

Gleig, Ann. *American Dharma: Buddhism Beyond Modernity.* New Haven, Conn.: Yale University Press, 2019.

———. "Sexual Violations in American Buddhism." On the Ten Thousand Things website, March 5, 2020.

Gordon, James S. *Golden Guru: The Strange Journey of Bhagavan Shree Rajneesh.* New York: Penguin Books, 1988.

Grof, Christina. *The Thirst for Wholeness.* New York: HarperCollins, 1994.

Grof, Stanislav, and Christina Grof, eds. *Spiritual Emergency: When Personal Transformation becomes a Crisis.* Los Angeles: Jeremy P. Tarcher Publications, 1989.

Gross, Rita. *Buddhism beyond Gender: Liberation from Attachment to Identity.* Boulder, Colo.: Shambhala Publications, 2018.

Guest, Tim. *My Life in Orange: Growing Up with the Guru.* New York: Harcourt, 2005.

Halser, Marlene. *Bhakti Marga: Just Love Documentary.* Documentary film available on the Rumble website, March 29, 2022.

Harrigan, Joan Shivarpita. *Kundalini Vidya: The Science of Spiritual Transformation: A Comprehensive System for Understanding and Guiding Spiritual Development.* Knoxville, Tenn.: Patanjali Kundalini Yoga Care, 2006.

Harris, Lis. "O Guru, Guru, Guru." *New Yorker,* November 14, 1994.

Harvey, Andrew. *The Direct Path.* New York: Broadway Books, 2001.

———. *Sun at Midnight.* Los Angeles: Jeremy P. Tarcher Publications, 2002.

Hassan, Steven. *Combatting Cult Mind Control.* Rochester, Vt.: Inner Traditions, 1990.

Heschel, Abraham Joshua. "Religion and Race." January 14, 1963 speech. Available online at Voices of Democracy: The U.S. Oratory Project website.

Hillman, James. *Healing Fiction.* Thompson, Conn.: Spring Publications, 2019.

———. *Loose Ends.* "Pothos." Washington, D.C.: Spring Publications, 1975

Hixon, Lex. *Great Swan: Meetings with Ramakrishna.* Burdett, N.Y.: Larson Publications, 1992.

Holecek, Andrew. "The Evolution of Abuse." Blog post on Holecek's personal website, first posted August 23, 2018.

Horton, Adrian. "'He Got Away with It': How the Founder of Bikram Yoga Built an Empire on Abuse." *The Guardian,* November 20, 2019.

Jackson, Peter A. "Non-normative Sex/Gender Categories in the Theravada Buddhist Scriptures." Working/technical paper, Australian National University Open Research Library, 1996.

Jain, Andrea. *Peace, Love, Yoga: The Politics of Global Spirituality.* New York: Oxford University Press, 2020.

James, William. *The Varieties of Religious Experience.* New Delhi: General Press, 2021.

Joy, Brugh W. *Avalanche: Heretical Reflections on the Dark and Light.* New York: Ballantine Books, 1990.

Jung, C. G. *Memories, Dreams, Reflections.* New York: Random House, 1961.

———. *Psychology and Religion: West and East.* "Imitation of Christ." Princeton, N.J.: Princeton University Press, 1969.

———. *The Psychology of Kundalini Yoga.* Princeton, N.J.: Princeton University Press, 1996.

———. *Psychology of the Unconscious.* New York: Dodd, Meade and Company, 1947.

———. *The Undiscovered Self.* Princeton, N.J.: Princeton University Press, 2010.

Kaleem, Jaweed. "Buddhist 'People of Color Sanghas,' Diversity Efforts Address Conflicts about Race among Meditators." HuffPost (online), March 31, 2015.

Karpinski, Robert D. "I Was Abused by a Priest. Then I Became a Priest." HuffPost (online), December 28, 2021.

Kempis, Thomas à. *The Imitation of Christ*. New Delhi: Delhi Open Books, 2019.

King, Russell. *Rajneeshpuram: Inside the Cult of Bhagwan and Its Failed American Utopia*. Chicago: Chicago Review Press, 2022.

Kohlberg, Lawrence. *The Psychology of Moral Development*. New York: Harper & Row, 1984.

Kohut, Heinz. *The Analysis of the Self*. New York: International Universities Press, 1971.

Kornfield, Jack. *After the Ecstasy, the Laundry*. New York: Bantam Books, 2000.

———. *A Path with Heart: A Guide through the Perils and Promises of Spiritual Life*. New York: Bantam Books, 1993.

———. "Sex Lives of the Gurus." *Yoga Journal*, July/August 1985.

Kramer, Joel, and Diana Alstad. *The Guru Papers: Masks of Authoritarian Power*. Berkeley, Calif.: North Atlantic Books, 1993.

Kristof, Kathy M. "Faith-Based Investment Scams Fleecing Followers of Billions." *Los Angeles Times*, September 16, 2001.

Lachkar, Joan. "The Psychological Make-up of a Suicide Bomber." *Journal of Psychohistory*, Spring 2002.

Lachs, Stuart. "For Whose Best Interest." Posted on The Zensite (online), July 29, 2015.

———. "Tibetan Buddhism Enters the 21st Century: Trouble in Shangri-La." Posted on the Open Buddhism website, 2019.

Lachs, Stuart, and Rob Hogendoorn. "'Not the Tibetan Way': The Dalai Lama's Realpolitik Concerning Abusive Teachers." Posted on the Open Buddhism website, 2021.

Lane, David C. *Exposing Cults: When the Skeptical Mind Confronts the Mystical*. New York: Garland Publishing, 1994.

Langenberg, Amy. "The Buddha Didn't Teach Consent." *Tricycle: The Buddhist Review*, February 23, 2021.

Lawton, Dan. "When Buddhism Goes Bad: How My Mindfulness Practice Led Me to Meltdown." Posted on Lawton's personal website, July 16, 2021.

Leonard, Linda Schierse. *The Wounded Woman*. Columbus, Ohio: Swallow Press, 1982.

Lifton, Robert Jay. *Losing Reality: On Cults, Cultism, and the Mindset of Political and Religious Zealotry*. New York: The New Press, 2019.

———. *Thought Reform and the Psychology of Totalism: A Study of Brainwashing in China*. New York: Norton Books, 1969.

Lion's Roar staff. "Confronting Abuse of Power." *Buddhadharma*, November 20, 2014.

Lockhart, Russel. *Words Are Eggs*. Thompson, Conn.: Spring Publications, 1983.

Lucia, Amanda. "Guru Sex: Charisma, Proxemic Desire, and the Haptic Logics of the Guru-Disciple Relationship." Journal of the American Academy of Religion 86, no. 4 (December 2018).

Masson, Jeffrey. *My Father's Guru*. N.p.: Untreed Reads, 2013.

Matousek, Mark. *Sex, Death, Enlightenment*. New York: Riverhead Books, 1996.

Matthews, Caitlin. *In Search of Women's Passionate Soul*. Montgomery, Ill.: Element Books, 1997.

McCormack, Win. *The Rajneesh Chronicles: The True Story of the Cult That Unleashed the First Act of Bioterrorism on U.S. Soil*. Portland, Ore.: Tin House, 2010.

Meissner. W. W. *Psychoanalysis and the Religious Experience*. New Haven, Conn.: Yale University, 1984.

Mikulincer, Mario, and Ilana Peer-Goldin. "Self-Congruence and the Experience of Happiness." *British Journal of Social Psychology,* March 1991.

Miller, Lama Willa. "Breaking the Silence on Sexual Misconduct." *Buddhadharma*, Summer 2018.

Nelson, John. *Healing the Split: Integrating Spirit into our Understanding of the Mentally Ill*. New York: State University of New York, 1994.

Newberg, Andrew, Eugene D'Aquili, and Vince Rause. *Why God Won't Go Away: Brain Science and the Biology of Belief.* New York: Random House, 2001.

Newland, Tahlia. *Fallout: Recovering from Abuse in Tibetan Buddhism*. Foxground, NSW, Australia: AIA Publishing, 2019.

———. "Wisdom Obscured by Devotion." *Tricycle: The Buddhist Review,* July 2017.

Newman, Andy. "The 'King' of Shambhala Buddhism Is Undone by Abuse Report." *New York Times,* July 11, 2018.

Nithyananda Facts (blog). "Nithyananda Contracts for Sanyasis, Adheenavasis, Volunteers, Participants to Be at Bidadi Ashram Dynapeetam." January 16, 2018.

North, Anna. "Seven Positive Changes That Have Come from the #MeToo Movement." Vox (online), October 4, 2019.

Oppenheimer, Mark. "Zen Predator of the Upper East Side." *The Atlantic,* December 18, 2014.

Owens, Lama Rod. *Love and Rage: The Path of Liberation through Anger.* Berkeley, Calif.: North Atlantic Books, 2020.

Preece, Rob. "Our Teachers Are Not Gods." *Buddhadharma,* Winter 2014.

Rauch, Mikele. *Healing the Soul after Religious Abuse.* Westport, Conn.: Praeger Press, 2009.

Religion and Sexual Abuse Project website; accessed January 5, 2023.

Remski, Matthew. *Practice and All Is Coming: Abuse, Cult Dynamics, and Healing in Yoga and Beyond.* Rangiora, N.Z.: Embodied Wisdom Publishing, 2019.

Robbins, Erin. "A Letter to the Osho Community." Posted on the Erin Robbins website, n.d.; accessed September 10, 2022.

Rochford, E. Burke Jr. *How Krishna Transformed.* New York: New York University Press, 2007.

Rodarmor, William. "The Secret Life of Swami Muktananda." *CoEvolution Quarterly,* Winter 1983.

Rolheiser, Ronald. *The Holy Longing: The Search for Christian Spirituality.* New York: Crown, 2009.

Rothbaum, Susan. "Sorting It Out." *Yoga Journal,* May/June 1980.

Rubin, Pamela. "Confronting Abuse of Power." *Buddhadharma,* Winter 2014, p. 49.

Rutter, Peter. *Sex in the Forbidden Zone.* Los Angeles: Jeremy P. Tarcher Publishing, 1991.

Sacks, Oliver. *An Anthropologist on Mars.* New York: Vintage Books, 1995.

Schneider, Robert G. *The Guru's Touch: A Novel.* Rockland, Maine: Strange Land Publications, 2017.

Scofield, Be. "Becoming God: Inside Mooji's Portugal Cult." *The Guru Magazine* (online), March 14, 2019.

———. "Master of Deceit: How Yogi Bhajan Used Yoga for Money, Sex, and Power." *The Guru Magazine* (online), March 5, 2020.

Shaw, Daniel. *Traumatic Narcissism and Recovery: Leaving the Prison of Shame and Fear.* New York: Routledge, 2014.

Siena, Catherine of. *The Dialogue.* Classics of Western Spirituality. Mahwah, N. J.: Paulist Press, 1980.

Simpkinson, Anne. "Soul Betrayal." *Common Boundary,* November/December 1996.

Singer, Margaret. *Cults in Our Midst.* San Francisco: Jossey-Bass, 1996.

Sipchen, Bob. "Tracking the Mystical Traveler." *Los Angeles Times,* November 1, 1994.

Sipe, Richard. *Sex, Priests, and Power.* New York: Brunner/Mazel, 1995.

Spong, John. *Why Christianity Must Change or Die.* San Francisco: HarperSanFrancisco, 1999.

Stein, Alexandra. *Terror, Love and Brainwashing: Attachment in Cults and Totalitarian Systems.* New York: Routledge, 2016.

Steinbeck, John IV, and Nancy Steinbeck. *The Other Side of Eden: Life with John Steinbeck.* New York: Prometheus Books, 2001.

Stork, Jane. *Breaking the Spell: My Life as a Rajneeshee, and the Long Journey Back to Freedom.* London: Pan Macmillan, 2009.

Storr, Anthony. *Feet of Clay: Saints, Sinners, and Madmen.* New York: Free Press, 1986.

Szabo, Marta. *The Guru Looked Good: A Memoir.* Woodstock, N.Y.: Tinker Street Press, 2009.

Tamm, Jayanti. *Cartwheels in a Sari: A Memoir of Growing Up Cult.* New York: Crown Publishing, 2010.

Teresa of Ávila, Saint. *Interior Castle.* Washington, D.C.: ICS Publications, 2010. Orig. pub. 1577.

Todd, Douglas. "Sai Baba: Holy Man? Sex Abuser? Both?" *Vancouver Sun,* April 26, 2011.

Tredwell, Gail. *Holy Hell: A Memoir of Faith, Devotion, and Pure Madness.* Maui, Hawaii: Wattle Tree Press, 2009.

Tworkov, Helen. "Zen in the Balance: Can It Survive America?" *Tricycle: The Buddhist Review,* Spring 1994.

Unicorn in the attic [pseud.]. "The Connected Abuses of Vishwananda, Nithyananda, and the Hale Clinic, Bhatkti Marga in London." Blog post on Medium, October 4, 2019.

Vaidya, Abhay. *Who Killed Osho?* Uttar Pradesh, India: Om Books, 2017.

Van der Braak, Andre. *Enlightenment Blues: My Years with an American Guru.* Rhinebeck, N.Y.: Monkfish Press, 2003.

Watts, Jack. *Recovering from Religious Abuse.* New York: First Howard Books, 2011.

Webster, Katharine. "The Case against Swami Rama." *Yoga Journal,* December 1990.

Weiner, Herbert. *9½ Mystics: The Kabbala Today.* New York: Simon & Schuster, 1992. Orig. pub. 1969.

Wilber, Ken. *Integral Psychology.* Boston: Shambhala Publications, 2000.

———. *Integral Spirituality.* Boston: Shambhala Publications, 2006.

———. *The Religion of Tomorrow.* Boston: Shambhala Publications, 2017.

———. *Sex, Ecology, Spirituality.* Boston: Shambhala Publications, 2011.

———. *Up from Eden.* Boston: Shambhala Publications, 2007.

Wilber, Ken, Terry Patten, Adam Leonard, and Marco Morelli. *Integral Life Practice.* Boston: Shambhala Publications, 2008.

Williams, Reb. Angel Kyodo, Lama Rod Owens, and Jasmine Svedullah. *Radical Dharma: Talking Race, Love, and Liberation.* Berkeley, Calif.: North Atlantic Books, 2016.

Winell, Marlene. *Leaving the Fold: A Guide for Former Fundamentalists and Others Leaving Their Religion.* Berkeley, Calif.: Apocryphile Press, 2007.

———. "Religious Trauma Syndrome." Three-article series. *Cognitive Behavioral Therapy Today* 39, no. 2 (May 2011); 39, no. 3 (September 2011); and 39, no. 4 (November 2011).

Woodman, Marion. *Addiction to Perfection.* Toronto, Calif.: Inner City Books, 1982.

———. *Emily Dickinson and the Demon Lover.* Audio cassette. Boulder, Colo.: Sounds True, 1993.

Yandell, James. *The Imitation of Jung.* N.p.: Centerpoint Foundation, 1977.

Yenner, William. *American Guru: A Story of Love, Betrayal and Healing: Former Students of Andrew Cohen Speak*. Rhinebeck, N.Y.: Monkfish Books, 2009.

Zweig, Connie. *A Moth to the Flame: The Story of Sufi Poet Rumi*. Lanham, Md.: Rowman & Littlefield Publishers, 2006.

———. *The Inner Work of Age: Shifting from Role to Soul*. Rochester, Vt.: Inner Traditions, 2021.

Zweig, Connie, and Jeremiah Abrams, eds. *Meeting the Shadow*. Los Angeles: Jeremy P. Tarcher Publishing, 1991.

Zweig, Connie, and Steve Wolf. *Romancing the Shadow*. New York: Ballantine Books, 1997.

Index

action on our own behalf, reclaiming, 223–26

activism, 218

addiction, meeting the shadow of, 190–93

Adi Da, 99, 118, 164–65

advaita, defined, 55

After the Fall, 111–244

Alcoholics Anonymous, 190–91

alcoholic strategies, 171

al-Sadiq, Jafar, 103

Amma, 159–61

Ananda Church of Self-Realization, 132

An Olive Branch, xvi, 135

Aphrodite, 233–34

Archer, Rick, xiv

archetypes, 50

Arjuna, 96–97

Armstrong, Herbert W., 216

Association for Spiritual Integrity, xvi–xvii
  code of ethics, 251–53

Augustine, St., 60

authentic self, xxvii, 236–37

authoritarianism, 91–92, 95

Baal Shem Tov, 227–28

Baker, Richard, 136–37, 171, 195

Baran, Josh, 213

Basho, 200

Bell, Rudolph, 107

beloved
  as god, 70–77
  longing for the human beloved, 61–79
  as parent, 66–70

Bhajan, Yogi, 149–51

Bikram Choudhury, 151–52

Bill W., 190–91

bin Laden, Osama, 188–89

Bistami, Bayazid, 38

Black images of the divine, 235–36

Bodhisattva Buddhism, 40–41

body, reclaiming the, 221–23

Bogart, Greg, 211, 213

Boorstein, Michelle, 128–29

Booth, Leo, 172–73, 203–5

borderline personality, 185

Bourque, Judith, 162–63

bride (in Song of Solomon), 17

Buddhism, scandals in, 134–35, 139–47

Bullitt-Jonas, Margaret, 192–93

Butler, Katy, 178, 195, 203

Butterfield, Stephen, 80, 215–16

call of the beloved, 23

Campbell, Joseph, 241

Catherine of Siena, 104–8

Catholic church
  call for reform in, 204
  sexual abuse scandal, 123–26, 128, 170, 172, 180–81
Chetanananda, Swami, 168, 171
child development, 43–48
child survivors, 123. *See also* spiritual abuse
Chinmoy, Sri, 132–33
Chogyam Trungpa, 139–43, 172, 177, 215–16
Christ. *See* Jesus
Christianity, 30–31, 104–7, 114, 231–32. *See also* Catholic church
Christian Science, 170, 216–17
Clare of Assisi, Saint, 229
Cohen, Andrew, 165–66
community healing, 203–10
complexity, 20
confession before the community, 203
consciousness, how it grows, 65
consent, xx, 157
Conway, Timothy, 140, 164–65
cosmic consciousness, 52–53
couple in their twenties, 68–70
covert abuse, identifying, 120–23
covert dependency, 182
crazy wisdom, 140–41, 172
creativity as practice, 237–41
Cushman, Anne, 205–6

Dalai Lama, xxii, 143–46
Dalbey, Gordon, 30–31
Dante, 63
darkness, the way of, 114
darshan, 103
death, 193–95, 223
de Fuentes, Nanette, 180, 205

Deikman, Arthur, 182
denial, 170
dependence, need for, 182
dependent personality, 185
Desai, Amrit, 205–7
development, stages of, 42–48, 78–79, 189–90, 225, 237
dhikr, 114
Dickinson, Emily, 68
disillusionment, 117–18
  a guide for disillusioned believers ("After the Fall"), 111–244
diversity, 234
divine human, spiritual teachers as, 102–9
divine mother, 99
Dostoevsky, Fyodor, 9, 112
doubts, 120–23, 217
Downey, Jessica, 116
Downing, Christine, 46
downward arc (involution), 21–22
drinking, 114
Dürckheim, Karlfried Graf, 27
Dyson, Damcho, 131
Dyson, Pamela Sarah, 149

Eastern culture, shame-based, 177
Eckhart, Meister, 20, 54
Edinger, Ed, 226–27
ego transcendence, 175
Eido Roshi, 134–35
Ein Sof, 28
Elder, Sean, 161
Elkins, David, 221
Emerson, Ralph Waldo, 53
emotional integration, 209–10
epaktasis, 30
Eros, 61–62

ethics, code of
  for Association for Spiritual
    Integrity, 251–53
  for Insight Meditation Society, 254
exile, 58

faithful believers, a guide for ("Before
  the Fall"), 15–109
feeling, reclaiming authentic, 219–20
feminine images of the divine, 232–35
Feuerstein, Georg, 175
Fox, Matthew, 115, 237
Franklin, Satya Bharti, 170
Freud, Sigmund, 25, 42–43, 46–50, 84
Freundel, Barry, 154

Gaia, 233
gender gap, 178–79
gender identity, xxvi–xxviii
god, 8, 39
  beloved as, 70–77
  longing for, 39–59
  longs for us, 27–31
  spiritual teachers as, 93–102
goddess, 232–35
god image, 39–41
  Black images, 235–36
  development in children, 43–48
  and evolution (up), 51–59
  feminine images of the divine,
    232–35
  and involution (down), 42–51
  reclaiming images of the divine,
    226–37
  and shadow, 41
Goethe, 12, 18
Golden Temple, 149–51
gopis, 17, 81
Gordon, James, 189

great return, the, 20, 51
Grof, Christina, 191
Grof, Stanislav, 116
growing up, and separating from a
  teacher, 211–12
Gurumayi Chidvilasananda, 147–49
gurus, nature of, 118
guru yoga, 94

Hades, 197, 199
Hare Krishna, 163
Harris, Lis, 148
Harvey, Andrew, 182, 214–15
Hasidism, 227–28
Heaven's Gate, 193
hero, myth of the, 20, 241–44
Heschel, Abraham Joshua, 20–21
Hillman, James, 12, 24, 38, 98
himma, 32
Holecek, Andrew, xv, xvii–xxviii
Hollis, James, 66
holy longing, xxix–xxx, 6–7, 16–37
  awakening to, 22–26
  banished by rationality, 59
  carries seed desire of a life story, 36
  effects of, 19
  god longs for us, 27–31
  for the human beloved, 61–79
  longing for god, 39–59
  longing for the divine human,
    81–109
  proper stance toward, 36
  two faces of, 35
"Holy Longing, The" (Goethe), 18, 61
Houston, Jean, 60
human beloved, longing for the, 61–79

identity crisis, global, xxvi–xxix
imagination, 40

"in" and "out" split, 225–26
independence
    establishing, 211–19
    reclaiming independent thinking,
        215–19
individuality, stress on, 176, 227
in-group issues, 121–22
ISKCON, 163
Islam, 31, 39–40

James, William, 10–11
Jehovah's Witnesses, 171
Jennifer (meeting with her teacher),
    81–83, 87–90
Jesus, 114, 228, 230–31
    a woman with a passion for, 229–30
Jewish mysticism, 28–29
Job, 112, 117
John Paul II, Pope, 186–87
John-Roger, 134
Joy, W. Brugh, 208–9, 211, 232
Judaism, 227–28
Jung, Carl, 10–11, 25, 60, 71, 227
    on being on fire, 18
    and Bill W., 190
    on Eastern teacher/disciple model,
        99–102
    on gods, 7–8
    on imitation of Christ, 230
    on longing for god, vi
    on mana-personalities, 97
    and patient with religious
        transference, 96
    on possession by an archetype,
        193–95
    and relationship to infinite, 93
    on religion, 23, 48–51
    on secret societies, 182
    and soul stones, 42–43

Kabbalah, 29
Kabir, vi, 60
Kalu Rinpoche, xvi, 166–67, 177–78
Kant, Immanuel, 227
Karpinski, Robert, 128
Kelsey, Morton T., 40
Kempis, Thomas à, 228
Kohlberg's stages of moral
    development, 225, 237
Kohut, Heinz, 86–87
Kook, Abraham, 22–23
Kornfield, Jack, 187
Kripalu, 205–7
Krishna, 27–28, 96–97
Kristof, Kathy, 126
Kriyananda, Swami, 132
kundalini, defined, 21–22

Lachkar, Joan, 194
Lachs, Stuart, 135–36, 139, 142–43,
    146
Landry, Sarah, 158–59
Larsson, Conny, 164
Layla and Majnun, 74–77
Lenz, Frederick, 133–34, 171
Leonard, Linda, 98
Levine, Noah, 161
Lifton, Robert Jay, 122
light, reclaiming the, 214–15
longing, defined, 12–13
love, 62
    courtly, 62–63
    and longing for the human beloved,
        61–79

Maat, 233
maenads, 17
Maezumi Roshi, 171, 209
Maharishi Mahesh Yogi, 162–63

Majnun and Layla, 74–77
Mark (Gospel), 83
Marpa, 239–40
Massaro, Bentinho, 154–56
Masson, Jeffrey, 104
Matousek, Mark, 219–20
matriarchy, 226–27
Matthews, Caitlín, 73
May, Rollo, 186
Mechtild of Magdeburg, 200
meditation, potential problems with, 116
Meera, Mother, 182, 214–15
Meher Baba, 112
Meissner, W. W., 48
Merton, Thomas, 200
Messiah, as object of longing, 227
#MeToo, xvii–xx, 144
Mikulincer, Mario, 185
Milarepa, 239–40
mind/body split, 221
Mirabai, 17
monotheism, 227
Mooji, 152–53
moral development, stages of, 225, 237
Muktananda, Swami, 102, 147–49, 168
myths, finding our spiritual, 241–44

Nachman, Rabbi, 29–30
narcissistic personality, 185
Nelson, John, 116
neuroscience, 11–12
Newberg, Andrew, 11
Newland, Tahlia, 130–32
Nietzsche, Friedrich Wilhelm, 80
Nisargadatta Maharaj, 118
Nithyananda, 158–59

nonattachment, 217–18
Norlha Rinpoche, 146–47
numinous, defined, 49

obsessive compulsive personality, 185
Oedipal stage, 45
Oracle at Delphi, 38
Osel Tendzin, 141, 171, 177–78, 187
Osho, 99, 137–39, 189
overt abuse, identifying, 123–26

Padre Pio, 228
paradise motif, 24–25
parent(s), 67–68
    beloved as, 66–70
    spiritual teachers as, 83–93
path of love, Rumi and the, 33
patriarchy, 178–79
Paul, 30
Peer-Goldin, Ilana, 185
Pentecostal story, 173–74
Persephone, 197
personality styles, and vulnerability, 185
Plato, 21, 70
Plotinus, 54
polytheism, 227
power, 92, 95, 112, 123, 157, 188
    and sex, xii, 116–17, 174
Preece, Rob, xxii
Premka, 149
priests. See also spiritual teacher(s)
    and spiritual abuse, 180–81
Prigogine, Ilya, 19
Procession, 180–81
projection, and spiritual teacher, 84–86
Psalms, vi, 16
psychological growth, 9–10, 42–44

puella woman, 98–99
puer aeternus, 98, 186

Radha, 27–28
Rajneesh, Bhagwan Shree, 99,
    137–39, 189
Rama, Swami, 130
Rama, Zen Master, 133–34, 171
Ramakrishna, 38, 51, 55–57, 101,
    108, 226
Ramana Maharshi, xiii
Ram Dass, 25–26
Rand, Yvonne, xxiv, 178
Raniere, Keith, 153–54
redemption, 99
relationships, 61–79, 71
    suggestions for, 77–79
religion, 10, 223
religious trauma syndrome, 183–84
religious unconscious, 202
remedial work, 195
Remski, Matthew, 151
Richardson, Marie, 235–36
Rilke, Rainer Maria, 65, 238
Robbins, Erin, 138–39
Rochford, E. Burke, Jr., 163
Rodarmor, William, 147
romantic union
    and collapse of projections, 77
    search for, 61–79
Rubin, Pamela, 166
Rumi, 17, 31–35, 80, 108
Rutter, Peter, xx, 157

Sacks, Oliver, 119–20
Sakyong Mipham, 141–43
samadhi, forms of, 54–55
Sasaki Roshi, Joshu, 135–36
Sathya Sai Baba, 163–64

scandals (of spiritual teachers), 88–89,
    126–67
Schneider, Robert G., 148
Scofield, Be, 149, 152
self, authentic versus true, xxvii
selfobject, 86–87
self-organization, 19–20
self-transcendence, as what we crave,
    62
senex, 97
separating from a teacher, 211–13
separation, as inherent in union, 64
service to others, and community
    healing, 209
sexual abuse. See also spiritual abuse
    in early life, 185–86
shadow
    accepting the, 201
    collective shadow, 121
    denial of our own, 114
    in higher stages of practice, 175
    the intention in exploring the,
        xi–xii
    as lodged in every chakra, xv
shadow-work for communities,
    203–10
shadow-work for individuals, xxvi,
    211–44
    meeting the spiritual shadow,
        113–67
shadow-work for spiritual abuse,
    201–44
Shambhala Meditation Center, 140
Shinge Chayat, 134–35
Simpkinson, Anne, 181
Singer, Margaret T., 174
Sipchen, Bob, 134
Sipe, Richard, 123
Sogyal Rinpoche, 130–32, 177

soul, what does the soul want?, 12, 22
Southern Baptist Convention,
    cover-up of sex abuse, 129
spiritual abuse
    and alcoholic strategies, 171
    in the Catholic church, 123–26
    consequences of, 179–84
    defined, 119–20
    identifying covert abuse, 120–23
    identifying overt abuse, 123–26
    and identity crisis, xiii
    non-denominational nature of,
        183–84
    responses to clergy misconduct
        (non-Catholic), 126
    sex and power in, 174
    shadow-work for, 201–44
    steps for congregational healing, 205
    tales of, 126–67
    understanding, 169–99
    warning signs of, 169–70
    who is susceptible to?, 184–90
spiritual emergencies, 116
spiritual justice, need for, xviii
spiritual marriage, 54
spiritual membership, positive results
    of, 181–82
spiritual myths, finding our, 241–44
spiritual practice
    goal of, 24–25
    psychology of, 83–93
    success or failure in, 176–77
spiritual shadow-work, 203–44
    beginning of, 236
    meeting the spiritual shadow,
        113–67
    as recovery, 9
spiritual teacher(s), xii, xxiii, 81
    as divine human, 102–9

financial fraud, 126
finding one's, 81
as god, 93–102
high spiritual development / low
    moral development, 179–80
inherent dangers of the
    relationship, 94–95
must recognize their own shadows,
    204–5
as parent, 83–93
potential abuse of power,
    116–17
and projection, 84–86, 108–9
separating from a teacher, 211–13
tasks of, 102
vulnerability to becoming
    perpetrators, 186–89
Spong, John, 226, 231
spousal mysticism, 228–29
stages of awakening, 245–48
Steinbeck, John, 140
Steinbeck, Nancy, 140
Sufism, Majnun and Layla, 74–77
suicide bombers, 193–95
Suzuki, Shunryu, 136–37
Szabo, Marta, 148–49

Tamm, Jayanti, 132–33
tanha, 192
Tanya, 28, 38
teacher/student relationship. See
    also spiritual abuse; spiritual
    teacher(s)
    advantages and disadvantages of,
        108–9
Teresa of Ávila, 53–54
terrorists, 193–95
teshuvah, 51
therapists, abuse by, 188

Tibetan Buddhism
  and god contemplation, 40
  scandals in, 139–47
Tisdale, Sally, xxvii
Todd, Douglas, 164
transcendence
  death and, 193–95
  will to transcend, 11
transference, xxi, xxiv, 93–94
Tredwell, Gail, 159–61
trickster, 99
Trungpa Rinpoche, 139–43, 172,
  177, 215–16
Tsultrim Allione, xvi
Tworkov, Helen, 117

upward arc (evolution), 21–22
Utter, Jeff, 31

values, defining our own, 219
Vishwananda, Swami Paramahamsa,
  156–58
Vivekananda Saraswati, Swami, 152
Vow, The, 153–54

Watts, Nigel, 193
Wendy Egyoku Nakao, Roshi, 209–10
Western culture, guilt-based, 177
whistleblowers, xxi–xxii, xxv
Who am I?, xiii
Wilber, Ken, xxiii
  on developmental stages, 44–47,
    78–79
  on doing our psychological
    homework, 101

on high spiritual development and
  low moral development, 189–90
on levels of consciousness, xiv–xv
on primary Drive, 51
on transpersonal experience, 52–55
on "up" and "down," 21–22
Williamson, Marianne, 214
Winell, Marlene, 183–84
Winn, Andrea, 142–43
women in spiritual practice, 178–79
Woodman, Marion, 68, 70, 107,
  191–92

Yandell, James, 100–101
yearning, defined, 12–13
yetzer harah, 175

Zacharias, Ravi, 128–29
Zen Buddhism, scandals in, 134–35
Zusya, 200
Zweig, Connie (author)
  biography, 274
  disillusionment, initial, 5–6
  disillusionment with practice, 115
  her awakened friends, 245–46
  her longing for the dark, 196–99
  her longing for the light, 1–13
  her questions about her spiritual
    community, 4
  learning meditation, 1–4
  leaving her community, 221–23
  and meditation, 174
  as new writer, 238–40
  spiritual experiences of, 247–48
  and Steve, 63–64

About the Author

Connie Zweig, Ph.D., is a retired psychotherapist, former executive editor at Jeremy P. Tarcher Publishing, former columnist for *Esquire* magazine, and contributor to the *LA Times*. She has been on a spiritual path, practicing and teaching meditation, for more than fifty years—exploring the light and dark side of contemporary spirituality.

Known as the Shadow Expert, she is the coauthor of *Meeting the Shadow: The Hidden Power of the Dark Side of Human Nature* (with Jeremiah Abrams) and *Romancing the Shadow: A Guide to Soul Work for a Vital, Authentic Life* (with Steve Wolf, Ph.D.). She is also the author of *To Be a Woman: The Birth of the Conscious Feminine* and a novel, *A Moth to the Flame: The Life of the Sufi Poet Rumi*. Her bestseller *The Inner Work of Age: Shifting from Role to Soul* extends her work on the shadow into midlife and beyond and explores aging as a spiritual practice. Published in 2021, this book won both the 2021 American Book Fest Award and the 2021 Best Indie Book Award for inspirational nonfiction.

For more about Connie and shadow-work, visit her website **ConnieZweig.com.**